PRAISE FOR *WORK, PARENT, THRIVE*

"This might as well have been called 'How to Be a Happier Working Parent'—and it will, indeed, help you do just that."

—KJ Dell'Antonia, the *New York Times* best-selling author of *The Chicken Sisters* and *How to Be a Happier Parent.*

"If you want life advice from a dry scientific text, put this book down now. But if you want a book that feels like a conversation with a smart, empathetic friend who's seen it all and helped countless clients improve their lives—and can help you with yours—read *Work, Parent, Thrive.*"

—Alex Soojung-Kim Pang, author of *Rest*

"This book is for every working parent who thinks they don't have the time to read it. Make time! Yael Schonbrun combines academic scholarship, clinical expertise, and personal experience as a mother of three to offer deeply wise advice on how to manage our inner lives while we wait for society to make the outer lives of us working parents more manageable."

—Barry Schwartz, author of *The Paradox of Choice* and *Why We Work*

"Parenting is hard. Working is hard. Caring deeply about both is even harder. In an area rife with judgment, hot-takes, and 'hacks,' thank goodness for Yael Schonbrun. She offers much needed nuance and complexity and provides an evidence-based framework to harmoniously integrate what, for many people, are the two most important parts of their lives—family and craft."

—Brad Stulberg, author of *The Practice of Groundedness* and *P..k Performance*

T0015221

"Reading *Work, Parent, Thrive* is like chatting with a knowledgeable best buddy, one brimming with fascinating stories, cutting-edge science, and practical tips from the therapy room. Yael Schonbrun offers a way to accept our working-parent reality and use elements from both worlds to our advantage. It's just what every working parent needs!"

—Michele Borba, Ed.D.,
educational psychologist and author of *Thrivers*

"You likely picked up this book to find a way forward as a working parent. That's a fine start, but not just any solution will do. You are a living, breathing human being, not a broken dishwasher. A truly effective way forward needs to help you become aware of your own self story, to focus on how you relate to your own insides, and to aid you in finding meaning and purpose. Those are the kind of processes that pay off in every area of life. It will take both knowledge and practice, but this wise and well-written book will deliver scientifically sound know-how in clear, bite-sized units—you just need to supply the energy and commitment to learn and to grow. Ready when you are! I can highly recommend the journey."

—Steven C. Hayes, PhD, originator of Acceptance and Commitment Therapy, Foundation Professor of Psychology, University of Nevada, Reno

WORK PARENT THRIVE

12 SCIENCE-BACKED STRATEGIES TO
DITCH GUILT, MANAGE OVERWHELM,
AND GROW CONNECTION
(When Everything Feels Like Too Much)

YAEL SCHONBRUN, PhD

SHAMBHALA

SHAMBHALA PUBLICATIONS, INC.
2129 13th Street
Boulder, Colorado 80302
www.shambhala.com

Cover art: Clock and mug icons by kornkun / Adobe Stock
Cover design: Amanda Weiss
Interior design: Amanda Weiss
Author photo: Inna Chernysh-Govorov

9 8 7 6 5 4 3 2 1

First Edition
Printed in the United States of America

Shambhala Publications makes every effort
to print on acid-free, recycled paper.
Shambhala Publications is distributed worldwide by
Penguin Random House, Inc., and its subsidiaries.

LIBRARY OF CONGRESS CATALOGING-IN-PUBLICATION DATA
Names: Schonbrun, Yael, author.
Title: Work, parent, thrive: 12 science-backed strategies to ditch guilt,
manage overwhelm, and grow connection
(when everything feels like too much) / Yael Schonbrun, PhD
Description: First edition. | Boulder, Colorado: Shambhala Publications,
[2022] | Includes bibliographical references and index.
Identifiers: LCCN 2022011543 | ISBN 9781611809657 (paperback; alk. paper)
Subjects: LCSH: Parenting. | Work and family. | Work-life balance.
Classification: LCC HQ755.8 .S347 2022 | DDC 649/.1—dc23/eng/20220310
LC record available at https://lccn.loc.gov/2022011543

In loving memory of Raffy Chatav,
who showed me that finding joy in
our work and in our connection to others
is the embodiment of a life well lived.

CONTENTS

PART THREE: FROM THE HEART
How to Working-Parent Happier

THE PROBLEM OF WORKING PARENTHOOD

Nobody in the history of humanity has ever achieved "work-life balance," whatever that might be, and you certainly won't get there by copying the "six things successful people do before 7:00 a.m."

—OLIVER BURKEMAN

should have a solid hour and a half to get work done if I get going right away. I shuffle an untidy stack of research articles on sex trading among incarcerated women, pull out several relevant ones, and begin the work of revising the discussion section of my article. I've just gotten into a satisfying flow when a sweet song drifts over from the room next door: "Mommy, I'm awaaa-ake!" Without missing a beat, I finish my sentence and head to my angel's room.

I'm totally kidding.

It's more like this: With frustration bordering on rage, I curse everyone from my husband (for going to his office, seemingly guilt- and worry-free), the grandparents (for not being there to help out), my colleagues (for wanting this paper to go out), and my four-year-old (for being awake). Amid the frustrated rage, a seed of guilt quickly blossoms into a towering oak tree. I feel pissed off, guilty, and deeply conflicted over what to do. As my kiddo's sweet song transitions to a tyrannical "Mommy, COME NOW!" I take a deep breath, snap my computer shut, and head to his room.

What now feels like a hundred years ago, I expected to ace the whole project of working parenthood. I'd take advantage of childcare, a supportive partnership, and a flexible workplace to make sure my kids' needs got met while carving a path toward research greatness. At the time I became a working parent, I was only a few years out from my PhD in clinical psychology. I'd been awarded a grant from the National Institutes of Health to conduct research on treatments for couples in which one partner has an addiction, and throughout my pregnancy I had worked on a new grant application that, if funded, would allow me to get promoted to assistant professor. I fantasized about breaking enough new research ground to become so legendary that I'd be the first academic psychologist invited onto *Dancing with the Stars*.

But then my first son was born and something deep inside of me shifted. Especially in those early days, being apart from him tied me into existential knots. It wasn't simply the huge life transition, the sleep deprivation, and the hormonal swings (though I'd hazard a guess they didn't help). No, I was in a free-fall identity crisis.

Still the same ambitious person I had always been, I wanted to do interesting and important work, to apply my skills and drive outside of the privacy of my family life, and I was committed to providing financially for my growing family. Only now I was also drawn to gaze contentedly at my son for hours. I wanted to be the one meeting his needs, the one ooh-ing and ah-ing over every absolutely ordinary baby thing he did.

I was both the same and different, the results of which meant that no matter what I was doing, I felt like I could and perhaps *should* be doing something else. No matter how much I had done that day or week, I could only see what I had failed to accomplish and how I had shortchanged the people and roles I cared about. I had worked so hard to secure the presupposed "all." Now that I had it, I found myself stressed out, racked with guilt, pissed off that I didn't have more help, and overwhelmed with uncertainty about how to proceed in the life I'd worked so hard to build.

I'm in good company with my predicament. Dual-working-parent households increased from 25 percent in 1960 to 60 percent in 2012 among married couples with children.[1] In 2020, 95 percent of married couples with children had at least one working parent, and 60 percent of married-couple families with children were both employed,[2] while 72 percent of parents who lived without a partner were likely to be employed.[3] Working parenthood has clearly taken permanent residence in households of various shapes.

In the best of times, the privileged among us can take advantage of a huge infrastructure that includes teachers, day cares, and grandparents or other family members who help us stay productive in professional life while also ensuring that our kids' needs get met. Yet somehow, even under ideal circumstances, the demands of working parenthood feel relentless. There is too much to do and there are too few resources to do it.

Then there's the fact that working parents often live without commonsense supports. In 2020, for instance, we watched swaths of necessary infrastructure crumbling before our very eyes. Working parents navigating through the COVID-19 pandemic were suddenly expected to work without support from day cares, schools, or grandparents while parenting and homeschooling full-time. Those of us lucky enough to still be employed needed to make an unprecedented pivot to working remotely while acting as if parenting wouldn't interfere with our productivity. Others were expected to show up in workplaces with unknown dangers while being available to children who were scared, lonely, confused, and bored at home. We felt as if we'd been dropped onto a double black diamond ski run when we hadn't yet mastered the greens.

But impaired as we may be as a result of normal challenges or pandemic outbreaks, working parents have no choice but to struggle down the mountain. So we turn to the bookshelves, news media, blogosphere, friends, family, credentialed experts, and social media channels for guidance on how to make it through the trees, moguls, and icy terrain unscathed.

The solutions come at us, fast and furious. Just craft a better schedule. Negotiate more strategically with your partner, if you have one. Engage virtual support from grandparents and teachers. Do your work before children wake up or after they go to bed. Ignore your children. Disregard your colleagues' objections to email-blackout evenings. And so on. But no matter how we try to solve the painful challenges, we feel like we fail.

It's time to radically rethink how we approach the challenges of working parenthood. We can't continue to hinge hopes for our own and our families' well-being on infrastructure, social policy, marital renegotiations, or planning our schedules more strategically to save us from the conflict, guilt, burnout, anger, frustration, and overwhelm.

We don't need to.

Even though we must continue to advocate for better support for families—infrastructure, social policy, gender equality in the workplace—there is vast and often untapped power you already have within your grasp. I'll concede that this power won't give you more hours in the day or undo injustices. Even so, it can dramatically impact how you feel inside of a busy week and how workable you find the inevitable conflict of working-parent life to be.

Starting right now, you can take advantage of an ability to modify how you *think about* and how you *approach* your working parenthood. Core to this approach is the realization that the typical conversation about working parenthood has been missing something profound—it assumes that the problem only exists outside of our human bodies, mind and heart alike. As a result, we take an exclusively outside-in approach to solving the challenges of working parenthood. The logic goes something like this:

Problem: Workplaces and childcare facilities expect that working parents can neatly divide their work and parent time.

Solution: Workplaces need to increase flexibility around work time and offer employees access to childcare or actively support whatever forms of care can be made available. Childcare facilities, teachers, and grandparents need to increase the amount and reliability of support, and do so at a more affordable price point.

Problem: It's shameful that the United States is the only developed country in the world that doesn't offer paid family leave.

Solution: Policymakers must create reasonable parental leave policies at a national level.

Problem: Women can't continue to be the primary caretakers, diaper changers, and dentist-appointment makers if they are also breadwinners.

Solution: Partners (particularly men) must be compelled to more equitably split the domestic and childcare duties.

All of these outside-in formulations are logical. In fact, it is absolutely critical that we continue to push for more, and more rapid, reform. But while we wait for change to happen in the world outside our bodies or homes, we can reclaim some power by shifting how we approach working parenthood within our daily lives. In fact, from the perspective of a clinical psychologist (that'd be me), we often ignore the usefulness of tackling working parenthood from the inside out. For working parents to be less exhausted, overwhelmed, and torn between identities, we must also address working parenthood from a psychological perspective.

Before I dive into inside-out thinking, I want to be clear that I view *both* outside-in *and* inside-out approaches to be critical. Much as I love getting on my soapbox of psychology, it's evident that the external limitations of working parenthood won't and *can't* be undone with inside-out psychological practices alone. When all is said and done, no amount of clever thinking or action will allow you to fulfill expectations to be all in, all the time, for multiple roles— especially when each of those roles requires more energy, time, and patience than most humans can access on any given day.

Inside-out and outside-in approaches are both critical. In fact, they *complement* each other. And they are each more powerful when applied in tandem.

Now, here's the inside-out proposition: Despite problems aplenty in the world outside of our bodies, work-family conflict also lives inside our heads and hearts. Longing to master skills, to make public contributions, *and* to participate in deeply loving relationships are innately human drives. As early twentieth-century psychoanalyst Sigmund Freud once noted, "Love and work are the cornerstones of our humanness." But engaging in roles that are as demanding and different as work and parenting is hard, no matter how you maneuver it. That's true for everyone, even that Perfect Working Parent who loudly declares job gratitude, who shows up on time and unruffled for pickup, and whose car remains (miraculously) free of crumbs. Yes, it's hard even for *that* working parent.

Working parenthood requires vast amounts of resources—time, energy, attention—often sent in entirely different directions. If you aspire to sustain paid work, get your infant through the first six months of life, care for aging parents, or survive working parenthood under quarantine, you are certain to encounter struggle, discomfort, and internal conflict. If you could undo the challenges (say, by getting a nepotistic bump or by delegating all nighttime feedings, diaper changes, and mountains of laundry), you'd be less likely to feel the sweet reward that comes with overcoming the hurdles. Being at the top of the mountain feels satisfying, in part, because it is so damn hard to get there. Working parenthood offers a sense of purpose, growth, resilience, and joy because it's a taxing journey.

Thankfully, though, undertakings aren't powerful only because they are hard—most of us are not that masochistic! For example, work can be rewarding because you value what you get through your job, whether it's income or a chance to make contributions outside of the home. And you can foster meaning in parenting whether or not becoming one was a choice you voluntarily made. In other words, however difficult or easy, a project can have purpose when you connect it to something you care about.

Connecting to a sense of purpose isn't outside of your control—you have influence over how you relate to a project, a role, or a set of tasks you engage in. Maybe, for example, you were pressured to do a Couch to 5K program, even though you would've rather just rented *Brittany Runs a Marathon* (a great movie, by the way). Perhaps you initially thought running to be a silly waste of time and energy—the couch suits you just fine, thanks very much. But through your training, you might have opened up to the thrill of building your endurance, the magic of quiet streets at dawn, and the satisfaction in connecting with others who've joined you in getting off the couch. Tools from clinical psychology teach you how to become more skillful in both finding and creating meaning as you exert yourself.

If by choice or necessity you are on a working-parent journey, it isn't easy. But you don't have to hate working parenthood, despite the inescapable challenges and the structural supports that have been too long in coming. It is here that practical psychology offers tremendous power. You can learn to work with your mind, body, and heart to transform your working-parent experience.

A PEANUT-BUTTER-AND-JELLY APPROACH
TO WORKING PARENTHOOD

Practical psychology may not, at first, seem like the peanut butter to working parenthood's jelly. But the pains of our human bodies and minds need solutions designed for, you guessed it, our human bodies and minds. That may seem obvious, but our modern culture perpetually attempts to solve inside problems with outside solutions. Maybe it's a result of our consumer-driven culture, or maybe it's because we like to fantasize that there are simple solutions that can rid us of the uncomfortable experiences of living. Whatever the reason, we often find ourselves enticed by simple and outside solutions for complicated internal human experiences.

Follow me through this line of thinking:

Feeling sad? Fix it by buying something pretty to wear, shiny to drive in, or delicious to eat!

Worried you spent too much money on new clothes, transportation, overpriced lattes? Get yourself a new credit card!

Frustrated that you are accruing debt? Join the gig economy and put your shiny new wheels and cute outfit to work as a driver!

Feeling overwhelmed by the hours of work you've been clocking? Download an app or buy a book to help you improve your time management.

Overloaded with apps on your phone? There's a next-generation phone with more storage and more processing speed! You can add it to your new credit card and pay it off with your side hustle.

You get where I'm going with this, right? Trying to solve a problem inherent to being a living, breathing human being with solution strategies better suited for your broken dishwasher tends to create new problems and worsen the original problem. Solving uncomfortable human experiences, including emotions you don't like or internal conflicts you can't avoid, with linear, outside-in solutions is like trying to fight your way out of quicksand—the harder you struggle, the faster and deeper you sink.

Inside-out solutions are a cornerstone in psychology. From depression and chronic illness to partnerships and parenting, psychological and neurological research shows that how we think about and respond to very real challenges can make a huge difference in our experience in the world, how we relate to others, and how skillfully we navigate our life journeys. The same is true for working parenthood.

But, you might ask, why would working parenthood be any different if nothing outside of you changes? How can things get fairer, easier, or more pleasant if you have the same old boss who requires fifty hours a week at your desk, a day care that is unbending about snow-day closings, a job that expects you to punch in for the early shift while you're being subjected to sleep torture by your one-year-old, and a partner who doesn't know where you keep the mac and cheese even though you are supposed to have achieved a fifty-fifty division of labor? How the heck do you improve working parenthood with three children under the age of ten while you and your spouse both face ongoing demands for work productivity? (Asking for a friend.)

Those are good questions, and social science offers some surprising answers. Psychological practices can help you change your relationship with your thoughts, feelings, and experiences by teaching you how to unhook from unhelpful thinking and better tolerate unavoidable discomforts. They teach the power of clarifying values to provide direction and a reason to tolerate discomforts. They help you choose intentional actions informed both by your self-knowledge and the science of best practices in work and parenting. Practices from psychology can also help you harness more happiness by learning how to wisely define happiness for yourself, balance different forms of happiness strategically, and extract maximal joy from each of your life roles.

Engaging these psychological practices doesn't make working parenthood effortless. We're talking psychology, not wizardry, after all. But by changing your approach from the inside out, you can craft a better approach to the game, even while playing the same hand of cards you've been dealt.

Keep pushing your workplace, your partner, and society to make advances in expectations and practices. Sustain your optimism for an end to the working-parent horror of pandemics. But while you wait for more effective support, continue to live inside a body divided between multiple important life roles, and navigate impossibilities such as epidemics, unreliable childcare, unyielding bosses, financial stressors, and health problems, these strategies can help make you happier and more effective in your working parenthood.

TRANSFORMING YOUR WORKING PARENTHOOD

Strategies described in this book are drawn from acceptance and commitment therapy (or ACT, pronounced as one word), a scientifically tested treatment approach that I practice in the therapy room and in my life. The nature of being human sits at the core of all ACT ideas and strategies.[4] ACT embraces the fact that all humans experience the gamut of emotions and experiences. We all feel pleasure and pain, connection and disconnection, joy and irritation, terror and optimism, boredom and excitement. More relevant for the working parent, we will all hate our kids and our jobs, not to mention our partners and our bosses, from time to time, even if we mostly (occasionally?) love the heck out of them. Accepting this natural human truth helps us to not panic when feelings of frustration (or loathing) crop up. Allowing feelings to come up without panicking about them prevents us from layering more negativity onto ourselves and the whole working-parent experience. This, in turn, helps us appreciate the gifts that do come from raising our kiddos, engaging in the work sphere, and living full lives.

The discomforts of being human, whether unpleasant emotions or tension between conflicting desires, aren't in and of themselves a problem. They are simply part of the natural human experience. Problems grow, however, when we try to avoid natural human discomforts and conflicts and have only pleasant experiences. Paradoxically, the effort to avoid discomfort increases our suffering.

It may feel counterintuitive, but instead of trying to get rid of the miseries of working parenthood, this book will teach you to relate differently to them. Instead of trying to eliminate or avoid what we find unappealing or uncomfortable, we will change how we understand and respond to it. Again, this doesn't mean that we condone social structures that are unjust. We absolutely *must* continue to press for reform even as we sort out how we can best manage our current reality. Nevertheless, we can learn to accept the parts of working parenthood that cannot be changed (or which are slow as molasses to change) all the while learning how to relate to working parenthood in ways that are more tolerable, skillful, and even enjoyable.

THE WORKING-PARENT ACT

ACT has six core processes that are important in helping people to live more satisfying lives, even when realities are uncomfortable or downright objectionable:

1. Getting in contact with the present moment

2. Accepting—with equanimity—the thoughts, emotions, and experiences you struggle with

3. Becoming aware of your thoughts and stories

4. Learning to unhook from unhelpful thoughts and stories when you get caught up in them

5. Knowing what you want to stand for in this moment

6. Taking committed action to move your life in directions that matter to you[5]

These six core processes converge onto a skill psychologists call "psychological flexibility." Psychological flexibility refers to an ability to be self-aware and to have clarity in what matters most to you. It means choosing behaviors that reflect the person you'd most like to be in a given moment as you move your life in directions you find meaningful. Being psychologically flexible can mean sticking with something, even when it's uncomfortable. But it can also mean having the wisdom to quit what you were doing to pivot toward something different. Psychological flexibility is a skill that underlies psychological health and effectiveness in all life roles. Above all else, this book aims to help you develop this ability.

Of course, all working parents have moments when we feel ready to chuck it all and book a one-way trip to Tahiti. (Every. Single. Day.) There isn't anything wrong with having the fantasy, but acting on it may not fit in well with values we might hold, such as connecting to those we care about and to a sense of purpose in our life roles. Pausing to gain self-awareness about what you're feeling and unhooking from the stories of injustice, anxiety, exhaustion, and identity crisis give you an opportunity to reconnect with what matters most to you—*before* you book a nonrefundable ticket.

If you're working on psychological flexibility, you might take a deep breath and make room for the frustrations and fatigue, and even offer yourself some self-directed kindness. After all, working parenthood is hard—no rational person can deny that. In the pause, you can reconnect to your values. You might remember that you value being an adult who raises small people because you love to laugh and you love to hug. You might also remember that you value being an adult who does a job in return for income because, exhausting as it is, there is real satisfaction in doing work that gets recognized (and in being able to afford to house and feed your funny, huggy small people).

To be clear, being psychologically flexible doesn't mean you won't be pissed off, tired, frustrated, or in need of that trip to Tahiti. You are going to experience all those feelings and thoughts, no matter how skillful you are. But now, instead of getting sucked into a downward ruminative spiral, and instead of acting on negative thoughts and feelings only to experience regret and yet more anger, frustration, and guilt, you can more intentionally choose your response. You'll be able to respond intentionally instead of reacting reflexively. The more you practice doing this, the more you'll feel connected to the person you want to be in the life you want to build, and the less you'll feel at the mercy of working parenthood.

THE SCIENCE OF SYNERGY

Unhooking from the fantasy of what working parenthood *should* be also opens you up to explore what it *can* be. On a day-to-day basis we might feel that work and families are incompatible, that they are natural enemies. But just like peanut butter and jelly, work and parenting can make each other better. In fact, research from the fields of psychology and business has shown that work and family roles frequently benefit each other. Psychologists have labeled this relationship "work-family enrichment." Studies show that most working parents experience both work-family conflict and work-family enrichment, but that the enrichment is often quantifiably greater than the conflict.[6] This science offers up terrific guidelines, too, to better manage the conflict while amplifying the enrichment.

A synergy between conflict and enrichment is available in most complex areas of life. The Buddhist monk Thich Nhat Hanh offers a notion of "no mud, no lotus" in his book of the same name.[7] The idea here is that mud provides the beautiful lotus with needed nourishment. As sticky, dirty, and disgusting as mud feels, its existence is the reason floral goodness flourishes. Beauty and muck go hand in hand.

Let's take this metaphor to working parenthood because, yes, work-family conflict and work-family enrichment go hand in hand. This truth is evident in my personal life as a working parent, in my clinical training, in the psychological science, in my therapy practice, and in each of the many dozens of in-depth interviews I have conducted with working parents over the past several years for this book. I witnessed lotuses growing en masse as patients, colleagues, and friends working-parented their way through the devastating pandemic. The challenges and pains of working parenthood nurture growth, create opportunity to make meaning, and even hold the possibility of building greater happiness.

And you don't have to blindly hope for enrichment as you clamber about in the muck of working parenthood. You can strategically use conflict to nourish enrichment by employing ideas and strategies from social science and practical psychology. For example, we'll discuss how switching between roles can help you recharge. You'll learn how you can use each role to enhance creativity in the other. You'll be guided to experiment with shutting down your work email when you are with your kids and to deliberately refocus your attention on the meeting when your mind wanders over to whatever ball you dropped today.

Practices like these get easier as you begin to appreciate how your simultaneous engagement in work and parenting prompts the growth of wisdom, empathy, nonreactivity, and psychological flexibility—for both your kids and for you. You'll discover that skills transfer from one role to the other, that each role provides stress buffering and respite from the other, and that you can access additive effects of having multiple roles to deepen life experiences and satisfaction. And you'll learn how to balance meaning and pleasure—the two core ingredients of happiness—to increase working-parent success and joy.

I freely admit that I still feel regularly challenged by my working-parent experiences and that my challenges grow exponentially during tough patches of life. But misery doesn't dominate. Using the scientifically backed ideas I'll describe in this book, I have learned to find meaning in tolerating my own discomforts and the disappointment of my colleagues ("Isn't the new manuscript ready yet?"), patients ("You don't offer evenings, weekends, *or* early mornings?"), and my youngest son ("You bad boy, Mommy"). Things become even more tolerable when I perceive how participating in both roles enhances my creativity and wisdom (even as it diminishes my work time) and provides my children with more opportunities to develop independence, competence, and resilience. I have grown to see the merit of my choices, even while appreciating that I am giving up something. As life teaches us, there are always trade-offs. Our power comes not from being able to eliminate trade-offs but from having the clarity to choose them for ourselves.

So despite being an anxious, stretched-too-thin working parent with far less support than I'd like, I don't feel the inescapable grip of guilt, panic, anger, or hopelessness I used to experience when work-family conflict swells. The grip of those feelings has been relaxed as a result of the principles and on-the-ground strategies in this book. Now when I hear that school is shutting down and I panic about the work I won't be able to get done, when work becomes demanding and I sit my boys in front of a screen to buy myself time, or even when life's busyness robs me of needed sleep, I notice the unpleasant feelings, thoughts, and impulses. Then I take a deep breath and turn toward a calming faith that I can get through whatever lies ahead.

Thanks to this approach, I've grown more skilled in parenting and work, competent in managing challenges, joyful in everyday life, and more connected—to my work, my family, and to myself. I hope it will do the same for you.

PART ONE

FROM THE HEAD

*Transforming Your
Working-Parent Mind*

Raising kids may be a thankless job with
ridiculous hours, but at least the pay sucks.
—JIM GAFFIGAN

1

WHEN YOU'RE LOST, LET VALUES BE YOUR GUIDE

*I feel very blessed to have two wonderful, healthy
children who keep me completely grounded, sane,
and throw up on my shoes just before I go to an
awards show just so I know to keep it real.*

—REESE WITHERSPOON

On April 28, 2019, my sister lay in a hospital bed in the California Bay Area gazing with wonder at the beautiful infant she had just brought into the world. Thirty minutes away (when Bay Area traffic is light), my father also rested in a hospital bed. A combination of tough-as-nails Israeli war hero and deeply optimistic bright-sider, my father had never been one to give up when faced with challenges. But the past few months had revealed that his years-long battle with stage IV melanoma was a losing one. The cancer cells that had entered my dad's spine and brain rendered him persistently sleepy, unable to walk, and barely able to communicate. My sister had created new life just as my father's was entering its final act.

While my dad and sister rested in hospital beds, I sat perched on the edge of a plastic blue chair at the airport, mind and body anxiously humming. I was waiting to board the plane from Boston to California. Knowing that my dad was very ill and that my sister would want help with her new baby, I had decided to take a week off from my life as a working parent. My three children, then ages two, six, and eight, needed more care than my full-time working spouse could manage, so my mother-in-law upended her schedule to fly out and help. In the days leading up to my trip, I typed up a detailed document for them with complicated kid schedules and instructions on packing lunches informed by whose classroom had life-threatening peanut allergies and which child abhorred cream cheese on their bagel. And there were patients, colleagues, and podcast guests. I spent hours emailing to cancel appointments, reschedule interviews, and notify people of my absence and my wish not to be contacted during my time away. It was clear what I needed to prioritize. Now was the time to set aside work and parenting responsibilities and show up, body and soul, as daughter and sister.

But despite feeling confident in my choice to leave my children and work for a week, I worried. How would my boys and I manage our weeklong separation? Would patients and colleagues lose faith in my professionalism during my absence? How much would my husband struggle in my absence? How steep would the price for my time away be? As determined as I was to prioritize my sister and father during my week in California, I could not push pause on my identity or the demands of being parent, wife, therapist, podcast cohost, academic, and writer. I wanted to do well in each of my important life roles. I felt doomed to fail.

UNSOLVABLE

Before I became a working parent, I relished the satisfaction of being a (mostly) competent and effective person in both my personal relationships and professional life. I naively expected a smooth entry into working parenthood. So when I found myself crying every commute to work, constantly pissed off at my spouse (and colleagues, parents, and friends), and falling short in ways I hadn't expected, I sought out solutions. But I discovered that the kind of problem-and-solution logic that works well for many dilemmas didn't work for working parenthood. Being a clinical psychologist, I turned to the research to understand why.

Without a doubt, many of the solutions that have been spawned from a "repair-the-problem" perspective are valuable. There's no question that we need to be addressing problems of gender inequality in marriages and workplaces, inadequate parental support, and policies at the workplace and societal levels. Yet as the American journalist and cultural critic H. L. Mencken quipped, "There is always a well-known solution to every human problem—neat, plausible, and wrong."[1] Locating a tidy or simple solution to a problem with many complicated layers inevitably fails to solve the original problem. Instead, it creates new and sometimes much trickier problems.

The week I was in California, my father was discharged from the hospital for the last time. I was set to head back to Boston two days later. When our favorite nurse came to hug my mom and me goodbye, she told me not to take the instructions for his prescribed diet too seriously. She held my hands and looked deeply into my eyes, telling me we should give him whatever he wanted because quality of life was what mattered. I realize now that part of me didn't comprehend the finality of her advice.

That day, paramedics wheeled my dad on a gurney into my childhood home before transferring him to the hospital bed we had rented. I imagined my dad was happy to be home, and I was even optimistic that a good night's sleep outside of the stale hospital room full of beeping medical equipment would refresh him. But at 5 a.m. the following morning, I heard my mom's panicked shout.

My brother and I sprinted to the bedroom to see my father convulsing wildly. He looked terrified as my mom simultaneously wept and screamed for us to do something. The paramedics and firefighters came quickly, but by the time they arrived, my father had already slipped into a coma. I stood in a state of unreality beside my mom and brother as one of the firefighters explained that hospice patients no longer go to the hospital for care. The firefighter teared up as he watched our realization sink in.

When the hospice nurse arrived to check on my dad later that morning, I asked her the kinds of questions that get asked of all hospice nurses: What now, and for how long? She patiently explained that in his comatose state, my father would not be able to eat or drink. The process now involved waiting for his body to shut down. She told us that he could die the next day or he could continue this way for a month.

Perhaps you'll think me cold, but my rising terror was not only about my beloved father dying. I honestly didn't know what to do. I had three little boys who were missing their mommy, and I them—how would we handle being apart for up to a month when one week in I was aching to wrap my arms around them? Plus, my mother-in-law needed to head back to her home in Colorado the day after I was supposed to return to Boston. My husband and I had always managed to arrange our work schedules to allow us each to do our jobs and still ensure kid coverage. Without me or my mother-in-law there, my husband would be forced to neglect either his job or our children. And less consequential but more immediately pressing, my oldest son's ninth birthday was the day I was supposed to be arriving home, and my boy had been planning for months how we would celebrate his favorite day of the year. Then there were my work obligations. I had meetings with colleagues about projects with deadlines the following week. And I had scheduled sessions with patients struggling with their own crises who were waiting on me. A therapist does not generally share personal information because we don't want patients to worry about our emotional well-being. How could I explain to patients that I was pushing back appointments to an as-yet-unknown date?

Still, I couldn't fathom leaving my father's side and abandoning my siblings and mother. The past week of my dad's deterioration felt tolerable only because I knew we were in it together. Going back to Boston felt wrong. So did staying in California. The conflict over where I belonged and what role I should prioritize made me physically ill.

For the modern working parent, even one without a dying parent, the tug between roles and responsibilities tears our hearts apart. The conflict leaves us in perpetual turmoil over seemingly impossible choices. Part of the dilemma, of course, is our fear of letting people (including ourselves) down. As parents, we worry about our children: If we put work or other obligations before our children, are we damaging our relationship with them and therefore their ability to relate to others? And what does it mean about us as parents if we aren't prioritizing their care? As workers, we worry about our work lives: Can we do our jobs justice even when we end the workday before our childless colleagues? What does it mean about us as employees (not to mention our ability to sustain income) if we aren't always prioritizing our work? Plus, even if we are as committed to our jobs as our colleagues, how might we—particularly women, who are evaluated more harshly than our male counterparts when we leave work[2]—be judged for going to pick up our children? How might we be judged by those caring for our kids, our peers, and even our kids if we don't?

Researchers have sought to answer exactly these kinds of questions. Inquiries into the impact of childcare, for example, reveal that beyond the earliest months of infancy (and given a high quality of childcare—which, unfortunately, is not a given),[3] employment has little impact on children's educational achievement, behavior, or social-emotional well-being (notably, most studies have focused on mothers).[4] As the economist, parent-data expert, and author Emily Oster summarized in her book *Cribsheet,* being a stay-at-work parent or a stay-at-home parent "isn't the decision that is going to make or break your child's future success (if there is any decision that would at all)."[5] When it comes to the impact of parenting on work, too, our concerns often outsize the reality of the dangers—at least for the quality of our work. Constraints to work life caused by needing to go pick up Junior from soccer practice can even offer benefit, whereas overwork negatively impacts our well-being and work productivity[6] and increases turnover.[7]

Of course, many of us know someone (or for that matter, have *been* someone) who has been criticized by a boss, punished, or laid off for a decision to prioritize family. We don't need to beat ourselves up for having fears about the impact of family life on work—they are well founded and often formally or informally condoned. But we can remind ourselves (and our bosses, if it's safe to do so) that being pressed to develop work-life balance can benefit our work lives and the workplace itself.[8] We'll explore how to tap into these benefits throughout this book.

But even if working doesn't doom our children, and having children doesn't doom our work, a tension between roles that demand so much of us and that so deeply matter to our sense of self is inevitable. It's natural to try to reduce the pain and purge the conflict between our most important life roles. The trouble is, the fixes rarely get to the heart of what plagues us. Yes, of course there are real and practical concerns. But the conflict also resides inside our own heads and hearts.

Still, the longing to solve the pain is powerful. I found myself hunting desperately for the "right" answer to the question of whether to return to Boston. I texted close friends, interrogated the various hospice nurses that came to see my dad, did Google searches on "length of time one could remain in a coma before dying," and spoke to each of my siblings, my mother, and my husband. I repeatedly made the decision to stay until my father died, then panicked and reversed course. I was searching for the choice that would unburden me of internal conflict, a solution that would allow me to do the right thing by all of the roles that mattered most to me. I found none.

THE VALUE OF VALUES

I had been willing to extend my stay in California by a day or two, but an entire month? Could I really do that? My panic and logic were taking turns in urging me to find a way out of the danger zone of failure, disappointment, and heartbreaking loss. It was a fool's errand. My father was dying even as my working-parent life demanded my attention. Regardless of how wise or thoughtful or strategic the choice I made, and regardless of how much family and collegial support I made it with, the pain of being divided was unavoidable.

So I turned to a practice I often help patients with: clarifying values. Values have been defined by psychologists as the purpose or attitude we take regarding our chosen actions. A value is not a goal or destination but rather a compass that guides our journey toward a more meaningful, purpose-driven life. Values describe qualities of action, such as being curious, maintaining a sense of humor, persisting in difficult tasks, being kind, or balancing demands. They reflect the ways we most want to show up in the world.

In comparison to emotions, which come and go and sometimes mistakenly lead us into thinking there is danger, values provide a steady hand that reminds us about the kind of person we want to be. In comparison to logic, values do not require us to solve anything. They require only that we choose, with clear-eyed intention, how we take our life's journey. We can always choose to put our values in the driver's seat, even when we find ourselves on a path we didn't choose, don't much like, or that is truly unjust. We can put our values in the driver's seat even while experiencing the searing pain of guilt, shame, sadness, or anger.

Overwhelmed, I decided to ask myself the kinds of questions I ask patients to help them clarify their values. I asked myself what I wanted to stand for as I went through this painful series of events. I asked myself how I thought my father would want me to choose. I even asked myself what I'd advise my kids to do in the face of my own mortal end.

· · · · ·

Pause to Clarify *Your* Top Working-Parent Values

Values clarification is best done as a writing exercise. So if you feel up to it, grab a pen and paper, a computer, or even your phone and jot down thoughts that arise in response to these questions. But if that's not realistic for you, you might reflect on these questions during quiet moments—your commute, the minutes before your kids get up, between meetings, during a shower, or while folding laundry. However you do it, allow yourself to go deep in considering what you'd like to stand for as a working parent.

- Consider a particularly difficult patch of working parenthood. *What are you most proud of having done or having stood for in that period? If you didn't handle it well, how do you want to handle it next time?*

- Think about what you'd like your children to admire about you as a working parent. *What are the main ways you'd like them to see you or remember you?*

- Bring to mind a working parent you look up to. *This could be a friend, colleague, family member, a depiction of a working parent you have seen on TV, or even an idea that you've fantasized about. How would you describe the ways that this individual journeys through working-parent life?*

- Travel forward in time by thirty years and imagine your older self is looking back on the current phase of working-parent life. *Looking back, what ways of being would make you most proud?*

Values change over time and in different circumstances. And let's be honest—none of us ever lives up to them fully or consistently. But by clarifying your top working-parent values, you can build a better compass to guide your choices through some of the thorniest working-parent terrain.

· · · · ·

THE VALUE OF EMBRACING LOUSY

Living life according to our values can sometimes feel pretty lousy. That's because things that matter to us often put us in direct contact with tension, internal conflict, and uncomfortable feelings. While we might not find slopping about in the discomfort appealing, it is often from these kinds of experiences that we flourish. Discomfort, conflict, and tension offer us nourishment. Sometimes that nourishment arrives quickly, like a lightbulb moment of insight or a skill that gets strengthened through an uncomfortable experience. But the gifts of conflict can also arrive much later or in less obvious ways. Though the speed and size in which they appear varies, once you start looking for gifts, you're bound to see them emerging. That's because opposing forces prompt balance, growth, creativity, wisdom, health, and, yes, even happiness.

Using values as a guide helps you get the most out of the discomforts. It's like playing chess, a game my oldest son is obsessed with. He wants to play, and he loves to *win*. But he knows he won't get better if he doesn't challenge himself. And he knows that if he challenges himself, he will lose sometimes. The losing, of course, can feel crummy.

Accepting the lousy feelings as he connects to his values is critical for my kid. For one, he gets a thrill out of connecting with experienced and talented chess players, which motivates him to play games with them (even when they decimate him on the board). His values also guide him in moving the pieces moment to moment. He has learned to shift between values that guide mental or emotional focus in productive ways, for example by choosing between:

- Focusing on present joy in playing or the game's outcome

- Having curiosity or disinterest about an opponent

- Sticking to what he knows or trying something new

- Focusing on learning from loss or moving on quickly from a bad game

Connecting to our valued way of being can guide how we orient mentally, emotionally, and behaviorally. As one small study of elite international chess players showed, acceptance of discomfort and value-aligned playing can help chess players play better over time, even when playing feels uncomfortable.[9] Researchers assigned the chess players to two groups. In the experimental group, players completed a four-hour ACT training that emphasized acceptance of uncomfortable experiences and values clarification. Players in the other group received no ACT training. Seven months after the intervention, players from the ACT group performed significantly better in competition. They were less likely to be unhelpfully distracted by uncomfortable thoughts and feelings that arose during competition compared to those in the group without ACT training.

From chess to working-parent life, striving to accept discomfort as you connect to valued ways of showing up can help you make wise choices. That's true even when you don't get to enjoy the delights of a win or other immediate gratifications. Just as in chess, sacrificing immediate pleasure for long-term purpose can give you access to deeper and more enduring forms of satisfaction. Research on people struggling with addiction, for instance, shows that the urge to succumb to cravings becomes less dominant when people clarify and connect with their values.[10] The same can apply to people working through many kinds of difficulties. We get better at transcending discomfort when we are clear on what we want to stand for.

Of course, we'd all like to achieve our greatest life goals without encountering pain, anxiety, or losses. But as I mentioned previously, engaging in activities we care about tends to put us directly in contact with those uncomfortable experiences. Chess losses sting for my son *because* he cares about chess. Being passed over for a promotion at work unsettles you *when* you care about climbing the ranks. Your kid being angry that you weren't able to attend the school talent show bothers you *because* you care about how they feel. Experiences in life often feel uncomfortable—or downright painful—*as a result* of our caring.

Beyond being an indicator of what we care about, discomfort has an additional embedded advantage: it provides the breeding ground for profound joys. Victory is even sweeter when we work hard, confront pain, and overcome what seemed to be insurmountable obstacles to arrive there. Just like learning chess, getting in shape, setting an ambitious work goal, or even getting through the first sleepless year (um, years?) of parenting, part of what makes achievements so very meaningful is how hard we have to work to achieve them. If it were easy, we wouldn't feel as enlivened by our efforts to be persistent, focused, fearless, and full of wonder.

Of course, a sense of purpose can be available when things feel good, too. We don't need to experience pain to connect to what matters most to us. Yet being connected to what matters to you will invariably bring up discomfort at some point. This realization can help us deliberately connect with our values during the muckier parts of our working-parent journey.

This view of challenges, conflicts, and discomforts does more than show you that you can stand for something meaningful. It can make you *better* at the things you care about. When you respond to discomfort in a value-aligned way, you can almost always locate an opportunity to learn more about yourself and others and grow skills that can make you more successful in each of your life roles. You can use those experiences to foster a deeper connection with what matters most to you, too.

As a couples therapist, I often observe that partners in conflict with each other overlook the ways that discomforts arising from their conflicting ideas, styles, and priorities can offer advantage. A spontaneous partner brings some joie de vivre to the relationship, while a reliable one brings calm stability. An introverted partner presses the couple to take time to listen, and an extroverted one pushes the couple to get out into the world. Sure, frustration can grow because of differences. But when partners learn to appreciate their complementary pressure, they discover that they independently and jointly benefit.

Frustrated with the pains of working parenthood, we can become oblivious to the complementary benefits. We can default to struggling against the conflict. Yet thinking that we should not have to tolerate conflict between work and parenting roles makes it much harder to . . . yep, tolerate the conflict between work and parenting roles.

The paradoxical effect of resisting uncomfortable experiences only to find discomfort growing is more common than most of us realize. As the renowned Swiss psychologist Carl Jung put it, "What you resist not only persists, but will grow in size." This effect can even be observed in laboratory studies, including one in which participants with diagnoses of anxiety and other mood disorders all watched an emotionally provocative video. Half of these individuals were told that "it is possible to experience emotions at lower levels if you really concentrate on controlling them" and that "you should not have to put up with more discomfort or distress than necessary." The other half of the participants was given a rationale for accepting emotions, and that "struggling against relatively natural emotions can actually intensify or prolong your distress." Those in the acceptance group displayed less negative emotion during the follow-up recovery period and had decreased heart rates, while individuals in the suppression group experienced increased heart rates.[11]

Our discomforts, emotional and otherwise, tend to subvert our efforts to control them. But allowing ourselves to experience the discomforts of internal conflict can help us become more effective in responding to them.

Unavoidable discomfort shows up in working parenthood, even for folks who work and parent in what might seem to be ideal circumstances. Lianne is a psychology professor at the University of British Columbia in Canada. She told me she would have loved to complete a postdoctoral fellowship in Los Angeles, but she wanted to have a child with the kind of maternity leave her native country offered. So she headed back to Canada, where an eighteen-month maternity leave is standard. But after having her daughter, Lianne realized that the generous leave on the books didn't quite match reality. She told me, "If you have an active lab, you can't really leave. If you did, you'd have to shut down the lab. Most of those on leave continue to work at least part-time." At home with her five-month-old daughter during our interview, Lianne admitted, too, that she missed work. "I like my job, research, writing, and clinical work. But that's all kind of gone right now and got replaced with doing laundry, which I like less."

Well resourced or not, working parenthood foists uncomfortable role conflict upon us all. By using your values to guide your response to internal conflict, you can land on wiser paths. Your values can guide you in creating a life lived skillfully and with purpose.

SOME IMPORTANT TRUTHS

In considering the complexities of the relationship between our life roles, we encounter a few important truths. First, the conflict between our important life roles exists as a natural part of being human. It lives inside of our hearts and souls because these roles matter so deeply to us, and because they activate unique parts of our souls that offer vitality and meaning. Tension between roles and desires is part and parcel of being alive. My preschooler offers me regular examples of this, as in our typical breakfast exchange:

ME: "You want oatmeal?"
HIM: "No, no oatmeal! Yogurt!"
ME: "Okay" (*putting away oatmeal*).
HIM: (*breaking into tears*). "I want oatmeal!"

According to the evolutionary psychologist Steve Stewart-Williams, "Whatever we do, we're left with unfulfilled desires. Human beings are chronically conflicted animals. And that's because that's what selection made us."[12]

The very fact of work and parenting each mattering so deeply and demanding so much leads us to a second truth: outside-in solutions alone won't solve work-family conflict. No matter how we approach working parenthood, we will feel tension around and between these roles.

But take heart because a third truth is that conflict isn't a bad thing despite the fact of it being painful (or simply irritating—see note above regarding preschoolers). Internal pains can serve important purposes. For one, they offer information. Significant pain cues you to seek medical attention where insensitivity to it would prevent you from knowing you needed care. And pain doesn't always mean something disastrous has happened. When you push yourself, as you might during exercise, discomfort invariably arises. This kind of discomfort—when you pay attention, don't overreact, and reconnect to your values—helps you to determine your best response. This could include going to the doctor, of course. But if you feel confident that no tendons or joints are at risk, values can guide you in pushing through the discomfort, adding new strength training to your workout routines, or incorporating additional rest time to promote healing and recovery.

Like many forms of discomfort, conflict between roles can inform and guide us. For one, internal conflict can be an indicator of how very much we care about participating in each of our different life roles. And while it may be practically challenging and emotionally uncomfortable, the discomfort is often accompanied by opportunities to develop greater wisdom, resilience, creativity, grace, and happiness. That growth emerges *because* we are tugged in multiple meaningful directions. Our incessant and sometimes painful internal conflict evolved because that conflict benefits us.

The steps to using conflict to your advantage are simple. Don't fight the conflict. Pause in it. Take an open and curious stance toward your discomfort. In doing so, you will develop a more nuanced relationship with it. You will learn to appreciate its natural complexities. You may learn more about what is bothering you and why. You will be better able to deliberate about what values you'd like to elevate as you endure this challenging piece of life. And as you pause and reflect, you may discover gifts amid the pain and complexity. Your values can help you gain greater access to those gifts.

WITH VALUES AS YOUR GUIDE

The day after my father went into a coma, I had a choice to make. I needed to decide whether I would prioritize my role as daughter to a dying father or my role as working parent with expectant patients, colleagues, children, and a spouse with similar parenting and professional demands. There was no solution without pain, no choice I felt good about. Recognizing this truth, I allowed myself to be guided by my father's values of prioritizing the grandchildren he adored and persisting in the work ethic he had been so proud of.

The hospice nurse had told me that hearing is the last sense to go. The evening I left, I held my dad's hand and explained that I was returning to Boston for his eldest grandson's birthday. I told my dad that he would be there in spirit for the birthday and that he would be there for me every day in my boys' passion for mastering complicated tasks, in their impish smiles, and in their love of slapstick humor. Finally, I told him that he would continue to inspire me to work hard, to believe that challenges make us stronger, and to know that finding joy in our work and in connecting deeply with those we love is the very embodiment of a life well lived. Then I kissed my dad's cheek and headed for the airport.

My husband and the birthday boy picked me up at the airport and my relief in seeing them was palpable. But the birthday celebration felt hollow. My mind and heart seemed to be hovering somewhere between California and Boston. When my phone rang the following morning at 3:15 a.m. Boston time, I knew before my sister said a word what had happened: my father—the man who for me had symbolized vitality, strength, and optimism—had died.

In our problem-and-solution-oriented culture, it's hard not to view emotional pain as a personal failing, a problem to be conquered, or an indication that we made a poor choice. But years reflecting on the nature of internal conflict provided me much needed wisdom and practical strategies to weather the events surrounding my father's death. Did I wish I had stayed for my father's final day? Of course I did. To this day I replay my choice and wish I had done it differently. But I also remind myself that I acted on my values as best as I could. And I can see that no matter what choice I made, a conflict between my most important life roles and a profound sadness resulting from the loss of my father were inevitable.

On that predawn morning, I sought to maintain perspective that my emotional responses did not mean I lacked morality or wisdom. They were simply information that could guide learning, growth, and meaning-making. As the psychologist and cofounder of ACT Steven C. Hayes writes, "Perhaps the most valuable gift we get from accepting our emotional pain is that of rediscovering what we deeply care about."[13] I realized how important it was to me that my husband and I book the five overpriced tickets so my entire family could travel to California that very day. I wanted my three little boys to meet their beautiful new baby cousin, to bring laughter to my grieving mom and siblings, and to honor and celebrate my dad's life with me.

By the time we arrived back in the Bay Area late that night, my California family was in chaos. My sister had been checked back into the hospital as a result of a severe infection. Her husband was with her. They hadn't been able to secure a room in the maternity wing and so had left their week-old infant with my mother. My mother had just lost her spouse of forty-four years and was going on several days with no sleep. She was jittery and beyond exhausted. So I took the baby while my mother headed to bed and my husband put our boys to sleep. It was strange to realize that I could offer a watchful eye over my newborn niece because, as tired as I was, my brief time away from California had given me more sleep than either my mom or siblings had. My choice to leave had provided this small but valuable gift.

And I knew to be on the lookout for other gifts. Despite the haze of grief and exhaustion, I saw them everywhere. Time with my sister's infant daughter and dying father had interrupted my therapeutic flow with patients and pressed me to share personal information. But being a good therapist requires more than intellect—it demands wisdom and empathic connection. The sadness of losing my father and the intense role conflict I experienced all deepened my ability to connect to the painful emotions and powerful internal conflict many patients want help with. These gifts will surely help me to parent more wisely and empathically, too. And I benefited from other tangible gifts that I write about in this book, including creative surges, strengthened clarity in essential versus nonessential work and parenting activities, and greater insights into the meaning of a life well lived.

A practical and existential conflict is bound to emerge when we participate in multiple meaningful life roles. While we desperately need outside support, we can't only solve this problem from the outside in. To transform our experience of working parenthood, we also need inside-out solutions to guide our minds, our feet, and our hearts in managing our human experience. We need to get clear on our working-parent values and allow them to act as our wise guides through the roughest patches of working-parent life. Clarifying and connecting to our core values can help us make thoughtful choices in impossibly complicated situations. Our values will guide us in learning, growing, making meaning, and getting the most out of each of our important life roles.

. . . .

The TL/DR (Too Long, Didn't Read)

A VALUE-BASED APPROACH TO WORKING PARENTHOOD

Consider how part of work-family conflict emerges because you are engaging in two roles that matter deeply to you. That's a good thing since fulfilling lives involve both deep connections with those you love and connecting to purpose in your work. Accepting that conflict is a part of the package, shift from a focus on eliminating the discomforts of working parenthood to getting curious about what kind of working parent you want to be. This is the practice of clarifying your values. Ask yourself:

- *What kind of working parent would I like to stand for through the messy and sometimes painful parts of working-parent life?*

Consider how your values might guide you in intentional activities by asking:

- *When I experience work-family conflict, how do I want to handle it? Whether it's staying calm, learning something new each day, enjoying the moment, appreciating the challenges, or laughing when I drop the ball, what would I like to do more of in my working-parent life?*

2

CHANGE YOUR WORKING-
PARENT MINDSET

There is magic in letting the worlds overlap.
Unless you operate heavy machinery, then
maybe you shouldn't do that.
—ERIKA WELCH

In 1956, Ruth Bader Ginsburg enrolled in Harvard Law School as one of nine women in a class of over five hundred men.[1] Her husband, Marty, was in his second year at the same program. Their daughter, Jane, was just fourteen months old. The Ginsburg scholars made the arrangement work by hiring a nanny and coordinating their schedules so that one of them could always be home to relieve the nanny at 4 p.m. Then Marty was diagnosed with an aggressive form of testicular cancer. If things had been challenging before the cancer diagnosis, life suddenly became exponentially harder. With Marty fighting for his life, Ruth now carried the burden of her own coursework, caring for their young daughter and her sick husband, and coordinating academic support for Marty, who remained enrolled throughout his cancer treatment.

Incredibly, Ruth Bader Ginsburg didn't just stay afloat at Harvard Law School (which would have been impressive enough). No, the future Justice Ginsburg finished her first year of law school as a top-ten student, graduating at the top of her class at Columbia, where she transferred to complete her third year after Marty got a job in New York City. She also became the first woman to serve on two major laws reviews, the *Harvard Law Review* and the *Columbia Law Review*.

How did she accomplish this feat under such intense pressure? How did she do so well in her professional training while also balancing the high-demand needs of her family?

There's a lot of ways to answer those questions. For one, there's no question that Ruth had an exceptional mind and a dogged work ethic. She also had the benefit of support from extended family and financial resources. Then there's the fact that Ruth needed less sleep than the average human. During Marty's illness, Ruth adopted a work-through-the-night practice that she retained throughout her life. And even when Marty was sick or his career was the one governing their zip code, the two built an egalitarian marriage uncommon for their time and which remains exemplary even today.

Ruth was privileged in many ways. But it's worth pausing on something to which Ruth herself credited her successes. She believed that parenting was a key ingredient for her iconic legal career. In her own words: "I attribute to my daughter the responsibility for why I was such a good law student. I went home, played with Jane, had dinner and then I was ready to go back to the books. It was the pause that refreshes."[2]

During the hours that the nanny was with her daughter, Ruth would throw herself into her studies. But once back at home, she would devote herself to games, bathing, cleaning, reading, and just generally being fully present as a parent until her daughter's bedtime. It was only after Jane went to sleep that Ruth would return to her work. As she wrote in a *New York Times* essay offering advice for living, the combination of parenting and legal training offered more than reprieve. It offered invaluable perspective. She wrote, "Each part of my life provided respite from the other and gave me a sense of proportion that classmates trained only on law studies lacked."[3] Ruth believed her tremendous career success wasn't despite her status as a mother but rather *because* of it.[4] Extraordinary as Ruth Bader Ginsburg might be, I suspect that work and parenting enrich each other, no matter our circumstances.

But enrichment is rarely top of mind when it comes to working parenthood. Take Rob, a business and tax attorney and single father I interviewed for this book. Rob emailed after reading my 2014 *New York Times* piece[5] to point out that as a writer about working parenthood, I might consider changing "the tone of these articles from the difficulty of working mothers to the difficulty of working parents." After all, he said, "Men who care for their children do not have it any easier." The data don't perfectly agree with Rob's point— from tenure clocks to how chores get distributed along gender lines, considerable evidence suggests that working mothers encounter challenges that don't hit working fathers as hard.[6] Still, Rob's main point stuck with me: regardless of background or circumstances, working parenthood is no easy feat.

Rob shared in an interview with me that his own working-parent challenges grew after he and his wife divorced and he was thrust into the position of being both breadwinner and primary parent to his two young children. For Rob, a rarely discussed gender bias was a regular occurrence. As he explained, "It's more acceptable as a female than as a guy to say, 'I have to leave work to go pick up my kids.'" And, he said, "Dads have the same issues as their female counterparts with a few other issues mixed in," including a lack of common social supports such as the playgroup meetups readily available to moms.

Of course, there are the unique challenges that befall working parents of any gender, including racism, poor health, financial problems, marginalization, and job and food insecurity, to name just a few. These challenges range in form and magnitude. Suffice to say, I haven't met many (okay, *any*) working parents who call the whole rigmarole "effortless."

INTRODUCING ... WORK-FAMILY ENRICHMENT

But maybe effortlessness is overrated. Take the popularity of books about resilience, grit, and gifts of failure. Such books highlight an important truth that effort, challenge, and even adversity can offer a host of unexpected benefits. Studies show, for example, that people who have experienced some adverse life events are ultimately happier than those who haven't.[7] That's because tough experiences deepen us as humans, grow our wisdom, contribute to our creativity, connect us with people and ideas, and even heighten our happiness. Gains live right alongside our pains.

We might think Rob's story is the "truer," more typical one, but far from being an optimistic working-parent unicorn, Ruth Bader Ginsburg's story fits a broad verdict that delights live together with the blights. Scores of research, in fact, reveal that most working parents experience both the dreaded work-family conflict *and* the wonders of enrichment. They don't just live beside one another. Conflict *fosters* enrichment. Remember, "No mud, no lotus."

Researchers have long sought a simple answer to the question of whether role conflict depletes our resources or leads to an expansion of energy, skills, and even life satisfaction.[8] As is often true in psychological science, there's evidence for both sides. In other words, tension that naturally exists between these two demanding roles can indeed lead to depletion. It can also serve as fodder for something a bit more appealing. That something is work-family enrichment.

Work-family enrichment is the extent to which experiences in either work or family improve quality of life in the other. For example, your irritating and emotionally immature boss may help you hone your negotiating skills with your two-year-old—that's enrichment. And your two-year-old can provide greater meaning to your work, whether the meaning comes from doing work that contributes to a greater good that includes her or work that keeps her solid on snack funds. That, too, is enrichment.

Work-family conflict and work-family enrichment aren't simply two sides of the same coin—they are separate and unique phenomena.[9] Think of them like the flavors of salty and sweet. Flavors occupy their own unique taste receptors on our tongue, and many of us prefer one over the other. But regardless of which you prefer, the science of gastronomy proves that learning the art of *combining* flavors can lead to masterworks.

The artful combining of roles also helps us achieve a much more satisfying working-parent experience. Like a chef in the kitchen, we can each learn how to skillfully combine work and parenthood by establishing an optimal mindset, transferring skills between roles, and managing the tension between them more skillfully.[10]

Getting to Enrichment

For decades, Jeffrey Greenhaus has been one of the most influential researchers in the field of work and family. As Jeff told me in an interview, the enthusiastic response to his landmark review on work-family enrichment in 2006,[11] written with his colleague Gary Powell, suggested that both academics and the general public were "ready to acknowledge that it's more than just conflict."

Jeff told me, too, that he enjoyed teasing his MBA students about how to deliver a knockout blow to conflict. He'd egg them on, saying, "I really believe people should avoid a conflict between work and family, and here's how to do it." He'd instruct them to take notes on this advice: "*Don't* get married, *don't* have kids, *don't* care about other family members, *don't* take a responsible job, *don't* seek to develop new skills. In other words, don't be involved in life. That's the best way to avoid conflict." They'd get his joke by then, so he'd shift to explaining how conflict and enrichment can coexist: "Being actively involved in different parts of life is going to bring some interference between the two. And the question is keeping it managed so that positive experiences in different roles outweigh the negative."

Jeff and Gary's milestone review of work-family enrichment also offered the revelation that in almost every case in which a study assessed enrichment and conflict, "the average enrichment score was at least as high as the average conflict score, and generally was substantially higher."[12] It's a striking point worth pausing on.

. . . . .

Pause to Connect to Your Work-Family Enrichment

It's easier to call up negative thoughts, memories, and emotions than positive ones. That's because our hardwired human tendencies prioritize survival rather than happiness. Thankfully, getting eaten by a predator isn't the pressing concern it once was. In modern life, with safety more often a given, we can choose to override our survival-oriented negativity to instead focus on enrichment. Accomplishing this feat begins by taking a moment to deliberately unhook from the negative to get curious about the positive. When we do, we might discover that the positive is available—sometimes in surprisingly large amounts.

To locate the enrichment in your work and parenting life, ask yourself:

- *How did my professional life help me parent better today?*

- *Where did my parenting role help me do a better job in my work this week?*

- *How did either (or both) role(s) help me grow as a person?*

- *In what ways did one of my roles help me feel more posi-tive emotions: joy, satisfaction, connectedness, excitment, relief, gratitude, hope, inspiration, contentment?*

- *In what ways did one of my roles help reduce stress in the other?*

- *In what ways do I feel a greater sense of meaning in my life because I engage in both roles?*

If you have a moment, write down your answers in a journal or in your phone. Writing it down helps to concretize it in your mind. Plus, looking back at your notes about working-parent goodies in the future will help you access more enrichment, even in the face of work-family conflict.

. . . . .

THE MINDSET SHIFT

If you began reading this book believing that work makes you a bad parent and that parenting makes you a bad worker, you're not alone. If you thought that work and family are bad for each other and that they naturally—and exclusively—conflict, you're in good company. These common notions represent what I'll call a "work-family–conflict mindset."

Mindsets are overarching beliefs that shape how you understand a very complex world around and inside of you. They represent what you believe to be accurate, natural, or achievable. Mindsets guide how you organize information, help you to quickly resolve complexity and uncertainty, shape how you ascribe meaning to events, orient your attention, and make many decisions automatic. In other words, mindsets are useful because they keep your brain from exploding.

Examples of common mindsets include:

- Personality is fixed versus malleable.

- Effortful activities deplete my energy versus effort is invigorating.

- Happiness is genetically determined versus happiness can be intentionally grown.

- Work and parenthood only conflict versus work and parenting can enrich each other.

Much of the thinking around mindsets comes from the work of the pioneering Stanford psychologist Carol Dweck.[13] She began her decades of research focused on the impact of mindsets on student outcomes, though she's since expanded into many other content areas. But regardless of the content of the mindset, Dweck's major distinction is "fixed mindsets" versus "growth mindsets." Fixed mindsets are defined by the assumption that we have built-in capacities that can't be changed, whereas growth mindsets assume that through effort, experience, and interest, where we start can contrast starkly with where we end up.

The differences between a fixed and growth mindset set the stage for divergent responses to the very same challenges. Imagine that you're being set up with a challenge of looking for a lost sweatshirt. And imagine that it's pitch dark. You might think of a fixed mindset as a searchlight that can only point in one direction. You'll find the sweatshirt quickly if it's in the line of the light beam. But if the direction your searchlight is pointing doesn't contain the lost sweatshirt, you'll likely give up on your quest to find it. A growth mindset, on the other hand, would be more like a searchlight sitting atop a swivel. It may start out in one spot, but it can pivot in various directions, spending more time in areas that seem fruitful for searching.

When it comes to learning in academic settings, a student with a growth mindset might not yet know or understand a concept or skill (certainly not any better than someone with a fixed mindset). But a student with a growth mindset will swivel about until learning is accomplished or a better approach is adopted. *Yet* is an important word and concept for someone with a growth mindset, setting them up for the possibility to be willing to fail but continue to try harder and smarter.

Our mindset—growth versus fixed—has powerful ripple effects. If we believe we can't learn math and we don't try, we can quickly prove our own inability. But if we believe we can sort out geometry (even if we failed a test or dread the class), we might set out on the path to find a good teacher, break down hard problems into easier ones, find the fun, and practice, practice, practice. With a growth mindset, we'll discover that our mind, our skills, our personality, our beliefs, our interests, and our compassion can grow. In fact, researchers have shown that mindsets can positively impact areas as wide-ranging as physiologic responses to food and exercise, personal characteristics, illness recovery, and, yes, even happiness.[14] As Dweck summarized in a 2012 review, adopting a growth mindset can increase conflict resolution (even in long-standing rivalries), resilience, chronic aggression, and willpower.[15] Mindsets matter.

Mindsets matter in working parenthood, too. A work-family enrichment mindset suggests that working and parenting can enrich each other and our lives, whereas a work-family conflict mindset suggests that the two roles cause us to do worse and be inescapably miserable. Just like a growth mindset in academic pursuits, thinking that goodness can emerge through strategic effort (versus effort being futile) sets you up for the kind of ripples most of us would prefer in working parenthood.

As evidence for the power of an enrichment mindset, consider a national survey of working and nonworking mothers. In this study, mothers were compared on beliefs about whether their employment status (working or not working) was good for their children. Mothers with more positive attitudes about their work status—regardless of which status it was!—had healthier psychological well-being. The children of mothers who had more positive attitudes about their work status also had better social and emotional outcomes.[16] It was the mindset about the work status, not the work status itself, that mattered for well-being, both for mothers and children.

That mindsets matter doesn't mean circumstances don't. Real life is never that cut and dried, and circumstances clearly matter a great deal. For instance, no mindset could have allowed me to write this book if I had lived in a time and place where Jewish people—or women, for that matter—weren't allowed to be educated or to work outside the home, where egalitarian marriages were unpopular, or if I didn't have good health and other resources needed to read and write while raising a family. There's no question that circumstances like mine make it easier to cultivate a growth mindset since daily experiences drenched in racism, misogyny, violence, poverty, or debilitating illness make it hard and sometimes impossible to overcome challenges. But though mindsets can't entirely undo rotten realities, there's growing evidence that they can make a difference. For example, mindsets can reduce inequalities in academic outcomes,[17] help to foster cross-cultural and cross-race relations, and motivate social justice action.[18]

Growth mindsets help us adjust to lousy realities and constraints we sometimes live with, and they can help us find the motivation and strategies to work to change them, too. A growth mindset is ideal for students because it suggests that whatever challenges you face in learning, you'll be better able to learn once you find the appropriate learning strategies and supports. Similarly, an enrichment mindset is ideal for working parents because it suggests

that enrichment can emerge even while you encounter conflict between your roles. In other words, an enrichment mindset doesn't
assume that you'll delete tension between roles. Rather, an enrichment mindset opens you up to finding the good that already exists,
the strategies to tolerate (or make an impact in) what sucks, and
the motivation to learn how to get the most out of your working
parenthood.

CANCEL CONFLICT CULTURE

A mindset of embracing conflict may not appeal to many of us. Alan
Watts, a British philosopher whose life's work was interpreting and
dispersing Eastern philosophy for Westerners, summarized that
"the whole enterprise of Western technology is 'to make the world
a better place'—to have pleasure without pain, wealth without poverty, and health without sickness."[19] Efforts to undo the pain and
enjoy only pleasure are boons for many industries, including the
wellness industry that promises happiness and vitality if you try
this pill or that mantra. A failure obviously means you tried the
wrong panacea—on to the next! But (spoiler alert) this approach
doesn't actually work for wellness. To tell the truth, marketing be
damned, it doesn't work for most human problems.

The ancient Chinese philosophy of Taoism offers a time-tested
and more workable approach to pleasure and pain. According to
this philosophy, difficult and easy are interdependent. They both
complement and sustain each other. Or as it's written in the second
chapter of the Tao Te Ching, "Hard and easy complete each other."[20]
Contradictory forces aren't a problem to be solved. Rather, they are
critical for the health of complicated systems.

Nature offers countless examples of seemingly oppositional
forces underlying health and sustainability. On a recent visit to the
New England Aquarium in Boston, I saw a sign posted above one
of the huge kaleidoscopic tanks that said "Healthy Communities

Rely on Diversity." Human diversity differs from marine diversity, of course, but some general truths apply. For one thing, diverse communities suffused with assorted colors, shapes, and sizes are magnificent to behold. The contrasts between movement and stillness, bright and neutral, big and small, smooth and spiny, top and bottom, and quick and slow are breathtaking. From a sustainability perspective, those elemental differences between fish and plants keep an ecosystem thriving. Oceans thrive when there are top-feeders keeping the action alive near the surface and bottom-feeders consuming decaying matter on the ocean floor. Without kelp and other sea plants to produce oxygen, fish would suffocate. Healthy systems rely on the tension between contrasting forces of nature.

PATHWAYS TO ENRICHMENT

In nature, as in many kinds of ecosystems, harmony relies on tension. Making space for opposing forces like those of conflict and enrichment helps you manage that tension more skillfully. Healthy outcomes of role conflict arise through three unique pathways that take advantage of this inherent tension:

1. *Transfer effect.* Tension between roles means you regularly need to step away from each. But as you step away from parenting (or work) to tackle work (or parenting), you are being pressed to develop resources, skills, perspectives, or knowledge in a different area of life. Another role you must drop into means more learning that needs to happen. The resources you develop in one area of life (whether work or parenting) can then be helpfully applied back to the other.

2. *Buffering effect.* Having multiple roles involves lots of different places to be. This offers an opportunity to have stress in one part of life complemented by a different

(sometimes even positive!) experience in the other. On the most painful of work (or parenting) days, the slog will get interrupted as you step into the less-rotten role of the day.

3. *Additive effect.* Multiple roles pull us in many different directions. Participating in multiple meaningful roles contributes to greater breadth of life experiences and greater opportunity to create meaning through living.[21]

Let's dive a bit more deeply into each of these pathways.

The Transfer of Skill

Athletes, gamers, and experts from pretty much any discipline appreciate the benefits of cross-training. Football players have been known to take ballet, scientists become passionate about rock climbing, and I've interviewed many an impressive author with an ardent knitting habit (I prefer crocheting, myself). These pairings may not appear synergistic. That is, until you consider the skill transfer potential. Ballet helps football players with balance and coordination, rock climbing builds neurological pathways and habits for zooming out to plan next steps, and the yarn arts help a busy mind learn how to get quiet so important ideas can get noticed.

Spreading your resources between roles does, of course, reduce what you can send to either. Yet that spreading has huge benefits. For one, it helps you acquire new perspectives on long-standing, sticky problems. Many scientists struggle to zoom out on a narrow problem inside the laboratory. But rock climbing requires flipping back and forth between the immediacy of where you'll put your foot to the broader topography and route you're tackling. Building the muscle of toggling between focused thinking and broad perspectives can occur on a cliff and then be applied in a laboratory setting.

The different kinds of activities you might participate in as a part of your working-parent day help you build skills that serve you well, even in roles the skills aren't designed for. Working parenthood itself can help you parent better because as you juggle and struggle, you teach your children a whole host of important values and behaviors (like, say, juggling and struggling).

John, a pizza shop owner and father of two boys, explained to me that he uses his job to teach his kids "that you gotta work hard to get where you want to be in life." Jamila, a customer complaints representative at a utility company, sees her work as means of providing financial stability to her family but also as a place where she builds self-esteem. Jamila finds that her work helps her overall mental health because she feels pride in her income and has built competence and confidence in her job. She uses these workplace advantages as a teaching tool, modeling for her son how one can develop self-care skills that are useful at practical and psychological levels.

Not only can work help you parent better but parenting can also benefit your work. The development of interpersonal skills that often accompany parenting—patience, empathy, and tolerance, to name just a few—can be superpowers in the workplace. As Elizabeth Corey, a political science professor and the director of the Honors Program at Baylor University, told me, "Being a nurturer helps me as an administrator. That is not the tenure track way of thinking, but part of my current job is making the department function well." Simone, an exotic dancer, told me that she learned a lot about how to more skillfully handle her customers when her daughter was a toddler. She told me, "Now that I am a mom, the way I interact with customers is a little bit different. I have more empathy and skill when they misbehave. I talk to them the way I talked to my toddler. I say, 'Honey, that's just not how we behave here.'"

The Stress Buffer

You know those days when work seems like one failure after another or parenting means a front-row seat to the meltdown of the century? You might be wondering, "How might this rosy concept of work-family enrichment show up there?" Now might be a good time to mention that there are times it doesn't. If you had a rotten morning with the kids and then your client shows up unwilling to work with you, the junky feelings of incompetence, frustration, and general pissiness can grow faster than your kid's birthday wish list. Sometimes a crummy day is just a crummy day.

But often the buffer effect can help you make something out of a rotten day. Each role can help take the edge off of the stress in the other.

Intentionality serves us well in stress buffering. When we deliberately step away from one role and enter fully into the other, we give ourselves permission to loosen the grip of the stress or unhappiness we were feeling. One working parent described that this can look like having "a hug on a tough workday, and a place to feel competent on a tough parenting day." That hug serves us better when we show up for it, body and mind. When we mindfully step into (or away from) each role, we can, as statistician Tracy described it, "have two mountains to be on top of." For her, as for many working parents, the dual roles can "make the highs higher and actually buffer the lows."

And as Tina, a professor in child development psychology, told me, "Having the multiple aspects of identity makes each one feel less threatening. Like last night, my husband and I were trying to get dinner together for our daughter and she was testing our patience. If she were my entire identity, I would see those moments as more threatening." Balancing time as parent with time as professional means Tina can avoid placing all of her self-worth eggs in one basket.

Add 'Em Together and What Do You Get?

There is yet another way that work and parenting roles enrich each other, and it is perhaps the most important: the additive effect. Research confirms a cumulative effect on our overall well-being when we have more roles in life.[22] We can also understand this notion from the perspective of Taoist philosophy, which suggests that the whole is greater than the sum of its parts. *Taijitu*, the graphical symbol for the concept of yin and yang, is, in fact, translated as the "supreme ultimate." It's the *combination* of yin and yang that results in harmony. After all, what is light without dark, effort without rest, quiet without noise, femininity without masculinity, or expansion without contraction? Health and wholeness result from balance and contrast between opposing forces.

Incorporation of different parts of the body, areas of the brain, and aspects of our interpersonal self help us become more whole and also more flexible and psychologically healthy. As Daniel Siegel, the author of bestsellers such as *The Whole-Brain Child*, writes, "Harmony emerges from integration. Chaos and rigidity arise when integration is blocked."[23] Integrating roles offers this same kind of benefit.

The benefits of having many life roles was first published in the late nineteenth century by the French sociologist Emile Durkheim. Durkheim researched various social factors that contributed to suicide. He collected data from across Europe and conducted comparisons of soldiers versus civilians, Protestants versus Catholics, women versus men, partnered versus unpartnered, those with children versus those without.[24] No matter how he grouped the data, individuals who had *more* obligations and constraints were *less* likely to commit suicide.

In the 1970s, researchers dug deeper into the various ways that having a greater number of roles creates stress *and* offers benefit. Despite the possibility of role overload, the stress that arises from participating in multiple roles is more often outweighed by a net gratification. Working parents who take part in multiple important and even highly demanding roles can thus understand that the exhaustion or other stressors that arise are a part of the chaotically wrapped gift package that is a meaningful life.

I interviewed Robin Romm, the author of several books including *Double Bind*,[25] which includes a chapter from me on—you guessed it—working parenthood. Robin is unapologetic about the value of ambition, asserting, "There is a rich reward in pushing yourself and mastering your skill." Professional life was the focus for Robin during her twenties and thirties when she worked intensely hard to achieve professional success as an academic and author. But even as she committed herself to her work, Robin yearned to have a baby.

Getting pregnant wasn't easy for Robin. It took years of effort and medical intervention to have her first baby at the age of forty. Now she is mother to two sparkly-eyed daughters. She is intoxicated with motherhood, telling me they are "the best thing I've ever done."

Robin worked hard and managed to achieve a bonanza kind of success with a career that is flexible, a supportive partner, and a sincere dual commitment to professional and parental life. But there are plenty of moments when she struggles. She admits that there are constant practical challenges—like getting enough sleep!—and that her professional focus isn't now what it once was. Yet, Robin said, "having a baby is an incredible gift because it tosses you right into life in such a powerful way." And it turns out, she added, "parenting and writing enrich each other."

GETTING TO HAPPY WHEN WE CAN'T ELIMINATE CONFLICT

There is a bit of a contradiction here. On the one hand, living a life full of meaning and purpose helps you feel happier. On the other hand, so much meaning and purpose can wear you out and leave you conflict-ridden. Are you happy or unhappy? And if you're unhappy, can you turn that into happy?

The field of positive psychology explores these very questions. Sonja Lyubomirsky, a professor of psychology at the University of California, has spent her career focused on exploring the question of why some individuals are happier than others. Her and her colleagues' work identifies three distinct drivers of happiness: genetics, life circumstances, and intentional activities.[26]

Our genetics seem to account for a good chunk of happiness. In other words, a sizable portion of happiness belongs to the DNA lottery. But life circumstances, which we often assume to be the largest piece of the happiness pie, tend to account for much less than other factors.[27] We mistakenly think life circumstances matter more than they actually do because we overestimate the intensity and duration of our emotional reactions to them.[28] The third predictor of happiness is what happiness researchers call "intentional activities." These include activities such as acceptance, cultivating growth mindsets, gratitude, acts of kindness, and growing skills in work, parenting, and well-being—concepts we focus on in this book. Though estimates vary widely on how large an effect our intentional activities have, it's clear that we have considerable influence over a good chunk of our happiness by practicing these kinds of activities.

Social science helps us understand which intentional activities serve us best at work, as parents, and in the balance of our roles. It helps us learn how to manage our minds, our behaviors, and learn where it's useful to invest resources and where we should simply let go. Practicing these kinds of activities helps us build toward a better, happier working parenthood, even when our circumstances and genes won't budge.

WHAT ABOUT ROB?

Let's return to Rob, our single working-parent attorney who struggled to raise children while maintaining his professional life. The very struggles Rob experienced also helped him create more working-parent success and happiness. Maintaining that single working parenthood "is just about the hardest thing there is," Rob pointed out that his experiences gave him "a better sense of understanding and patience," which has been hugely advantageous when working with his clients. Single working parenthood made him a better parent, too. Parenting alone was painfully hard, but it also created opportunities to emotionally connect with his children that Rob doesn't think he otherwise would have had.

There's no question that work-family conflict showed up often. But Rob had also remained open to work-family enrichment. His enrichment mindset allowed the sometimes painful combination of experiences to help prompt the development of skills and a deeper happiness that he now enjoys in and outside of working parenthood.

. . . .

The TL/DR (Too Long, Didn't Read)

DEVELOP YOUR ENRICHMENT MINDSET

Work-family enrichment gets overlooked in our modern conversation about working parenthood. But as you get to know enrichment, you can learn how to elevate its influence and have its gifts shine more brightly.

Begin to shift toward a working-parent mindset of enrichment by asking yourself:

- *How does each role strengthen skills in the other? How does each make me more creative, skilled, or engaged in life in ways that offer benefit to the other?*

- *When things get rough in one domain, how does the other help to lessen the stress? How does having access to both work and parenting give me helpful perspective?*

- *In what ways is my life richer, fuller, and filled with a greater sense of purpose because I participate in both work and parenting?*

3

UNHOOK FROM
UNHELPFUL LABELS

It may be that which we call "a rose by any other
name would smell as sweet," but I should be loath to
see a rose on a maiden's breast substituted by a flower,
however beautiful and fragrant it might be, that
went by the name of the skunk lily.
—ALEXANDER HENRY

In the time it took her to read an essay I had shared about the gifts of work-family conflict, Erika was interrupted by her nine-year-old, asked to make pizza for her ten-year-old, got hungry and decided to join him for a slice, and responded to the knock on the door from a Jehovah's Witness offering a heads-up that Armageddon was coming. Erika neglected to read the final paragraphs in order to avoid murder by her youngest, age six, who was waiting for a bedtime story. Erika, a popular Boston-based comedian and mother of three, actively seeks humor in most of life's situations.

Work makes Erika both funnier and happier. She finds meaning in helping other people write jokes and in pointing out the absurdity of everyday life, most particularly in her life as a parent. She says, "I remember the exact magical moment when I decided I wanted to have lots of kids *just* so I could argue about screen time for 95 percent of my day."

Erika works on her writing during her kids' school hours, and she leaves for comedy shows before her kids are ready for bed. When she leaves for a gig, her son often points out that she is abandoning her children in favor of laughs in seedy bars. He is, after all, the child of a sarcastic comedian. But for Erika, that sharp wit cuts. Every time she activates her professional self and leaves her parenting self behind, guilt eats away at her. The belief that work makes her a "bad parent" also makes it much harder to be a funny one.

ACCURACY VERSUS WORKABILITY

Labels help us navigate a complex world by helping us to categorize roles, experiences, relationships, beliefs, feelings, and people. But attachment to labels, such as "bad parent," can interfere with seeing useful possibilities. Labeling our biggest challenges and most painful experiences—like, say, "work-family conflict" or "worst parent in the world"—drops us right into that fixed mindset we discussed in the previous chapter. For this reason, the workability of a label often trumps its accuracy.

Workability refers to how well a label works for you. What do I mean by "works for you"? Your label is workable if it helps you move *toward* the kind of working parent you most want to be. It fails to be workable if it causes you to move away from your best working-parent self.

For instance, labeling yourself as "the worst working parent" or working parenthood as a life "doomed to conflict" can drive you *away* from what my podcast cohost and friend Jill Stoddard calls "the me you want to be."[1] Formulated by the ACT experts Joseph Ciarrochi, Ann Bailey, and Russ Harris, this choice model shows that getting hooked on labels can propel you toward your less-than-ideal self—not what most of us are aiming for.[2]

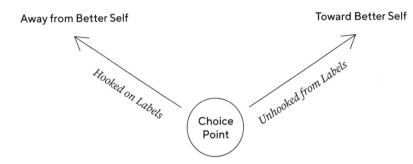

Let me explain how this works using a personal example. After my father died, I felt desperate for emotional support, and I turned to my closest friends, including my friend Alexandra. When Alexandra didn't reach out for weeks, I was deeply hurt. Then I became furious. My mind took a cue from my feelings and labeled her as "unreliable," "thoughtless," and "selfish." My actions followed suit. When she called a few weeks later, I didn't call her back. When she texted to say hi, I responded curtly that I was very busy. Ultimately, a third close friend intervened to let me know that Alexandra had been struggling mightily with her own recent life events. And, it turned out, she had been worried about me all along but thought that giving me space was the loving thing to do. Now she was frantic and losing sleep over how to make things right with me. I had been so wrapped up in labeling and my own emotional pain that I hadn't considered what was going on with her or that my behavior was causing her tremendous pain. Labeling her as a rotten friend had caused *me* to act like a rotten friend.

But there's no stopping our brains from labeling. Categorizing, a preverbal form of labeling, can be traced back to early human brain evolution. Research has localized some of the neurological activity that takes place when we label (or, in preverbal terms, categorize) items, experiences, and events to the more primitive areas of the brain.[3] Our tendency to notice and label maximizes efficiency and survival. Early human brains that easily got hooked on negative labels were much more likely to survive and reproduce than brains attaching to optimistic ideas were. Greater survival rates meant that those sensitive to negative labels were more likely to mate with other labelers and breed babies that were—you guessed it—increasingly predisposed to label. The conclusion of this evolutionary tale is that the brain we've evolved over millennia has a thinking style that skews toward perceiving, categorizing, and labeling danger or problems (even when there are none) and exaggerating the negative when it exists.

A tendency to focus on the negative was adaptive in early human times. It's far less helpful in a world where concerns over survival are less dominant than concerns over how to engage fully and effectively in complex, demanding roles. Harsh labels not only cause us to think in fixed-mindset ways but also make it much harder to focus on whatever it is that you're doing, whether it's work, parenting, or anything in between.

Sian Beilock is a cognitive scientist, president of Barnard College, author, mother, and an expert on performance and brain science. In her book *Choke,* she explores how negative labels interfere with our ability to perform in tasks and roles that matter to us.[4] In a podcast interview, she explained that pessimistic labels occupy our working memory—the part of our brain that helps with on-the-go thinking and decision-making.[5] Working memory, even for those with high cognitive horsepower, has a finite bandwidth. Negative labels lead to worries about our weaknesses, anticipation of failure, and thought-spirals about catastrophes sure to follow from our failures.

As Sian details in her book, the cost of negative labels for task performance has been shown across studies of athletic performance, work performance, and test performance. For example, when students from groups at the receiving end of negative labels are reminded of those bogus negative labels—for example, "Girls can't do math" or "Black people aren't very smart"—before an exam, their test performance drops significantly.[6] Neurological research confirms that negative labels actively occupy working memory, reducing our mental capacity to focus.[7] Harsh labeling causes mental resources that would otherwise be thinking through complicated tasks or connecting mindfully with small people we love to get diverted by anxious, pessimistic thoughts.

When negative, bogus, and generally unworkable labels weaken your performance, they can easily contribute to a vicious cycle. If you think you're a failure and then perform poorly, you've now confirmed to yourself that you indeed are a failure. Buying into your inherent failure as a worker, parent, or working parent then demotivates efforts to learn new skills (you'll fail, so why bother?) or ask for help (for fear of revealing your incompetence to others). The more you avoid tasks you feel incapable of doing, the fewer opportunities you have to become skilled in those tasks and the more you confirm what you originally feared.

But let's not jack up the negativity by harshly judging our harsh judgments. Be kind to your mind! Your cynical brain is trying to do you a solid by helping you survive. The self-directed mudslinging represents an ancient impulse to protect yourself from saber-toothed tigers. It's just that your brain's wiring doesn't account for the fact that saber-toothed tigers have gone extinct. That's why strategies to unhook from the harsh labels your mind generates come in handy.

CHOPPED

I love the Food Network hit *Chopped,* and not because I'm a great cook (you'd be wise to take me at my word). In the show, skilled chefs are charged with making tasty dishes with outrageous ingredients. The contestants create gastronomic delights with items such as goat brains, leftover pizza, marmite, and whole chicken in a can. The sound of the chicken coming out of the can alone will make you lose your appetite, so it's a good lesson in making delicious out of disgusting.

Making delicious from wacky or revolting items begins, of course, with a mindset of possibility. But the chefs have to get from point A (bizarre ingredients) to point B (high-end cuisine). That pathway requires viewing the ingredients in productive ways. Consider, for instance, that canned chicken can be viewed as "slimy" and "smelly" or "nauseating." Those labels might leave a chef feeling pretty stuck. But canned chicken can also be labeled as "protein." That label change can open up a whole menu of possibilities.

PRACTICE UNHOOKING

Like *Chopped* contestants, we working parents might not get to choose our ingredients. But even when we begin with components that are far from ideal, we can create masterpieces by learning to chop our labels wisely. It begins with unhooking from labels that aren't workable for us. Remember, workable labels are those that help you to move toward the kind of working parent you most want to be.

In my private practice, I frequently see working parents with unforgiving, conflict-oriented mindsets. "I'm a complete failure," one working mom recently declared to me. Nina had arrived for her therapy session ten minutes late and it was, for her, another sign of her many inadequacies and inabilities. As a high school teacher and single parent to two-year-old daughter Alynn, Nina's days needed to start early. Nina would be rushing out of the day care by 7:30 a.m., often leaving Alynn weeping and reaching out for her in vain. Nina would drive away, absorbed in shame, wondering what Alynn's adult therapy sessions would reveal about her parenting blunders. By the time she got to school, Nina would feel incompetence oozing out of her every pore. Her mind would get caught up in labels of "incompetent" and "failure," setting her on a course for feeling unfocused at work and snappish with her students.

Our work began by examining her thoughts with a touch of distance. The ancient Greek philosopher Aristotle noted, "It is the mark of an educated mind to be able to entertain a thought without accepting it." When you notice a thought about your working parenthood without accepting it, you open up an infinite number of possibilities for response and growth. First, though, you need to recognize that thoughts or feelings don't need to direct all that follows.

. . . . .

Try This

SIMON SAYS THOUGHTS AND FEELINGS
DON'T DICTATE YOUR CHOICES

Simon Says teaches young children the power of choice in whether to trust a direction given by someone with a voice of authority. In other words, kids learn that they can make choices different from what directives tell them. We can practice the same freewill response to the directions our own minds give us. Consider the following examples:

While you read these words (preferably aloud), do the *opposite*:

- "Make a fist with your hand."
- "Open your mouth."
- "Raise your shoulders."
- "Close your eyes."

Note that you can read and think these thoughts, then choose to do the exact opposite action. That's because thoughts don't dictate or predestine action or inaction!

. . . . .

Next, you can shift how you relate to your thoughts. This practice begins with unhooking, and it can be done through a variety of practices. One of them is quite simple: remembering that labels are words, not facts. Remember, too, that words don't predetermine your behavioral choices. When you notice a common label, remind yourself that thoughts are just thoughts by using the preface, "I'm having the thought that . . ." or "I am using the label of . . ." This simple strategy creates distance between what psychologists call the "observing self" and the thought itself. You're letting your mind notice that it lives in a compendium of thoughts.

From there, strive to pay less attention to fixed-mindset descriptors such as "unbearable" and "impossible" and orient your attention toward more measured, enrichment-mindset terms such as "uncomfortable" and "challenging." Loosening the hold of rigid labels—particularly those that prevent you from seeing the good things that come out of the conflict or that discount the complexity of your reality—is an important step in changing your working-parent mindset.

For the really sticky thoughts, you can go a step further with a word game called Milk, Milk, Milk.[8] Here's how it goes: Think about the word *milk*. What image comes to your mind? What reactions do you notice in your body? If you enjoy a cold glass of milk, maybe you find yourself salivating. If you dislike it, maybe you get a bit queasy. Just *thinking* of four letters associated with the sounds and the image we associate with a white liquid we pilfer from our bovine friends causes a distinct, observable reaction in your body. Such is the power of our attachment to words. But we can reduce the reaction in our minds and bodies to words by unhooking from the literal meaning of the word itself. To unhook, say the word *milk* out loud. Repeat it as fast as you can for a full minute. Go ahead, set your timer and do it. (Try it! This exercise will surprise you with a realization of how bizarre language is.)

Once you've completed that exercise, you'll notice that the word *milk* has lost its oomph. Now it just sounds like . . . sounds. Maybe the sounds even seem nonsensical. The link between those sounds and the idea of that cool glass of white liquid has relaxed. You can apply the same word game strategy to the word or words that you most commonly associate with your working parenthood.

FLEX YOUR LABELS

Labels serve you best when they help you engage in strategic ways. The most workable labels leave room to sort out a value-consistent path forward, no matter where you begin. They're the kinds of words that will motivate you to keep trying when things get hard or to quit what isn't working in order to experiment with different strategies. They will also help you to be resourceful and willing to tolerate discomfort in the learning process. Such labels link up with an enrichment mindset because they assume that you can end in a different place than you started. They suggest that it's worth it to continue trying until you do.

Shifting which labels you put your attention on can result in rapid changes to how you endure challenges, as it did in a laboratory study where college students were asked to submerge their hands in ice-cold water.[9] Researchers manipulated the experimental condition by casually revealing a folder with either the label "Pain Study" or "Discomfort Study" to participants. Those shown the "Discomfort" label reported less subjective unpleasantness and were more willing to withstand the cold water. The more benign label reduced both the experience of discomfort and the willingness to withstand the discomfort. Labels shape our mindset, impacting our experience and behavioral choices.

Incredibly, labels impact us at the neurological level, too. You've probably heard of the placebo effect: when an inactive treatment, such as a sugar pill, is believed to contain active medicine, many individuals have a response akin to taking active medicine.[10] For instance, in a study in which fake pain relievers were given to study participants, fMRI analysis revealed decreased brain activity in the areas of the brain associated with pain sensitivity.[11] Buying into labels that acknowledge discomforts in workable ways creates neurological adaptations that result in a less painful experience.

Labels matter because they shape our mindsets. Or as William James, the father of American psychology, noted, "My experience is what I agree to attend to." We can use this idea to our advantage by carefully choosing which labels we pay attention to.

. . . . .

Pause to Take Note of Your Working-Parent Labels

This curiosity exercise seeks to help you identify some of the words your mind regularly attaches to working parenthood. These might be words associated with working parenthood generally or words associated specifically with your working parenthood. Be on the lookout for words such as:

- *Conflict*
- *Impossible*
- *Unfair*
- *Wrong*

And don't overlook more positive or nuanced words, such as:

- *Meaningful*
- *Busy*
- *Full*
- *Interesting*

Noticing both gives you more choice in which to attend to. Then try out the following steps:

STEP 1: *Pause.*
Our mind is constantly chattering away, clouding our ability to notice particular thoughts. To achieve greater clarity, you're going to have to pause. Use the brief moments on your commute, after your children go to bed, during a transition between tasks, or even while you pop your little imps in front of an electronic babysitter, while folding laundry, just before you get out of bed in the morning, or during a shower.

STEP 2: *Notice your body.*
Fish discover water last. You know, because it's always *there.* The same thing goes with thoughts. The practice of noticing what's going on in your mind begins by taking a step *away* from the mind. Exit the fishbowl of your thoughts so that you can notice them. Shift attention away from your mind into your body. For example, if you are sitting, *notice* that you are sitting. Notice the sensations of the chair under your bottom, feel the pressure of the ground on the balls of your feet. If you are showering, pay attention to how the water feels against your skin. Spend a minute or two just noticing your body, and return to noticing whatever sensation you've chosen when your attention returns to thoughts. (This will happen repeatedly for most people!)

STEP 3: *Note your thoughts.*
After spending a few minutes noticing sensations, you are more likely to return to your thoughts with greater

awareness. You'll be the wise fish who knows you live in the water. Note the kinds of thoughts that arise when it comes to working parenthood. Ask yourself:

- *What words do I associate with working parenthood?*

- *What labels do I apply to myself as a working parent?*

- *What are my common assumptions about what it means to be a working parent?*

- *What do I get most incensed or anxious or guilty about in my working parenthood?*

. . . . .

COURAGEOUS ACTS OF SELF-COMPASSION

Once you've begun to identify and unhook from your stinkin' thinkin', it's time to get courageous in action. Action is where the rubber meets the road on well-being because, for one thing, you have more influence over your behavior than you have over your thoughts and feelings. And actions matter because they are the imprint you leave on the world. Consider this: we wouldn't remember Martin Luther King Jr., Mahatma Gandhi, or Mother Teresa if they had only *thought* about changing the world but never had the courage to *do* anything with their ideas. It turns out that the individuals who changed the course of history each experienced sadness, anger, worry, and self-doubt. They acted in courageous ways even when uncomfortable internal experiences were along for the ride.

Like these titans of history, you, too, can make choices to act in ways that align with your values—even when harsh thoughts and uncomfortable feelings show up.

Perhaps paradoxically, one of the most effective ways to get courageous in action is to engage in practices of what psychologists call "self-compassion." It may seem like a meager response to great injustices, but self-compassion has been explored extensively in social science and revealed to be powerful in inducing optimism, happiness, and effective engagement in various life roles.[12] Self-compassion feeds the psychological reservoir necessary for persisting in what you care about, including fighting for justice.

Self-compassion consists of three core components. The first is being kind and understanding toward yourself. It's easy enough to offer kindness to people you care about, including your children or close friends, but it can be challenging to offer it to yourself. Self-compassion involves building that muscle. You can ask yourself what sorts of kind statements you might make to a friend in your same situation and then repeat those phrases for yourself. Or you can talk to yourself in the third person, acting as if you were your own close friend coming in to offer reassurance and compassion. Find ways to treat yourself kindly as you endure what's hard.

The second component of self-compassion is common humanity. Though you may feel alone, pain is an unavoidable part of the common human experience. Ironically, so is loneliness. When you recognize that painful feelings, even those of isolation, occur for everyone, you can use them to connect to others. For instance, you can grow connection by remembering that in the very moment you are reading this, working parents the world over are feeling guilty, pissed off with their bosses (and partners, and parents-in-law), and like their brains might break from pressure. Remember that as a working parent, you are part of a huge tribe of people struggling to get through a complicated life that requires a lot of you. You are not alone.

The final element of self-compassion is holding your painful experiences, feelings, and thoughts with mindful awareness. That might sound like a corny bromide, but allowing yourself to experience your sadness, the unhappy story, your incapacitating exhaustion, and maybe even fury can help you manage those experiences more strategically. When you hold those feelings with kindness and a sense of common humanity, you allow yourself to *feel* your feelings before you take any kind of action.

Think of self-compassion like an alternative way to respond to a painful stubbed toe. Where you might feel compelled to scream profanities at no one in particular, you could instead take a breath and feel the pain with a sense of self-kindness. You might pause to notice how the pain moves through you, growing more intense before it begins to diminish. No matter how you respond, of course, that toe will hurt. But with self-compassion in hand, you're less likely to feel like a jackass in your response. And if despite your best efforts you do act like a jackass, self-compassion offers tools for responding to yourself with grace and kindness. Giving yourself some time to breathe, to feel the pain, and to be gentle with yourself makes it easier to eventually return to whatever else you need to do.

In our work together, Nina, my tired working-parent patient, loosened the grip her mind had held of "failure mom and teacher" labels. Whenever those thoughts came up, she'd practice observing them and then note to herself, "I'm having the thought that I'm a failure. It's just a thought." She'd follow up the "I'm a failure" label with more helpful and nuanced ones, such as "I'm a working parent who multitasks pretty well, considering . . . life," and "I'm a working parent committed to loving my kid and doing my job, even if it feels messy sometimes."

This new way of approaching her old, unforgiving labels opened her up to working-parent enrichment. She began to turn her attention toward the various ways that her working parenthood benefited her daughter, including by allowing her daughter to create a closer bond with other caregivers and by modeling for her daughter how loving adults navigate demands in multiple realms of life. And she began to see the benefit for her students in her ability to model the challenges and gifts of participating in both work and parent roles. This enrichment mindset loosened the hold that her harsh thinking had on her and helped Nina get more comfortable with asking for help when she needed it.

But, Nina told me, not everything changed just because her mindset had shifted: "I still feel like Alynn is a handful, I'm still always short on time, and I still haven't figured out how to take a much-needed break." Nina put self-compassion into practice in those rougher moments—pausing, noticing, and taking a soothing breath of self-kindness to remember that, like many working parents, she carried a load that sometimes felt unbearable.

Nina also reflected on the areas that she had more control over. With a kinder attitude toward herself, she began to contemplate specific ways she could make things easier on herself, and she had the insight that being more present wherever she was would help her feel less overwhelmed and guilty. At home, she developed a routine of placing her phone and computer out of reach in a kitchen drawer between the time she got home and when Alynn went to bed. At school, when she would notice thoughts straying to her daughter, she would use an imagery technique of placing those thoughts in a box and then gently closing the box and setting it aside until a time she could more mindfully open the box to study them.

It wasn't easy, but Nina found her frustration and self-criticism shifting as she turned toward the labels of pride, effectiveness, and strength she had built through her working-parent journey.

THE WOPO FLOW

Back to my comedian friend Erika. Although she didn't have time to read the last few paragraphs of the essay I had sent her, Erika absorbed the idea that changing her own label of working parenthood might have some value. Perhaps instead of seeing the relationship between her professional and parenting roles as wholly conflicting, she could begin to reframe it as a synergistic relationship. Perhaps she could begin to develop an appreciation of the flow between work and parenting roles, or as she coined it: *WoPo Flow*.

I love the term that Erika came up with because the flow of water is a central theme in Taoism, an ancient Eastern philosophy that, as I mentioned earlier, guides much of my thinking on working parenthood.[13] Water embodies both a soft passiveness in its tendency to flow to the lowest place and a persistent assertiveness as it carves a path for itself, even in the harshest environments. Water does not fight with forces that oppose it but instead willingly moves toward the places where its flow will be maximized. Sometimes this movement lands it in surprising paths, and sometimes this movement results in the creation of awe-inspiring wonders (like, say, the Grand Canyon). A label like *WoPo Flow* can open our eyes to the various ways that we can move more fluidly and capture unanticipated gifts.

By shifting your labels, you can more actively cultivate the enrichment mindset that helps open up new possibilities for how to engage in working parenthood. Whether you're a fan of *WoPo Flow*, work-family enrichment, work-parent enhancement, work-family balance, or anything else, choose labels that open more options than "work-family conflict."

Erika tested this for herself, texting me to share the results of her one-woman experiment. The next time she absented herself from the role of parent to do a comedy show, she made a deliberate choice not to apologize for leaving. Instead, she asked her sarcastic son if he was proud of her. He surprised her by saying that he loved that she did comedy. Her change in label lead to a different action from Erika, which created an opening for her son to respond in a new way to her work. Erika told me that the effect of changing her label was "like a weight lifted."

The important take-home message isn't generating any specific label. Rather, your awareness of how labels can rigidly orient your mind in unhelpful ways empowers you to use *your* preferred vocabulary to move away from labeling rigidity and toward greater flexibility. Loosening the hold of rigid labels—particularly those that orient you toward a conflict mindset and prevent you from seeing the good things that come out of the conflict—is an important step in changing your working-parent experience.

* *

The TL/DR (Too Long, Didn't Read)

UNHOOK FROM UNHELPFUL LABELS

The next time you notice guilt, overwhelm, or rage in working parenthood, use your discomfort as an opportunity to practice unhooking from rigid and unhelpful labels using a three-step approach:

STEP 1: *Notice common labels.* Notice how you label your most uncomfortable working-parent experiences. What are the words that float through your mind as you experience or reflect on your working parenthood?

STEP 2: *Create distance between you and that label by describing the words as labels, thoughts, or descriptions.* Practice adding the preface "I'm labeling myself/my child/my working parenthood . . .," "Giddyap [thought]," or "I'm having the thought that . . ." to common labels. Apply the exercise Milk, Milk, Milk to your most powerful labels.

STEP 3: *Turn your attention away from unhelpful labels and toward alternative, flexible labels for your working-parent experiences.* Consider modifying "I can't" to phrases like "I haven't yet figured out," or "I'm still learning how to . . ." Experiment with switching out "hopeless" and "insurmountable" to "painful," "tricky," or even "educational," "folly," and, for fun, "catawampus."

4

SPIN YOUR STORY

Story, as it turns out, was crucial to our evolution—
more so than opposable thumbs. Opposable thumbs
let us hang on; story told us what to hang on to.

—LISA CRON

Shel Silverstein's classic story *The Missing Piece* tells the simple tale of a circle that is missing a piece and is unhappy. Seeking to make itself whole, the circle sets off to find its missing piece.[1] As it journeys, it sings a sweet song, meets friends, and has exciting adventures. Eventually the circle finds its perfect piece. But instead of feeling content, it discovers that it can no longer enjoy singing (its mouth is now full of the perfect piece) or stop to talk to its old friends (it now rolls too efficiently to slow down). It realizes that finding its missing piece created a new set of desires and problems. So it gently sets down its missing piece and returns—this time with delighted awareness—to its original quest of searching for its missing piece.

Like the circle, the stories we develop to understand our experiences contribute to our emotions and reactions. In other words, the events in our lives matter, but they don't dictate the outcomes. While circumstances have less influence than most of us assume,[2] the stories we tell ourselves have *far more* influence than we realize. Stories guide how we feel, what we do, and even how skillful we become. They have huge influence over our lives. Luckily, we have a hand in designing those stories.

But telling a happy story in order to feel good isn't easy. Plus, it's not a magic bullet that can transform working parenthood into a simple or stress-free life. That's okay though, because a happier story isn't the ultimate goal. Instead, our goal is to craft stories that are more workable. That is, we aim to edit our working-parent stories into narratives that guide us toward more meaningful and effective living.

If this notion sounds similar to ideas presented in the previous chapter, that's because stories are extensions of labels. While labels are single (or several-word) descriptions of an experience, feeling, or event, stories offer a bit more. Most stories have a beginning, a middle, and an end. They also have main characters and side characters, and there's often a moral or other lesson learned. Stories have enormous importance in our lives because they help us make sense of our circumstances, crises, the people in our lives, and the meaning of it all. The stories we tell about our lives help us understand where we've been, where we are, and where we'd like to go next.

OUR DEFAULT WORKING-PARENT STORIES

The stories that permeate working parenthood often focus exclusively on the challenges. I'll admit to a reflexive story line of my own that goes something like this: "Working parenthood shouldn't be this hard," and "If I had more support, then everything would be so much easier." The familiar story of "Everyone else is doing this better than me and most of them are judging me for my performance" crops up pretty often for me, too. Not surprisingly, when I get caught up in these story lines, they leave me feeling angry with the people who "should" be helping me, pitying myself when they don't, feeling anxious around peers, and yelling at whatever moving body happens to be crossing my line of vision.

Not to sound defensive, but I'd like to point out that the problem of my narrative is not one of accuracy. As a parent who carries much of the mental and task load of parenting, plus my work responsibilities, I really *could* use more help and I really *do* feel overwhelmed much of the time. My anxiety, overwhelm, and anger are not inaccurate, nor are they problems in and of themselves. Anger, for one, is a natural and healthy part of the human experience, and it's an emotion that can point to real injustice. I don't want to ignore my emotions because they might offer important information and elicit productive action.

I do, however, want to pay attention when my emotions spur a story line that doesn't help me out. Or worse, when my story causes me to act in ways that move me away from the kind of person I want to be or life I want to live. In other words, I need to recognize when stories aren't workable for me.

My reflexive story line of injustice, for example, overlooks the important fact that my spouse is overworked in a job that is often inflexible. It also neglects to account for the reality that he rarely (as in, never) responds to my expressions of white-hot rage by offering more help, changing his career path, or even giving me a sympathetic hug (word to the wise—righteous rage seldom breeds compassion from most partners). Getting caught up in the "shoulds" often leaves me right where I started, just a whole lot crankier and less likely to act like the kind, motivating, and compassionate parent, spouse, and therapist I most want to be. Perhaps worst of all, my default story line causes me to overlook one of my greatest gifts:

a life so jam-packed with meaningful roles and responsibilities that I get worn out.

SPIDERS SPIN WEBS, HUMANS TELL STORIES

Evolutionary scholars explain that the human brain developed the capacity for storytelling because stories themselves are critical for functioning in a collective society. Whether common stories were about religion, the value of money, or expectations around acceptable village behavior, buy-in to shared narratives allowed large numbers of humans living together to cooperate successfully.[3] Those stories matter for individual functioning too, guiding us in understanding the complexities of our environment and making strategic choices in each of our life roles.

Jonathan Adler, a professor of psychology at Olin College of Engineering, studies narrative identity. He explained to me that storytelling is core to what it means to be human, saying, "Spiders spin webs, bower birds build bowers, and humans tell stories. That's the thing we do, and stories are actually an incredibly efficient and effective tool for navigating our extremely complex niche." Work from Jon and other narrative researchers has revealed that the way we tell our stories impacts our well-being.[4]

Jon is a working parent of two elementary-aged children. Knowing the power of stories, he prioritizes the skillful telling of them. He reflected that his own narrative identity underwent a shift once he became a working parent. For one thing, as he explained, he came out as gay relatively late in life because he wanted other features—such as his passion for stories, for scientific inquiry, and for having a positive impact through his work—to be the lead descriptors of his public reputation. But, he said, "being a gay dad feels like *yes*. That gives me the right level of 'that does make me feel like an outsider to mainstream society to the right degree' and makes me feel landed in mainstream society to the right degree."

Jon is intentional about reflecting on his personal narrative and seeking out purpose inside of difficulty because he knows it's important for his own well-being. In fact, research from Jon and his colleagues consistently shows that how you make sense of what has happened to you through your narrative is incrementally more predictive of your well-being than the events themselves.[5] In one study, Jon and his colleagues showed the power of storytelling for parents who had a child on the autism spectrum. These parents, not surprisingly, experienced chronic stress. But developing a narrative that more effectively integrated meaning into caregiving was associated with less DNA damage and greater biological stress resilience.[6]

Telling stories in which we identify opportunities for personal and interpersonal growth inside of challenges, as well as connection to meaning through difficult experiences, can help us tolerate difficulty and transform it into something worthwhile. Helping individuals accomplish this narrative task is, in fact, one of the main objectives of psychotherapy.

Finding the Workable Threads

Having an unhappy working-parent story, often a perfectly accurate one, brings many patients into therapy. Consider the following common unworkable working-parent stories:

- I'm falling short everywhere.

- Everyone at the school playground and in the office is judging me.

- I'm failing my kids in ways that will damage them permanently.

- I'm doing badly enough at work that my career and my friendships are sure to go up in smoke.

Your mind, like all human minds, is a storytelling machine designed to keep you safe and make sure that you do a good job. It's also worth noting that your mind likes to entertain you. A boring show isn't likely to keep you engaged for long—not when there's salacious reality shows, provocative politicians, and antagonistic sports rivalries to captivate you! Against your better judgment, entertaining and unworkable stories are more likely to absorb you than the dry stuff. But getting absorbed in an unworkable story is something you can influence once you learn how to relate to your story. Once you take a pause to notice what the story is, you can develop intentionality about where you choose to rest your attention. Then you might try designing more workable stories to get absorbed by.

· · · · ·

Pause to Reflect on the Workability of Your Working-Parent Story

To explore whether a working-parent story is workable for you, ask yourself the following kinds of questions:

- *What story or stories am I telling myself about working parenthood?*

- *Does the story my mind is telling me help guide me toward becoming the best version of myself?*

- *Does the story motivate me to engage in the world in ways that I'll look back on with pride and purpose?*

- *Does my story keep me on track in moving toward meaningful goals in my life?*

· · · · ·

If you discover that your story isn't helping you as much as you'd like, then your job is to tweak your relationship to the story as well as the story itself. Or as Jon explained to me, "There are different ways of telling the same series of events." In other words, choosing the narrative that supports your well-being and your effectiveness at work and in parenting is something you can work toward.

The steps to doing this can be simple. You can begin by recognizing that while you are a character in your story, you're also the narrator. As narrator, you can make choices about which plotlines are worth emphasizing, what tone to take, and even which characters and circumstances you might move to the fringes of the central plotline.

From there, you can actively seek to view your story in more workable ways, as individuals in one laboratory study were prompted to do. Participants who had experienced recent stressful events were brought in to watch film clips. They were coached to view the video situations in a more "positive light." The instructions asked participants to "imagine advice that you could give to the characters in the film clip to make them feel better" or to "think about the good things they might learn from this experience." And participants were told to "keep in mind that even though a situation may be painful in the moment, in the long run it could make one's life better or have unexpected good outcomes." For individuals with higher levels of stress and stronger ability to rework their story, fewer depressive symptoms arose after the film clips compared to those who were less skilled in doing the story edits.[7] Growing your ability to see things in a positive light, practicing generating ideas for how to bear difficulties when things are hard, and working to see the possibilities of growth and other good things coming out of difficult circumstances define the skill of spinning workable stories.

But seeing "good things" doesn't just mean roses and sunshine. Even if there aren't gifts of gratitude to uncover inside of your circumstances, you might still have helpful opportunities to learn about yourself, others, and your connection to the world. For instance, you might probe more deeply into what your emotions and personal values say about your life story. You can use the following questions to guide this reflection:

- What are my feelings telling me about how I'm experiencing this event?

- Can I learn more about what's important to me?

- What have I learned about my triggers that can be helpful for managing myself or my situation better in the future?

- How do I want to integrate this information into how I understand myself?

You might also use your difficult experiences to learn about how you want the story of relating to others to read. Ask yourself:

- What is my internal experience telling me about what is missing or isn't going well in work relationships or in parenting my child?

- What am I wishing were different in my relationships?

- How can I use that information to understand what kind of a relational world I want to build?

Finally, you can use your experiences to learn about what you value and reflect on how you want to show up in the world:

- If I'm having big feelings or painful thoughts, they might be pointing to the fact that there is something very important to me about this situation. What is important here?

- How can I use that information to flesh out a story that better guides me toward what I care about most?

Editing Horror Stories

Editing a working-parent story infused with injustice and impossibility can feel like being advised to shut your eyes tightly, stick your fingers in your ears, and sing loudly in order to convince yourself that your infant's screams sound more like a mellow tune than nails on a chalkboard. But we can beneficially edit stories without denying painful realities.

This kind of editing can even be applied to life experiences as extreme as surviving a Nazi death camp. The psychiatrist, neurologist, and Holocaust survivor Viktor Frankl explored the value of a meaningful life story, even in the most barbaric of circumstances, in his book *Man's Search for Meaning.*[8] Frankl had already begun to develop his treatment approach, called logotherapy, before World War II began. The treatment was based on the idea that finding meaning in life is the primary motivating force for humans. Like millions of Jews across Europe, Frankl was forcibly removed from his home and his work and interned in unfathomably inhumane conditions of the concentration camps. There, he reflected on whether searching for meaning under conditions of severe deprivation and daily brutality still held value. Perhaps surprisingly, Frankl concluded that it might be the most important thing any victim could do. After all, as the German philosopher Friedrich Nietzsche observed, "He who has a why to live can bear almost any how." A good story provides you with that "why."

Of course, it would have done concentration camp victims little good to pretend to themselves that life was just as it should be. But even in conditions like those of extermination camps, Frankl suggested that it was useful to suffuse the world around and inside of you with meaning. And he explained how you could.

First, a person could find meaning by being aware of how they made a difference through everyday actions, sometimes by impacting those encountered in daily interactions or through work done to better the world. A person could find meaning, too, by looking for and emphasizing connection to others or connection to something far bigger than any one individual (as some do through spirituality or through work and hobbies). A person could even find meaning by expanding their ideas about what suffering itself signified. For instance, you might find meaning in suffering by using your attitude as a model for others dealing with similar challenges, or by using your suffering to motivate making positive change in the world, showing compassion to others, or by growing your ideas or skills. Or a person could ask themself what lessons they could take away from the suffering they'd endured (or were continuing to endure). Using these strategies to flesh out your story line can help you clarify a sense of purpose, even inside pain.

What to Do When Reality Is a Sow's Ear

The horrific conditions of Nazi extermination camps are, thankfully, far removed from most modern working parents' lives. Yet there are powerful lessons we can adopt from Frankl's experiences. As the lovable television chef and author Julia Child once noted, "You can't turn a sow's ear into a Veal Orloff. But you can do something very good with a sow's ear." We can learn to find meaning and write helpful stories, and we can and should do so while acknowledging our reality. The alternative—pretending challenges away—puts us in danger of not asking for help, not taking restorative breaks, or not fighting for marital, political, and cultural progress. Plus, our brain isn't likely to buy into a bold-faced lie of ease and happiness while our body endures the reality of daily struggles.

Even if you could somehow suspend your disbelief, that might be counterproductive. Psychologists have termed the pressure to do so "toxic positivity" because this kind of thinking denies, minimizes, and invalidates negative thoughts or emotions. Attempts to disregard all negative feelings and thoughts makes you feel bad about feeling bad. You add shame, hopelessness, and alienation from others to the negative experience you started with. In other words, rigidly looking on the bright side is not the recommendation for a story edit. Instead, take Frankl's suggestion to find the meaning—even inside of horror stories.

Mark, a cruise ship room attendant, brought to life how to craft a story that appreciates the silver linings and the quest to find a "why." At the time of our interview, Mark's two children were ages six months and four years. As we chatted about parenting, I shared with Mark the idea of finding gifts inside of work-family conflict. He eagerly responded by telling me how he had worked hard to change his working-parent story.

Mark had been employed as a cruise ship attendant before he married and became a parent. The job was easier before he became a family man because for Mark, "going to work" means being apart from his small children and his beloved wife for several months at a time. And the work itself is emotionally hard and physically taxing. Mark is charged with being responsive to guests around the clock, making sure they feel well cared for, no matter how demanding they might be.

After becoming a father, Mark grappled with a difficult decision of whether he would continue in this line of work. But in the Philippines, where he lived, it can be hard to earn a living wage, let alone a wage that provides for a good quality of life. Mark shared that a close friend of his lived with his mother because he couldn't make ends meet on a nursing salary. Mark, on the other hand, had been able to use the income he earned on the cruise ship to buy a house for his wife and children, and he recently invested in a small taxi business that he hoped would eventually allow him to retire from work on cruise ships.

In the meantime, Mark was seeking to make the job fulfilling by finding joy in connecting with the children of families on the ship until he can return home to his own. Mark told me that he actively practiced thinking about the people on the cruise ship as his temporary family. He especially loved guests with small children because they reminded him of his own. And he regularly reminded himself that he was building a better life for his family by remaining in the cruise ship business and working as hard as he possibly could to provide his family with a better life.

Without a doubt, Mark longed for his family. His yearning to see his children and wife more didn't disappear under his ability to craft a story highlighting the silver linings of his work. But by finding meaning in his work, the challenges of his working parenthood become more tolerable and the gifts far more accessible.

ADAPTIVE STORYTELLING

All life stories are adaptable in their telling, and skilled storytellers take advantage of this. So do therapists. Successful psychotherapy often involves a patient articulating, dismantling, and then reconceptualizing their life story for the purpose of crafting a more life-enhancing version of that story. Reinterpreting your circumstances enhances your ability to transcend difficult circumstances in ways that can heal and empower you.

Strategic storytelling has been proven to help patients with a wide range of painful conditions and experiences. For example, in a study that examined the effect of letter writing, patients with chronic pain conditions who made meaning of their anger through their narratives experienced improvement in pain severity.[9] Research with individuals experiencing a recent breakup found that adopting stories that emphasized positive outcomes, instead of focusing on the negative circumstances, led to decreased post-breakup distress.[10] More broadly, studies have found that the edits to patients' life stories that occur through therapy are predictive of treatment gains.[11] Outside of therapy, too, a large and growing body of research shows that making meaning through expressive writing strengthens our physical and mental health. James Pennebaker, a University of Texas professor of psychology, and his colleagues have spent decades demonstrating how the process of writing helps individuals find meaning in painful experiences through the development of a coherent story.[12] Through dozens of studies, these researchers have shown that expressive writing—the form that helps individuals refine their narratives about hardships—leads to improved well-being.[13] We can each edit our life stories written, aloud, or through deep reflection, and in- or outside of a therapist's office.

A STORY OF ACCEPTANCE AND CHANGE

Remember that a good story edit takes the nuances of your circumstances into account and keeps workability as the guide for what to retain and what to set to the side. We've also come to understand that effective story editing needs to account for whether change is possible.

Good storytelling can, for instance, help you make changes when it's time to do so. Maybe your story edit helps you see that you need to renegotiate household chores with your partner, take a vacation, or up day-care hours. Or perhaps your story is highlighting that your job is not a good fit and that it's time to consider applying for a new one. When you can influence your life circumstances, making a change is more important than accepting a situation as it is.

But research shows that when stressors are outside of your control, acceptance of what can't be changed (at least for the moment) and highlighting silver linings are the most productive way to work with your story. Silver linings can include connecting to deeply painful emotions (which help us connect to ourselves and others), looking for the "helpers" (as the beloved Mister Rogers recommended), or finding meaning in the challenges you endure.[14] Making changes when change is possible and finding the silver lining when it isn't reflect the wisdom of the Serenity Prayer. The Serenity Prayer guides us to accept the things we cannot change, change the things we can, and learn to recognize the difference between them. It's this wisdom that should be applied as you formulate your story edit.

Like Mark, you can reflect on what can and can't be changed in the common stories of your working parenthood. For the domains where change isn't currently possible, consider how you can make meaning from challenges or how you might locate positive outcomes to emphasize. For the domains where change is possible, consider how your story can help you connect to a valued way of acting or toward making a change that helps you build your life in ways that matter to you.

. . . .

The TL/DR (Too Long, Didn't Read)

EDITING YOUR WORKING-PARENT STORY

Accurate as they may be, the way we tell our working-parent stories can be unhelpful. To begin, consider how well your story is working for you. If it feels as though it's getting in the way of your ability to act in line with your values or build toward a better life, consider the following kinds of edits:

- *Find the gifts.* In areas outside of your control, find the silver lining by considering how challenges and frustrations might yield surprising gifts. Know that there may be gifts available within the challenges that you have not yet considered (and get fired up to learn more in part 2, "From the Feet—How to Working-Parent More Strategically"). Use these realizations to cultivate a mindset that sees the possibilities for enrichment.

- *Connect to your values.* In areas where change might be possible, consider using your story to prompt actions aligned with your core working-parent values.

PART TWO

FROM THE FEET

How to Working-Parent
More Strategically

It is good to have an end to journey towards,
but it is the journey that matters in the end.
—URSULA K. LE GUIN

5

DO THE RIGHT HARD THINGS (THE RIGHT WAY)

I see your fear, and it's big. I also see your courage,
and it's bigger. We can do hard things.
—GLENNON DOYLE

In the first two years of being a working parent, I found my mind caught in a ceaseless refrain: If only we had family that lived closer, I wouldn't be such a guilty, overwhelmed disaster. I went green with envy when working-parent friends, colleagues, or even patients described being able to call on the grandparents for assistance in a pinch. I fantasized constantly about how my kid would thrive more and how I would be a Zen beacon of tranquility if only my energetic and loving mother-in-law were caring for my child while I worked, instead of the virtual strangers I paid.

The intensity of my working-parent guilt, overwhelm, and fear hit a new zenith when I became pregnant with my second child. I panicked about a practical conundrum—what to do with my two-year-old during the hours I was bringing his sibling into the world.

What if labor took so long that whomever he was with would need to be relieved? Would my husband have to leave to get him while I was in the throes of labor? And what would happen if I went into labor in the middle of the night? Would I have to wake my small child to take him to someone he barely knew (and who likely had their own children and a job) all while I was in enormous physical pain? My husband tried to reassure me that if all else failed, we could bring our son with us to the hospital. But the idea of having him nearby, nightmarishly exposed to the blood and gore of a baby being born, didn't sound awesome.

Feeling out to sea without a life raft, I tentatively began asking friends, babysitters, our day-care provider, and neighbors if they'd be willing to buoy me. Everyone responded graciously, allowing themselves to be entered into my painstakingly detailed document, with plans A through H. I was grateful, I really was. But still, I kept wishing I could rely on my own family. I hoped against hope that the onset of labor would be well timed and take long enough that my parents could complete a cross-country flight to be with my older son while I brought his new brother into the world.

Three weeks before my due date, a leaky feeling woke me at midnight—my water had broken. I wasn't experiencing contractions yet, but the doctor on call told me to come in for an examination. Thinking I had a gift of time, I called my parents in California to ask about the possibility of them coming to Boston that very night. My dad responded without hesitation—in the wrong direction. He told me he had a work obligation, so they couldn't come. I was left deflating in both body and spirit.

After my exam, the doctor told me to go home until the contractions began in earnest. I spent those predawn hours emailing patients and colleagues to let them know all meetings would be suspended until after my maternity leave ended. And I spent time reflecting and *feeling*.

I was a seasoned-enough psychologist to know I was mourning not having the family support I wanted during a significant life moment. I knew it would be wise to make space for my feelings. They offered important information about what mattered most to me. It was pretty obvious I wanted emotional support and a way to ensure that my toddler was well cared for while I attended to the business of our newest family member. So I let myself feel sad, worried, even deserted. Then I took a breath and asked myself some reorienting questions: "Could I access a feeling of being cared for, even if the setup wasn't my ideal one? What options actually were possible for this delivery? And among the options that were possible, what was the best, most value-aligned path forward for my growing family and me?"

At 6 a.m. I checked in with my husband, took a breath, and initiated plan D—"the weekend, daytime plan." Just seconds after texting my working-parent friend with two little ones of her own, she wrote me back: "Yes, bring him over! We would be so happy to watch him as long as you need!"

That day, while my two-year-old played at my friend's house, I brought my second boy into the world. I remember holding my velvety soft infant, glorying in what I had accomplished. I felt like an Amazon for transcending the various pains in the lead-up to this miraculous moment! True, many people shared credit for the achievements: my sweet friend who so generously watched my toddler, my husband who soothed me throughout the intense laboring process, and the incredible nursing staff in the maternity ward. But for a moment, I connected to an overpowering pride in myself. From a place of feeling entirely adrift and without a lifeline, I had tapped my strength and built a support raft. When things felt bleak, I had recruited my inner wisdom to chart this course.

We working parents do hard things. We are often without any alternatives than to figure out how to chart a course through choppy, uncertain waters. Accepting that uncertainty, fear, overwhelm, frustration, sadness, anger, self-doubt, and all kinds of pain will accompany us on our working-parent journeys helps us to show up for those hard things. Connecting to what matters to us provides a reason to weather the discomfort and do them. And the actual *doing* of them? Now that's where we procure superhero-level wisdom.

PRACTICAL WISDOM

The wisdom that grows through varied life roles is a special kind of wisdom—it's practical. Professor of psychology Barry Schwartz and professor of political science Kenneth Sharpe taught about the concept of practical wisdom together at Swarthmore College, which led to the writing of the book *Practical Wisdom.* They define practical wisdom as "figuring out the right way to do the right thing in a particular circumstance, with a particular person, at a particular time."[1]

Practical wisdom results from experience. Diverse and numerous experiences through which we learn how to perceive, assess, deliberate, and then act teach us in ways that no blog post, book, teacher, or inspiring movie could (though don't tell my youngest, who claims to have learned how to snowboard by watching an episode of *Paw Patrol*). As a direct result of participating in various roles and gathering information about what works well and what does not, we become increasingly adept in making our way through complex situations, even those that we've never encountered before. For example, if you're reading this book, I'm assuming that you are a highly skilled reader. Even if it's your first time on these pages, you're likely skimming the words with ease, barely even thinking about how you're doing it. But reflect back to the joy (and agony!) of watching your child learn to read—they got stuck on whether the *g* should make a sound like in *giraffe* or as in *geyser*, leading to tantrums and thrown books.

Letters often refuse to gel into anything logical for a new reader. Making meaning out of a sentence requires intense effort accompanied by uncertainty in landing on the right outcome. But with experience, practice, and plenty of trial and error, reading becomes more effortless. Now, when your preteen reads what looks like indecipherable messages (texts), barely legible font (anything handwritten), and even words with missing letters or typos, they can glean the meaning. So can you.

Yer ah reedeng eggspart!

Your reading wisdom is steeped in diverse experience, attunement to context, and the skills you have grown and strengthened over time. This is what wisdom looks like.

EXPERIENCE AS TEACHER

As Albert Einstein once said, "Learning is experience. Everything else is just information." Practical wisdom grows when we allow experiences—such as interactions with our kids and our colleagues/customers—to teach us. Researchers find that expertise in disciplines ranging from firefighting to software design to parenting results in stronger holistic and conceptual thinking.[2] Working parenthood, of course, offers a huge diversity of experiences.

The affable and wise Barry Schwartz is an academic who changed students' lives through teaching, the world of science through his highly cited academic papers, and the nonscientific world through TEDx talks that have garnered millions of views and bestselling books such as *The Paradox of Choice*.[3] But Barry shared with me that his wisdom also grew from being open to lessons from working parenthood. For example, he told me, "One of the things that parenting taught me is really about the uniqueness of individuals. You know, my two kids have more or less the same genetic material," but, he said, "they couldn't have been more different!" Being open to the feedback from those two unique individuals helped Barry and his wife expand their parenting repertoire wisely. That learning had useful crossover effects. As Barry explained, "Although I suspect very few physicians would say 'I learned how to treat patients by raising children,' it might turn out that they've learned more than they realized about treating patients by raising children." We become wise when we allow our life experiences to teach us.

Taking on perspectives foreign to our own, learning to listen carefully to different people, and practicing sorting out what options work best for which situations are important wisdom-building agents of working parenthood. But in focusing exclusively on skill-building, we can miss something core to practical wisdom—that is, knowing what we value, as we considered in chapter 1.

Working parenthood offers clever ways to connect to values. Barry offered me a one-sentence script to make that connection, suggesting working parents "ask this one question: 'Would you tell your children?' If the answer is no, don't do it, and if the answer is yes, then do it!" Kids naturally raise the stakes. Parents often yearn to build a better world that their children will benefit from, as well as be the kind of person that their children will admire. Grow your wisdom by connecting to your role as parent. Consider what matters most to you in contributing or modeling how to act in the world, knowing your children are watching and will eventually inherit that world.

GROWING TOUGHNESS

To do the right thing for the right reason, we often must persist through difficulty. Life has ups and downs and wisdom helps you manage the bumps in the road. Two psychological forms of toughness feed into practical wisdom: resilience and grit.

The Resilience Factor

The ancient Chinese philosopher Confucius said, "Our greatest glory is not in never falling, but rising every time we fall." When life throws a curveball that knocks the wind out of you and you take a moment to find your breath and then get back in the game, that's resilience. Resilient people tend to have higher general well-being and an ability to weather the difficult periods of living (which no one gets to avoid), and they tend to be protected against the development or worsening of mental health problems.[4] Working parent or not, resilience serves you well as you travel through life.

Working parenthood offers a daily dose of adversity as you juggle multiple demanding roles. This turns out to be good news since growing resilience isn't about avoiding difficult experiences but rather using them to learn to respond more adaptively. The usefulness of adversity applies across experiences and even living organisms, as my family and I discovered one depressing Boston winter. With little to occupy us, my husband crafted an indoor hydroponic vegetable garden setup that provided the plants with water, light, and minerals. Then we waited for the magic to happen.

Sure enough, our little tomato plants grew. But they were worryingly frail, knocked over with barely a tap. With a bit of research, we discovered that we had failed to consider the value of botanical adversity. Wind, rain, and even hail motivate plants to develop strength, to drive their roots deeper into the soil and to grow sturdy stalks. At the other extreme, of course, the plants would have died quickly had they been exposed to the harsh Boston winter. Hardship, though not too much, helps us to grow tough. There is, indeed, a scientific basis for the adage that what doesn't kill us truly does make us grow stronger.[5] With this knowledge in hand, my husband installed a small fan to regularly blow on our fragile little plants.

Resilience naturally gets built up in working parenthood *because* we encounter challenges. While too much adversity can be incapacitating, it's worth pointing out that humans are capable of far greater adaptations than plants and other creatures. Having a growth mindset and adopting an optimistic perspective, self-talk that helps you endure, and behaviors that are adaptive will help you grow more resilient.

. . . . .

Pause to Build Resilience

Strategically building resilience will help you grow it more efficiently and effectively. Read through the following practices that have been studied and shown to work. Pick two to try out for the next two weeks. Then track how resilience grows through your daily challenges.

- *Maintain perspective.* Unhook from unhelpful labels and rigid story lines and turn instead toward growth-oriented stories (see chapters 3 and 4).

- *Manage your energy.* Enduring crises day in and day out is exhausting, making it hard to grow anything—including resilience. Be deliberate about taking breaks to optimize growth. Consider meditation, walks, art, talking with a friend, long baths, or a good night of sleep in lieu of alcohol, overeating, or numbing out with screen time (see chapter 6 for more on how working parents can take breaks).

- *Learn.* Resilience requires learning and growing. Get clear on those lessons by asking yourself: "What do my challenges have to teach me? What can I try out the next time this challenge arises?"

- *Cultivate gratitude.* Individuals who experience gratitude tend to bounce back from difficult experiences more quickly. To build gratitude, begin a daily practice of writing down three things you appreciate (these might include things about you, your work, your children, or the world at large).[6]

- *Strengthen relationships.* Resilient individuals have strong social support networks that bolster their ability to bounce back from difficult experiences. Spend time and energy nourishing important relationships in your life (see chapter 9 for ideas on growing connection).

- *Choose a valued response.* In the most stressful of moments, it can feel like there is only one option. This is rarely the case! Practice pausing and reconnecting to your values before choosing among the options available to you (see chapter 1 for more on value clarification).

- *Practice bouncing back.* When your kid loses their mind just as you're headed out the door and already late, take a breath and offer yourself some self-compassion. Then return to what you need to do. On the drive to school and work, consider how you could try the morning routine more effectively next time. For example, start the departure process earlier, pack bags the night before, or just set lower expectations for mornings.

* * * * *

Getting Gritty with It

Resilience and grit can be easily confused because both are associated with toughness. But grit has more to do with the qualities that we bring to our efforts than with bouncing back from adversity. Angela Duckworth, the author of *Grit,*[7] talked with me during a podcast interview about the "never give up attitude" that defines grit. Because gritty individuals rarely give up, they tend to be extremely successful. In fact, the combination of passion and persistence that defines grit allows it to be *twice* as important as talent when it comes to success!

But why do some people develop a gritty attitude, while others give up more easily? Angela explains that persistence is tightly linked to what you care about *and* what you find interesting. As Aristotle observed, "Pleasure in the job puts perfection in the work." We transcend uncomfortable experiences such as failure, disappointment, grief, embarrassment, fatigue, boredom, and even physical pain when we have clarity on why our actions matter or when we locate enjoyment in our efforts.

As a proof of concept, Angela and her colleagues surveyed sixteen thousand adults, asking the standard grit questions and about their orientations toward purpose and pleasure.[8] They found that the contrast between grittier and less gritty people wasn't in seeking pleasure or avoiding pain. That's no surprise. Gritty or not, pleasure entices. I rate high on grittiness, for example, though I recently chose *The Tiger King* over an educational documentary. That's not a bad thing and certainly it's nothing to be ashamed of (well, maybe a little shame would be appropriate). The point is that gritty people like pleasure, too. But pleasure isn't their exclusive motivator. There's also the desire to pursue a meaningful, interesting life.

As the incomparable media mogul and philanthropist Oprah Winfrey said, "Purpose is the thread that connects the dots to everything you do that leads you to an extraordinary life." A meaningful, interesting life is available to each and every one of us when we connect our actions to what we care deeply about and what we are curious about. This idea gets to the heart of the bricklayers parable. The parable is rooted in the true story of Christopher Wren, an architect charged with rebuilding St. Paul's Cathedral in London after the Great Fire of 1666. According to lore, Wren approached three bricklayers on a scaffold and asked each what he was doing.

The first answered that he was laying bricks to feed his family. The second responded that he was a builder and thus was building a wall. But the third—the most productive one of the three—replied that he was a builder tasked with erecting a sacred structure for the Almighty.

Like the bricklayers parable, research from the psychologists Amy Wrzesniewski, Barry Schwartz, and their colleagues suggests that people tend to see their work in one of three ways:

1. A job
2. A career
3. A calling[9]

Two important things emerge in this research. First, though we might think it's merely a fable that a bricklayer could see his job as a calling, evidence suggests seeing work as a job, career, or calling can happen in nearly any line of employment, regardless of income or work-related prestige. For instance, hospital cleaners can either see their work as a necessary but unpleasant way to pay the bills or as a way to make a meaningful difference in the lives of patients and their loved ones.[10] Second, when you relate to the work as a calling rather than a job, you are more likely to find satisfaction in the work and to work in ways that are more effective. The research of Adam Grant, a Wharton professor and author, shows that having either interest or a larger sense of purpose can help us persist in our work. Better yet is having *both*. In a study of municipal firefighters and fundraisers at a university call center, Grant asked individuals what motivated their work. He also assessed how many hours they worked or calls they made. Those who both wanted to help others and who found the duties enjoyable worked more hours and raised more money.[11] In other words, cultivating interest and purpose in our tasks helps to make us grittier. In turn, being grittier helps us become more skilled.

Working parenthood supports the development of grit by offering you a bounty of options to connect daily actions to your interests and to a larger purpose. You have a veritable buffet of purpose and interest! If your work isn't inherently meaningful or thought provoking, you can find purpose or fascination in your role as parent. If you struggle to find parenthood meaningful or interesting, look to your role as a professional. You can even aim for the deluxe combo package—a working parenthood that offers purpose and interest *because* you get to do so many different kinds of activities. You can, as Wrzesniewski and her colleagues point out, shape, mold, and redefine your life roles with more meaning.[12] You might even switch off where you seek purpose and interests depending on the phase of your work life or on the developmental stage your kids are in.

. . . . .

Pause to Get Gritty by Finding Your Purpose and Interest

Experiencing meaning and interest in working parenthood isn't magic—it's something to pursue and grow with deliberate intention. Here are some tips for cultivating grit from meaning and interest in either (or both) of your roles:

- *Connect activity to service.* Connecting actions to service can help efforts feel more purposeful. Look for where you meaningfully serve others in each of your roles.

- *Create work you* want *to do from the work you* have *to do.* Being compelled to do tasks—whether it's filling in an Excel spreadsheet or wiping a dirty bum— brings less joy than freely choosing activities. Find the wiggle room to adapt required tasks to serve your own purposes. Next time you're entering data in a spreadsheet, turn on some tunes to see if your efficiency increases with a beat. Next time you're wiping a tushie, see if you can refine your comedy routine and make your kiddo giggle.

- *Invest in relationships.* Relationships are core to our happiness, flourishing, and even financial success. Tend to relationships at work and at home, finding opportunities to have positive experiences with people around you.

- *Remember your why.* Yes, of course you work because you need an income and you parent because your children need you to give them dinner. But there's almost always more to it than that. Ask yourself *why* you care about your work and *why* you care about being a parent. Keep your why in mind as you move through your day.

. . . . .

Of course, it's entirely possible that neither work nor parenting represent the ultimate connection to something greater than yourself. Each role may fall short in offering you an interesting activity. There's no requirement for work or parenting to be your raison d'être. Use what you can from them until you find a why that better suits you.

When Toughness Comes Hard, Start Small

I also want to take a moment here to note that grit requires more than simply muscling through what's hard in the service of purposeful living. Trying your heart out and getting nowhere can result in a feeling of hopelessness and a belief that no amount of effort will change anything. The renowned psychologist Martin Seligman first labeled this concept as "learned helplessness."[13]

Seligman studied how learned helplessness develops by placing dogs in different conditions. Some of the dogs were given electric shocks. This first group of dogs could turn the shocks off by pressing a panel but the second had no means for stopping the shocks. The third lucky group was not shocked. Later, all three groups of dogs were placed into boxes they could exit from by jumping over a short wall. When shocks were applied here, the dogs that had been able to stop the shocks and the dogs who were never shocked quickly exited the box. But the dogs that were taught they could not escape being shocked simply lay down in the box whimpering. These dogs had learned that no matter what they did, they could not escape the pain. They had been taught to believe there was no point in trying. That fixed mindset fed into their stuckness, causing them to miss workable approaches to managing a painful situation.[14]

The key to turning learned helplessness into grit is *not* to self-blame. Helplessness isn't your fault. Whether it's basic human rights, health issues, or financial stress, many circumstances can limit your ability to engage in action that gets you anywhere different. Feeling helpless is only natural. Offer yourself self-compassion while you reboot. Remember from chapter 3 that self-compassion is about taking a moment to make space without judgment for your feelings, offering yourself some self-kindness and then connecting your experience to common humanity (you're in good company with many other working parents).

When you feel ready, set your intentions toward seeking an experience of mastery, pushing yourself to, well, think outside of the box. Most important here: start *small*. Find the low-hanging fruit amid the bounty of working parenthood to get a win. Even a very small win counts. Try looking for moments where something like the following happened:

- You were kind to your child, even when your buttons were being pushed.

- You completed a task on your to-do list even though you were fifty shades of weary.

- Your children ate dinner while you did an important work call (even if that dinner involved crackers with peanut butter in front of a screen).

Identify an experience where you accomplished something small, felt skillful, or connected to something or someone important to you and then really show up for that experience. Notice how it felt, narrate it aloud, or just take a mindful pause to be present in that moment.

As you experience daily adversities, be on the lookout for opportunities to learn, grow, and experience mastery, all while connecting to what you want to stand for in this phase of life. When you do, working parenthood becomes the natural feedstuff for building both grit and resilience.

READING THE ROOM

Though our society may discount them, relationship skills—including empathy, communication, persistence, impulse control, and reading nonverbal cues—may be among the most important skills for both work and parenting. These interpersonal capacities are often grouped under the umbrella of "emotional intelligence." Daniel Goleman, the author of *Emotional Intelligence,* argues that emotional intelligence has greater positive impact on success than other forms of intelligence.[15] While the more classically defined kind of intelligence might get you the interview (and even the job offer), it's emotional intelligence that helps you keep the job and gets you promoted. It's how you befriend your prickly boss, determine what your clients really want, and even creatively problem-solve. It's emotional intelligence that prompts you to teach your kids how to be a good friend and which helps you reconnect to them after they baffle you with a meltdown when you forbid eating the dog's poop.

Emotional intelligence impacts each of your life roles. It helps you tune in to the relational needs of your dawdling toddler and to the needs of forward-thinking task completion. By actively tuning in to the needs of the role you're currently engaged in, you can more effectively relate and respond to individuals and your environment.

Skills for reading the room increase your ability to get what you want, offer what others want, and find satisfaction in authentically connecting in important work relationships. Interpersonal skills—including personal presence, collaboration, and addressing conflict—facilitate greater success. A study of food service workers showed that managers' emotional intelligence was associated with their own job satisfaction and performance.[16] Another study, this one conducted with police officers, showed that officers who demonstrated greater emotional intelligence had higher job satisfaction and well-being and their emotional intelligence predicted engagement and commitment to the job over time.[17] Workplaces benefit when they have individuals with high emotional intelligence on staff.

That synergistic relationship between role success and emotional intelligence is available within parenting, too. Parents may not arrive at parenting with high-level emotional intelligence in hand, but it gets *learned* as we grow right along with our kids. As Barry Schwartz told me, our kids' "lack of cognitive sophistication is so transparent that you simply have to struggle to see the world as they see it." Being forced to see things from a child's perspective naturally strengthens your ability to perspective-take. Lucky for you, that ability will conveniently transfer and help you relate to the hard-to-understand adults in your workplace.

Emotional intelligence naturally grows as your children grow. Where you feel clueless about what your infant wants in the early days, you'll eventually learn to interpret their cries, understand their circadian rhythms, and familiarize yourself with their emerging preferences. In toddlerhood, your child's wants shift dramatically from one moment to the next, taking you by surprise. Here, too, when you allow the experiences to teach you, you'll grow emotional intelligence and learn to better navigate the relationship with the small person your toddler is becoming. The more you continue to increase your knowledge base and ability to engage with your kids, the better off they will be and the stronger your relationship with them can become.

Of course, no matter how emotionally intelligent you are, you won't know the perfect response every time. Breaking news: there isn't actually one perfect response, and sometimes, despite your best efforts, you'll fail to figure out what the heck your kid or colleague wants from you. Emotional intelligence isn't about perfection, though. It's about being attuned enough to yourself and others to adjust course based on the needs of the situation.

· · · · ·

Pause to Grow Skill in Reading the Room

Emotional intelligence almost always comes back to awareness and interpersonal skill. To be emotionally intelligent, tune in to your own emotions, the needs and emotions of others, and practice adjusting communication style to maximize connection to others.

- Notice yourself making emotional and interpersonal pivots as you go through your day.

- Ask yourself what works well and what works less well in each situation. Ask yourself what kinds of behaviors foster connection (versus creating distance), help you get important work accomplished (versus causing you to feel stuck), and allow you to be the kind of person you want to be (versus acting out of line with your better self).

. . . . .

THE WISDOM TO PIVOT

I interviewed Anne, a senior director in a corporate legal department, between meetings. In addition to her demanding career, Anne is the mother to two children, ages four and seven. She shared a quintessential story of working parenthood. The Saturday before, her family had planned to arrive at their annual neighborhood block party together before her husband went to a movie with friends. But shortly before heading out, Anne received an urgent text from her boss. He needed to present an update on an evolving situation to the board of directors in one hour and requested that she prepare a slide deck to guide the discussion. Anne agreed with as much grace as she could muster, tweaking her plans to stay at the house to work while her husband and kids left for the block party. Anne finished the deck, made it through the presentation, then shut down her computer and joined her family down the block. Her husband soon headed off to his movie.

Anne told me, "I am drinking a beer and having a great time talking to my neighbors when I get a text and I literally stop mid-sentence and stare at it. The text says, 'We need to have another meeting at 6:30 p.m.' I call my boss and he says there was a mistake in the deck—in *my* deck—and my heart just drops. He says 'We have to reconvene, can you do it?' And I say, 'I'm at a block party, my husband's not here, and I have both of the kids.'" At just that moment, Anne saw her four-year-old son go from jumping jubilantly in the bounce house to crying after crashing into another child. Anne quickly reviewed her options, took a breath, and told her boss that she would get the job done. She tapped a neighbor on the shoulder to ask if she could watch her older daughter because something important had come up and that she'd return as soon as possible.

Anne rushed her son home and calmed him before turning on *Transformers* and getting to work. Just as the second meeting was nearing its conclusion, Anne's son came over to her crying—he had wet his pants. Trying to attend to her son but remain professional with her boss and the others, Anne put the call on mute and in a stage whisper said, "Take off your pants, honey! Take off your pants and keep watching *Transformers*! I'll be there in a minute!" Anne then unmuted herself, and in a more professional voice said, "So, do we have a consensus?" They did, and she gratefully ended the call. Feeling spent, Anne cleaned up her son and headed back to the block party to pick up her daughter.

Charles Darwin, the originator of the concept of natural selection, once noted, "It is not the strongest of the species that survives, nor the most intelligent, but the one most responsive to change." There is immeasurable strength in being able to respond flexibly, adapting our behaviors not just generation to generation but moment to moment to fit the needs of our situations. In other words, we need to know what to do, and just as importantly we need to know *when* and *how* to pivot toward doing it. Wisdom gives you the "what to do elements." Psychological flexibility gives you the "how."

Psychological flexibility has been defined as the ability to pivot depending on your internal and external circumstances and values. Researchers argue that psychological flexibility undergirds psychological health because it allows you to adjust to situational demands. Repeatedly and rigidly getting stuck in negative or otherwise unhelpful thinking or behaviors is what it can look and feel like to be suffering with a mental health problem.[18] In contrast, being psychologically flexible helps sets the stage for mental health.

For working parents, persisting and desisting often occurs on a moment-to-moment basis, as when we switch from one role to another. Building psychological flexibility can mean learning to stay cool under pressure, shifting focus when it is useful, persisting in a task even when it is difficult, or discontinuing our efforts when it no longer makes sense to endure. Psychological flexibility can look like transition after transition, as in Anne's day of block-party work stress. But remember, flexibility can involve either continuing *or* stopping a behavior. The decision is the right one when it is connected to a way of being that matters to you in that specific context. Consider the following psychologically flexible moves:

- Giving your kid a tight hug before turning on *Caillou* (so you can attend a Zoom meeting)

- Bringing your attention back (a dozen times over) to being in conversation with your child about *Caillou* even though you find *Caillou* annoying (and work stressors demand your attention)

- Noticing your fatigue and going to sleep instead of responding to urgent emails

- Hiding in the bathroom so you can take a few breaths and reengage your caring parent self

- Persisting on a work assignment late into the night even when you feel ready to quit the gig entirely

- Pausing in a moment of chaos or failure to reconnect to what matters most, here and now

The ability to pivot toward value-aligned action is characteristic of people who are wise, and it sits at the heart of effective working parenthood (and elsewhere in life). When you put together all the ingredients of psychological flexibility, you'll find yourself continuously taking in new information, noticing when behaviors aren't serving you, deciding to tolerate unavoidable emotions in the service of your valued way of being, and deciding to adjust course when it's effective to do so. Psychological flexibility lubricates the cogs and gears of practical wisdom. But psychological flexibility is not a given. It's something we must deliberately grow and maintain throughout working parenthood.

A PARKING LOT LESSON IN PIVOTING

Growing and refining psychological flexibility is part and parcel of the day-to-day machinations of working parenthood. Switching between roles spurs you to activate the personal attributes and mindsets most useful to each role. For Simone, an exotic dancer and mother, shifting between parenting and professional roles is one head-spinning example of this kind of pivoting. But, she explained to me, practice has made her incredibly strategic and skilled in making the transitions.

Simone wisely developed a car meditation practice outside of her club, just before her shift begins. Concentrating on her breath, she leaves behind her homelife and fully immerses herself in her work persona, transitioning from soft-spoken mother into a powerful and sexy exotic dancer. Like Simone, the more we practice these kinds of transitions, the more skillful we become in making them. We working parents can thus become true pivot masters, just like bilinguals who can near-effortlessly transition from one language to another. Studies of task-switching show that not only do lifelong bilinguals incur less switching costs than monolinguals but they also do task-switching in tasks unrelated to linguistics with less effort than do monolinguals.[19] Pivot practice makes you more pivot proficient. As you shift from maternal to erotic, industrious to relaxed, meticulous to easygoing, task-oriented to heart-centered, working parenthood can naturally strengthen your psychological flexibility.

Working parenthood also helps us support our children in developing psychological flexibility, through modeling it and through the opportunities we foist upon kids to respond adaptively to situations they didn't choose. As the biologist Fatima told me, the times when she has to focus on grant writing to the exclusion of some of her parenting duties provide opportunities to help her daughter build flexibility. During grant season, for example, her daughter knows that work has to come first. The little girl has learned to entertain herself during grant-writing season, anticipating that she can turn back toward deeper engagement with her mom after the grant is submitted. Teaching our kids that they, too, can tolerate discomfort in the service of parent and family values and pivot between behaviors to be their most effective is a powerful early life lesson. It's one that helps our children grow not only psychological flexibility but also their practical wisdom.

As Barry and I ended our conversation about practical wisdom in working parenthood, I asked him if working parenthood had helped him cultivate his own practical wisdom. "I think without knowing it, I subjected myself to two very substantial long-term laboratories and the cultivation of wisdom. Whether I was a good pupil is another matter, but I certainly got a lot of lessons," he said with a broad smile.

The TL/DR (Too Long, Didn't Read)

STRENGTHEN YOUR WORKING-PARENT WISDOM

Practical wisdom means knowing the best thing to do in a given circumstance, with a given person, and given your core values. Build practical wisdom by using practices from each of the following domains:

- *Persist strategically.* The next time you are bombarded with distractions or frustrations, take a deep breath and connect to what you value, what you find interesting, and what you can learn from this experience.

- *Read the room.* Actively try on perspectives of others (children, bosses, colleagues, partners) in each of your roles. Intentionally adjust communication style as you transition from parent to worker and from worker to parent, reflecting on what communication strategies work best in each setting and with each type of relationship.

- *Practice pivots.* Begin to see transitions from one role to the other as opportunities to practice and build your skill in making switches. Allow your values to guide whether you continue on or change course. Appreciate that regardless of what choice you make, you're practicing the skills that underlie practical wisdom.

6

RETHINK YOUR REST

Almost everything will work again if you unplug
it for a few minutes, including you.
—ANNE LAMOTT

vividly recall one winter when my boys' schools had three consecutive snow days. The first one was great—I happily called off
meetings with patients and colleagues and prepared for a day of
kid fun. We made snow angels, had a playdate with neighbors, and
drank hot cocoa with mini marshmallows. I enjoyed my boys' goof-
iness while they basked in the glow of my undivided attention. The
second day was a little less exciting and a little more frustrating. I
felt work pressure mounting as I ran out of patience for the three
beasts bouncing off the walls and into each other. I gave in to hours
of screen time and prayed schools would reopen quickly. The third
snow day found me calling every babysitter we had, and by the time
one arrived, my shoes and jacket were already on. I jetted over to

a local coffee shop where I spent the morning releasing my work pressure valve and savoring my thinking time.

Through the alchemy of coffee and a few hours of productive work time, I found myself happy to head home to the children I had been irritable with the previous afternoon. The alchemy wasn't entirely magic, though. I am well aware that parenting without reprieve and working without pause drain me. Through my work as a social scientist and parent, I've developed a set of regular practices for everyday life grounded in the science of rest. I strive to keep additional strategies in my back pocket for less typical situations (snow days, pandemics, weeks where day care unexpectedly shut down) so that I don't run out of parenting or work steam over the long haul.

It may seem improbable, but even the busiest working parents can learn to take a break. The busiest working parents are the ones most in need of doing so! A heart can persist in pumping blood around the body twenty-four hours a day only because it rests between beats. Similarly, you can only sustain the high-intensity effort required by work and parent roles if you, too, learn to rest strategically.

GETTING BURNED

As Alex Soojung-Kim Pang, the author of the transformative book *Rest*, writes, "Rest is not work's adversary. Rest is work's partner. They complement and complete each other."[1] We might know this intuitively, but a modern truth often interferes with acting on this wisdom. In our culture, busyness and overwork have come to serve as a kind of status symbol.[2] In many jobs, we grow our cachet by showing how much we're working. When we aren't actively working, technological innovations keep us just a ping away from employers, colleagues, and customers. And thanks to a cultural expectation that "good parents" are available to their children at all times, parents face a persistent pressure to be responsive emotionally and physically to our offspring.[3] Huzzah for technology and a cultural ethos of all-in effort!

It's entirely possible that you've bought into this set of beliefs. You might believe that "good" workers don't ask for time off and always respond to clients, no matter the hour. And you might assume (perhaps correctly) that your boss would shoot down a request of setting limits on after-hours availability. Because you feel guilty for working so much, you might also adopt the belief that you must be "on" at all times you are with your children. That thought places pressure on the time you spend with your kids and causes you to neglect to consider what healthy parenting practices for working parents might be.

News flash: they involve rest.

Expectations (from yourself and the world around you) to work as if you don't have children and parent as if you don't work can cause burnout in both spheres. The World Health Organization (WHO) defines burnout as an occupational phenomenon resulting from chronic workplace stress and leading to a state of exhaustion, detachment, and reduced efficacy. These kinds of experiences crop up outside of the work sphere, too. Parental burnout is on the rise and is distinct from work burnout or depression.[4] Recent surveys showed that about a quarter of the American workforce feels burned out "always" or "very often" and three-quarters feels burned out sometimes.[5] Between 5 and 20 percent of all parents report parental burnout.[6]

Burnout isn't merely an uncomfortable inconvenience; it has grim psychological and physiological consequences. You might grow detached, even from people you love or work you generally care about (or work that you care to remain employed in). You can grow so exhausted that you struggle to "bounce back" after a tough week or a difficult exchange with your kiddo. You may begin to feel that no matter what you do, you can't access a feeling of effectiveness or accomplishment in completing tasks or engaging with colleagues or family. None of these consequences make for enjoyable days and weeks. And in case you need a more compelling reason to take burnout seriously, it doesn't just impact you. It impacts your workplace and your children, too.

You can review your burnout symptoms by asking the kinds of questions burnout researchers ask, which assess for these three general domains: (1) exhaustion that you are unable to bounce back from, (2) detachment or depersonalization, and (3) loss of ability to feel effective in your roles:[7]

- Have I been finding my work/parenting role emotionally draining recently?

- Have I been feeling detached and cynical about work and/or with my family?

- Do I feel emotionally distant from colleagues or from my children?

- Am I experiencing negative attitudes (including self-doubt) about my abilities in work and/or in parenting?

- Do I struggle to feel a sense of accomplishment at work and/or in parenting?

- Have I been having a hard time connecting to a sense of purpose in my life roles?

- Have I had more difficulty concentrating than usual at work or with my family?

- Has my performance, productivity, or creativity been diminished recently at work or at home?

If you find yourself experiencing symptoms of burnout, please remember you are not alone. Remember, too, that you *can* recover from burnout. Just be gentle with yourself and take your time with this chapter and the suggested strategies.

THE BLAME GAME

Working for a rigid, unsympathetic boss who demands after-hours responses (with harsh consequences for delays) or having children with special needs can increase risk for burnout. So can pandemics, your own health issues, financial bombshells, and a toddler who fights you all winter about wearing pants. Unfortunately, sunshiny thinking and sheer will aren't likely to change your circumstances or a set of beliefs that have been confirmed too often. Self-blame and blaming others are counterproductive, too.

An effective response to incessant pressures begins without detachment from reality and without finger-pointing—especially toward yourself. Through no fault of your own, accessing a true pause amid the chaos and demands of working-parent life isn't simple. If you've received a different message, you're in good company. For example, tips on better time use recommend staging leisure and making sure you engage in restorative activities such as better sleep hygiene, regular exercise, manicures, and dates with friends. Or, as a well-intentioned friend of mine advised in response to my long vent about everything feeling too much: "Join me for a yoga retreat in Costa Rica—it's what we all need right now!"

If you're like me, these recommendations make your blood boil. They don't account for realities such as not having parents, a partner, or a colleague who can cover for you or the financial means to sign up for a vacation that you "need." They fail to consider the baby who awakens early and isn't keen on giving you time to read/breathe/poop alone, and the fact that pressing work demands are accompanied by an onslaught of "life" demands (laundry, buying birthday gifts, grocery runs, and oil changes) that won't get done if you simply pull the plug on what's exhausting. So instead of wondering why you're failing to take breaks (or throttling your well-meaning friend), send yourself some kind understanding—for many of us, it's absurdly hard to take a break in working parenthood!

It can be helpful to send that understanding to others, too. To be sure, those time experts, as well as the old guard enforcing workweeks in excess of forty hours (even during summer school breaks), an imbalanced division of labor expectations at home, a lack of childcare and vacation time, and even those darn social judgments about resting, each play a part in the difficulty of accessing a real break. Still, many people you interact with are doing their best. Your childcare providers, your boss, the grandparents, your partner, and even your friend who's headed to that beachside retreat without you are each doing their best to get through their own challenging days. Additional burdens or assumptions placed on you are unlikely to be malicious.

That doesn't mean you should excuse others for adding burdens to your life. But beginning without blame relieves you of carrying a particularly heavy encumbrance: anger. A common Buddhist saying is that holding on to anger is like holding hot coals with the intention of throwing them at someone who has harmed you. The punishment you aim to exact causes *you* to get burned. Or, in the words of Mahatma Gandhi, "An eye for an eye makes the whole world blind."

The key is to cool anger so you can use it to more helpfully guide you. Easier said than done, I know, but two steps can help you respond wisely when you're angry: (1) calm your threat system, and (2) be deliberate in choosing your response.

Calming your threat system doesn't involve screaming about injustices or inhaling a bag of cookies. The theory of catharsis—the idea that we can "release" anger by yelling or punching a pillow—has largely been disproven. Contrary to this theory, discharging anger often reinforces the feeling of anger as well as the impulse to act on it.[8] And while finding solace through a sugar (or other substance) binge might feel good in the moment, it's the kind of bandage fix likely to lead to problems in the long run. Ultimately these kinds of solutions tend to ignite more coals.

To cool your coals, you need to work within your natural responses. First, it's useful to appreciate what anger does to your body. That is, it triggers your nervous system to prepare to keep you safe. Even though it's unlikely that you're about to face down a bear, your system will get ready to do just that. When your nervous system is activated in this way, your prefrontal cortex—the part of the brain that does good planning, makes choices, and evaluates logically—goes offline. By settling your nervous system, you can bring your more deliberate, thinking mind back online.

Here's how to begin: *notice.* Notice what kinds of feelings and physical sensations arise when a tornado of anger touches down. Get to know your angry red flags, whether they show up as a rapid succession of vengeful thoughts, tightness in your chest, or the desire to numb yourself with food, wine, or other distractions.

Once you notice anger coming on, *pause.* Use the pause to take calming action—*before* you take any kind of action that is exclusively driven by anger. You might try what psychologists call "grounding strategies," which are simple techniques to help calm your nervous system. Grounding strategies look like:

- Breathing long and slow

- Spending a few minutes noticing your feet

- Touching a cold surface, noticing the texture and temperature

- Describing an object in detail, such as a pen or a sock, detailing the material, size, texture, color, and so on

- Holding an ice cube for a minute

- Naming feelings or thoughts aloud or in writing

Once calmer, you can be more deliberate in how to best use your anger. Your anger matters and often indicates something important. So get curious. You might discover, for instance, that your anger is pointing to something you care about, a need that requires your attention (like getting some sleep), or even a cause that wants your deliberate action.

Consider reflecting on the following questions:

- What is my anger telling me is important here?

- How might my anger prompt productive action?

- If my anger isn't getting me anywhere helpful, what might I try doing differently?

Remember, too, we empower ourselves by changing how we *relate* to our realities, even if the realities stay exactly as they are. Sometimes as we do this inside-out work, we can—over time—effect change in the structural realities around us.

REDEFINING BREAKS

Alyssa, an intensive care unit nurse and mother, has a typical nursing workweek of three twelve-hour shifts. Her nursing workdays are intense, but the structure of Alyssa's week is pretty ideal for having time to parent. This is particularly important because Alyssa's son has special needs. For the past few years, Alyssa's husband adopted a stay-at-home parent role, taking the lead on the many weekly appointments of occupational therapy, speech therapy, ophthalmology, and behavioral groups. Still, Alyssa's physical and emotional presence matters to her and to her son. Because her son has such wide-ranging needs, Alyssa has grown to see her work as a useful break from parenting. She laughed as she told me, "Bless those who don't need breaks from their children. I am ready to go back to work after several days home with my child."

You might reject the idea that stepping into the demands of intensive-care nursing equates to a true break. Neither Alyssa's work nor parenting could be mistaken for a leisurely stroll on the beach, a peaceful cup of coffee, or getting a pedicure in one of those giant massage chairs. But it's helpful to consider the most useful way to define a break, perhaps adopting a definition that's more realistic for a busy working parent.

One such definition is offered in Alex Soojung-Kim Pang's *Rest*.[9] Soojung-Kim Pang does a deep dive into the science of rest and considers how prolific figures from Charles Darwin to the Spanish painter Salvador Dalí managed to sustain their efforts over time. One of his conclusions is that a break can mean *moving from one task to another*. If the second task is also demanding but uses a different part of your brain, that is indeed a useful break. A plumber putting away the drain wrench to paint, a museum curator leaving work to play soccer, and a worker heading home to parent are, by this definition, taking breaks. They are restoring energy for one demanding role by stepping into another.

STOP THE BURN BY DETACHING

Research out of the sociologist Sabine Sonnentag's laboratory at the University of Mannheim in Germany shows how useful detachment from demanding tasks can be. When people get away mentally and "switch off" from high-demand work to deliberately send their attention and energy to nonwork tasks, they tend to return with an ability to be more productive, get along better with others, focus more intently, and deal more effectively with challenges.[10] But not all transitions from one role to another are created equal. That's because we frequently neglect to fully activate a key ingredient: *psychological detachment*.

Psychological detachment refers to the mental disengagement from any role that occurs when we completely "turn off" and step fully away from that role. That means that we are not only not working but also not thinking about work or keeping an eye on our phone in case someone needs us at work. We are wholly detached from and completely unavailable to that role. Like entering into a deep restorative sleep, activating full detachment helps us restore our energetic reserves.

In a paradigm-shifting study, researchers showed how the restorative effects of role transitions can happen even when individuals go to war. Researchers followed Israeli employees working at one company, comparing employees who were army reservists to employees who were not active reservists but who were matched on job, age, seniority, and marital status. During the course of the study, reservists were called in for active duty lasting at least two weeks, while matched participants remained working their normal jobs. Amazingly, a *decline* in work-related stress and work burnout occurred for the workers who went on active army duty, while employees who remained at their regular day job experienced continued stress and work burnout.[11] Detachment from work was, in fact, critical for recovery. Because of detachment, going to war offered a respite from work with benefits akin to those of going on a vacation. Importantly, the effects of detachment aren't permanent—they fade within weeks. For this reason, it's important to detach regularly in order to reap the restorative benefits.

Counterintuitively, having two roles that demand your attention can naturally provide the breaks required to keep you from burning out on either. Lisa Doctor, a semiretired Hollywood executive, described it to me this way: "If you do too much of anything, it's like drinking water from a fire hose." During her Hollywood career, Lisa worked on movies, including Robin Williams's *Mrs. Doubtfire*. The work was intense, but for Lisa, having two important roles helped her stay healthy in both. She told me, "Had I stayed on the fast track professionally, I might have run out of steam, missed out on family time, and compromised my health. But had I left the business world altogether as a young mother, I wouldn't have the resume necessary for my current empty-nest career." The ways that work and parenthood pressed her to take turns disengaging from each role helped Lisa prevent work and parenting burnout over the long run. Psychological detachment helps reduce emotional exhaustion over time, and it buffers the impact high role demands can have on physical well-being.[12]

KNOW YOUR OBSTACLES

Of course, the positive effects of energy restoration that come out of being fully switched off are hard to access when you live in a culture that values overwork and intensive parenting. The judgments around departing work to pick up children from school or leaving children with childcare providers so you can work can rain down on us.[13]

A few decades ago, embedded expectations of work and family as distinct were more dominant, helping us sustain boundaries between these roles. For instance, religious practices dominated for many families. Those practices provided accountability to fully detach from work and set firmer boundaries between work and family life. For example, the fourth commandment in the Old Testament *requires* observing a Sabbath rest. On this day, work is firmly prohibited. Comparable kinds of boundaries between work and family, as well as an insistence on rest time, are found in religious teachings from all corners of the world.

But for better or worse (I'd argue both), religious guidelines have largely fallen by the wayside for many. As religion and religious doctrine moved to the background, progress in technology increasingly shifted into the foreground. These days, it's become ever easier to remain in continuous contact with all of our life roles. And in an environment of expectations and pressure to remain always available, detachment becomes much harder to activate.

A parallel shift in parenting thwarts psychological detachment from our kids. *The Cultural Contradictions of Motherhood* explored the rise in intensive mothering expectations in the late twentieth century.[14] The author and sociologist Sharon Hays described the evolution of a cultural contradiction in which women were increasingly expected to enter the workplace and earn income with simultaneous pressure to mother in increasingly child-centered, emotionally absorbing, and labor-intensive ways. "Good parenting" began to be understood as maintaining a persistent connection to your kids, no matter what other roles you occupied. That, of course, is the very opposite of what parental detachment requires.

Recognizing the value of detaching from work and parenting could help to equilibrate our sexist judgments about the number of hours spent in the office. And it can support parents—especially mothers—in taking healthy and productive breaks from the parenting role. After all, the evidence is clear: for both men and women, taking breaks from work and parenting to restore enthusiasm (or basic willingness!) and sustain effective engagement over time is good practice.

USE ROLE PRESSURE TO YOUR GUILTY ADVANTAGE

Most working parents have some point at which they must stop their work and transition to parenting. Most working parents have some point at which they must stop parenting and head to work (even if "heading to work" means sitting at the computer crammed in the back corner of your bedroom). It's one of the last vestiges of an accepted boundary between work and family life. The need to personally show up for our different life roles encourages detaching. At least for now, it's a boundary that can't be expunged by technology.

But, no, your boss isn't likely to love your leaving early to get your children. Nor will your children celebrate being the last at the after-school program. It's only natural that this might feed a sense of guilt. Guilt, though, isn't the problem in and of itself. Guilt serves an important function by prompting us to treat people we care about attentively, respectfully, and lovingly. When we don't, guilt cues us to this fact.

Notably, one of the most significant causes of guilt turns out to be not spending enough time on people or things we care about.[15] If you do feel guilty, allow it to serve as a reminder of how much you care about work. Allow it to offer a reminder of how deeply you care about your children. Then remind yourself of two additional truths:

1. Leaving your child to go to work and leaving work to go to your child will help you return to each with greater gusto.

2. When your guilt interferes with fully switching off whatever role you're not currently participating in, it creates a double whammy. You aren't showing up for what you are doing and you're not resting from the role you've stepped away from.

Guilt is natural—and often even helpful. We can't and shouldn't try to avoid it. But learning how to wisely make space for it (without buying into it, hook, line, and sinker) can help you detach from each role more effectively.

. . . . .

Pause to Manage the Guilt

This quick mindfulness exercise helps loosen the hold guilt may have on you. Start by taking a few breaths to center yourself in your body. Then notice what your mind is telling you. Notice any guilty thoughts cropping up. Then thank your mind for caring about all of your roles.

Next, take a deep breath and tell your mind that bringing yourself into the present role will help you engage more fully and more effectively. In fact, getting fully into your current role will help you be more effective (both in the role you're involved in and the one you've stepped away from).

Remind your mind that stepping fully away from the role you aren't actively participating in will help you reenergize for it. Set an intention for the next period of time to be more engaged where you are and less engaged where you are not.

· · · · ·

DELIBERATE REST PRACTICES

It isn't easy, but knowing that you're a more attentive parent and productive worker when you detach from each role can prompt you to be more deliberate, creative, and motivated in rest practices. The kinds of practices I describe have been tested and shown to work well in diverse settings. And they can easily be modified, depending on your unique circumstances.

Midday Rest

As the parent with the more flexible job, I spend a lot of days with my kids. Most of those days, I also have work that needs to get done. Carrying the mental burden of that reality stresses me out and, by the end of the day, wears me out. But early in my working-parent research, I discovered how helpful an enforced midday "rest time" for my kids was in giving me a parenting break and for preventing my work stress from taking over my time with my children.

When my kids rest, I get work done. I simultaneously recharge for parenting. My kids have gotten used to this routine and use the time to nap, read, draw, or play quietly. (I'm also pretty sure that some days they keep themselves occupied by concocting plans for a rest-time coup and a toppling of the parent regime.) That midday hour offers a break from my small people and sends a jolt of energy to my parenting battery. And it helps me keep the ball rolling on work tasks, even when I don't have "enough" hours to devote to work. Parents whose kids thoroughly resist a rest time because they are too old or just haven't been raised with this practice can modify the midday rest. You can take a parenting break through the use of electronics, required outside time, reading time, playdates, or anything else that gives you an opportunity to detach from parenting during a long day of being with your kids.

You can use a similar approach at work. Whether it's your lunch break, a coffee run, or a walk around the building, see if you can find an opportunity to unhook from work for a chunk of time. To activate detachment from work, get yourself immersed in family life. Consider actions like emailing your kid, calling your partner, or even using visual imagery of time with your family to step fully away from work and into your familial role.

Don't forget, though, the process of detaching has an embedded agenda of reconnecting with more juice in your battery. When it comes to my parenting rest, my kids—even my youngest—have been informed of this rationale. Because they know that the break is supposed to help me show up in a more engaged way when we come back together, they expect it. That expectation ups my accountability to fully transition back to them, which pushes me to transition back to parenting and to psychologically detach from my work. When I'm back in parenting mode, I remind myself that stepping in fully helps to recharge my work battery.

Download Your Thoughts

When so much needs to be done, your mind wants to help out by reminding you what you aren't doing. This can be pretty distracting (not to mention a wee bit annoying). To get more effective with the time you have, reduce the impact of distracting thoughts by getting them out of your mind and onto an external device.

Research suggests that transferring worries or feelings out of your head and onto paper (or an electronic device) tames those worries and feelings. It reduces their ability to distract you from what you're trying to focus on because you've physically put them out of your mind space.[16] By downloading thoughts from your brain onto a notepad, phone, or computer, you create a reminder to come back to anything parenting-related at a nonwork time or to come back to work-related worries at a nonparent time. You also provide yourself reassurance that the ideas nibbling at your mind are going to be addressed but at a more suitable moment. So keep a notepad handy and move thoughts unrelated to what you're doing out of your brain space so you can reserve that space for focusing on the task you're engaged in.

Tech Turnoff

The biggest challenge to efficient work time, as well as focused parenting time, might be the distraction of phone, email, messaging tools, and social media. According to some reports, Americans check their phones between 80 and 90 times per day.[17] This constant checking results in a fracturing of attention and damns your opportunity to detach from whatever you aren't doing. If you're at work but checking kid-related email (so very many school emails, am I right?), you are failing to detach from parenting. If you're parenting and checking work Slack channels, you haven't effectively switched out of work mode.

Try out these tips from distraction researchers:

- Shut down any windows open on your computer that would distract you from your main focus.

- Put your phone out of sight.

- Silence all incoming reminders, notifications, and calls except emergency ones.

- Turn off your devices when you're attempting to focus on family—for example, during the time you're home and not working.[18]

Many digital devices are built to be addictive. Strive to reduce the time fracturing caused by technology whenever and wherever you can. Be mindful when it creeps back in (because it will!) and reset your intentions to turn down the disruptions of technology. Let your kids know your plan; they'll love helping you stick to it. By which I mean they'll glory in the game of trying to catch you with your phone in hand. More importantly, it'll give them an opportunity to learn about the addictive nature of technology and what tools they, too, can use to manage their use of it.

Micro-Rituals

Micro-rituals, or tiny habits, can cue your brain and body that you're stepping out of parenting mode and into work (or vice versa). Practicing various kinds of micro-rituals facilitates a more seamless, automatic, and full transition across roles.[19] Your body and mind learn to associate cues with role transition, including physical cues, scripts shared with others (like "Hello!" and "Goodbye!"), internal scripts you say to yourself, and behavioral rituals.[20] You can use these rites of passage to help you return to a task when you've been interrupted, as those of us who have small kids and large colleagues often are.

Moving from parenting to work, I often complete a three-minute mindfulness exercise. I spend one minute just being quiet in my body, one minute setting an intention for what I plan to get done, and a third minute on gratitude. I also use a hot cup of tea or coffee as a physical cue that it's work time. The ritual of making myself a hot beverage and the physical sensations of heat and scents emanating from the mug help my body get into the mode of work productivity. Transitioning back from work to parenting is easier. Hugging my boys feels great, and the connection with their little bodies fills me with overwhelming love. When I'm mindful during that reconnection hug, I can almost effortlessly drop back into parenting mode.

You can activate these kinds of micro-rituals whenever you get distracted, tired, or stuck on a difficult problem or parenting worry. Simply notice your wandering mind. Then practice whichever micro-ritual is most fitting before returning to the task at hand.

Dual Detachment

Bold as it may seem, I also encourage you to try detaching from both roles. Yes—at the *same* time! Of course, this dual detachment is hardest of all since the many demands are so very persistent. But inspired by the science supporting regular breaks from productive life, by some of my more religious patients, and by a repeated experience of my own burnout, I began committing myself to a Shabbat break a few years ago. I've found that the efforts to overcome my own productivity and technology habits were entirely worth it. And I've found that while I can't make it to a yoga retreat in a tropical location, I can still plug into rest.

My Shabbat break involves a prohibition of productive work and limited connectivity to those outside of my immediate family. I refrain from writing or podcasting, and I strive to keep my phone out of sight for the day. The best part of my day, though, is when my kids go to their rooms for midday rest time. During that hour (drumroll, please!), I take a nap. From Thomas Edison to Margaret Thatcher, renowned figures throughout history esteemed for their sharp minds and productive work took naps. I'm in good company.

The science of napping shows that a midday sleep, ideally lasting between ten and twenty minutes for healthy adults,[21] can improve self-control, emotion regulation,[22] and memory.[23] Napping also has a positive impact on task performance (especially for habitual nappers).[24] I can vouch for these data. My weekly nap restores me in a way that few other strategies do. I love my kids well on Saturday afternoons, and most Sundays (which, fatefully, happens to be the day I'm working on this section), I find myself raring to work once again.

I'm clearly an enthusiastic advocate of napping. So I surprised myself by blushing when my oldest son outed my nap habit to an adult I was just getting to know. I'm not alone in feeling discomfort around rest. Tricia Hersey, artist, activist, and founder of The Nap Ministry, is on a mission is to disrupt a system that views people as machines rather than divine beings. She explained in an NPR interview that most of us have been brainwashed to believe that rest is a luxury rather than a right. The prohibition of rest, argues Hersey, is an issue of social justice that's evident in the history of slavery, where Black bodies were viewed as tools of production not worthy of respite. With this in mind, she says, we can "see resting as a resistance movement, as a movement and a call for us to ignore the rush of productivity."[25] Working parents can join the resistance by reframing our embarrassment as the hangover from false messaging and ideals about rest. And the acquaintance my son outed my nap habit to? It turned out she was a devoted napper—a member of the resistance, too.

Of course, not everyone can nap at the drop of a hat like I can. (It's an enviable skill, to be sure.) But napping is just one strategy for dual detachment. Other options include meditation, long showers, daydreaming, solo walks, social time with friends, or time devoted to hobbies. Any way that you can build in time to fully detach from both work and parenting, even for brief chunks of time, can do good for your working parenthood.

· · · · ·

Pause to Deliberate Detachment

Get creative about taking breaks from both your work and parenting roles by:

- Unhooking from guilt
- Using role transitions to psychologically detach
- Engaging midday rest

- Downloading thoughts
- Implementing a tech turnoff
- Cultivating micro-rituals

Pick or generate one practice for each category above for detaching from work or parenting. Write it down and try it out for a period of two weeks. Take notes on how fully you were able to "switch off." Track how much you felt restored and ready to return to the role(s) you had detached from.

. . . . .

DELEGATE TO BREAK

Steve Stewart-Williams, an evolutionary psychologist and professor at the University of Nottingham, has written two books on evolutionary psychology. I turn to him with evolutionary questions—and because I love his New Zealand accent. On the topic of delegating parental responsibilities, Steve told me, "For most primates, the mother alone can care for the kids. For us [humans], that's just not possible. In fact, it's barely possible when Mum and Dad combine forces to raise their offspring. It takes a small army to do it comfortably."

The term *alloparenting* describes parent-like care provided for nondescendant young. According to the anthropologist and primatologist Sarah Blaffer Hrdy's "cooperative breeding hypothesis," humans are designed for alloparenting. In her book *Mothers and Others,* Hrdy writes, "Well might anthropologists and politicians remind us that 'it takes a village' to rear children today. What they often leave out, however, is that so far as the particular apes that evolved into *Homo sapiens* are concerned, it always has. Without alloparents, there never would have been a human species."[26]

Human parents rear children in groups because parenting alone works less well for both human parents and their vulnerable young.[27] That's why long ago in our history, all humans lived in villages where parents, grandparents, aunts, and uncles all participated in raising children. This cooperative care increased the reproductive success of biological parents by breaking up the burden of infant care. Parents could then invest in other kinds of activities—like, say, work—that increased resources needed to raise young children. Sharing care with others made sense in the context of villages with limited resources.

But alloparental care in modern society—even in places with abundant resources—has benefits, too. As Steve told me, "Alloparenting benefits kids by benefiting their parents. If the parental load is distributed more widely, parents will be less run off their feet, less tired, and less stressed out. That, in turn, may mean better parent-offspring relationships and a happier home." In fact, in a recent study of over eighteen thousand infants in Britain, care by alloparents was associated with a 15 percent reduction in hospitalizations during the first nine months of life. The researchers concluded that "the finding may have been driven by increased risk for infants of mothers caring for their infant during normal working hours with no other help, such as from the father or pay-for-day-care."[28] Research with young mothers similarly shows that whether from grandparents living with them or from visiting nurses, caregiving support led to improved health and development for children.[29]

These days, of course, many working parents live far from family and many working parents do the job of parenting and work without a partner. That working parenthood pressures you to install all kinds of supports turns out to be of benefit to you and your kids. For instance, you might feel guilty that you can't be there at pickup or for school performances in the middle of the day, and you rarely can "save" them when they forget their lunch or jacket at home. But your unavailability helps your children learn how to engage support from caregivers who aren't you—and learn to take responsibility for their jackets and lunches!

If you are partnered and you both work or if you are single, you'll have a rich opportunity to involve other caregivers in the form of day-care providers, teachers, and friends. I interviewed Megan, a research coordinator who had her son later in life, who worried that she wouldn't know how to parent. She found a remarkable gift in needing to share her parenting efforts with the day care her son attended during her work hours. In those early years, she told me, both she and her son "benefited from having a lot of adults who have loved him." She added, "Especially when he was an infant, they *taught* me how to parent."

When help is not easy to come by, you can get creative by building a support system of relationships with neighbors, babysitters, and the educational, recreational, or spiritual communities you and your kids are involved in. You might even consider getting integrated into a local retirement community. Many older adults crave contact with children, and giving someone a chance to care for your child can give them a gift of a new relationship while providing you with support. As the distinguished child anthropologist David F. Lancy explained to me, "It's kind of a myth to think of the stay-at-home, full-time mom as this angelic creature who is able to adequately fulfill her child's every need." And, he said, "From my experience as an anthropologist living and working in remote villages, I see how beneficial it is for children to have all these people to interact with."

Appreciating this benefit can help you let go of toxic working-parent guilt. After all, the delegation of caretaking activities isn't a weakness in modern working parenthood. It's something we are evolved to do as humans. It's a strength of our species. Or, as David wrote, "As long as a reasonably competent and caring individual is in charge, the more loving, intelligent, and dedicated helpers surrounding the nest, the better off the twenty-first century child will be."[30]

The constraints operate in the opposite direction, too, forcing working parents to delegate at work. This pressure is just as advantageous as delegating in the parenting realm. Delegating helps organizations improve task coordination, productivity, and the performance of individuals who can then focus on their unique specializations and skill sets. In other words, more delegation in the workspace helps workers increase their focus on tasks inside their wheelhouse. Workers can dedicate their resources to the areas of their highest output and skill. Allowing workers to delegate can prevent spreading attention and energy too thinly. And it can reduce turnover, since delegating increases the likelihood of feeling satisfied in your job.[31]

But delegating may not come easily to everyone. In fact, there are some notable gender differences in comfort with delegating tasks to others. Women tend to feel guiltier and thus benefit less when they assign tasks to others. But in a study looking at gender differences, researchers found that by reframing delegation as communally beneficial, guilt could be reduced, helping women experience the positive effects of delegation more.[32] In other words, women might delegate more—and get more benefit from the delegating—when they view doing so as good for everyone (which it is!).

Rather than getting hooked on feeling guilty about asking for help or delegating some of your tasks to others, seek to appreciate having allies in work and in parenting. You'll access more opportunities to recharge, specialize in work tasks, and grow the caring network for your children. You can seek out creative ways to take a break from work and from parenting when you set your sights on creating a village to delegate to.

. . . . .

Pause to Delegate

To get the most out of delegation, shift your mindset to appreciate its benefits. In parenting, connect to a value of giving your child more caregivers to love them and more support for yourself to be your best parent self. In work, connect to a value of assigning tasks to others that are not your specialization or where your efforts are less optimal.

Ask yourself:

- *What caregivers can I engage as allies in the job of parenting?* Consider day-care providers, babysitters, friends, neighbors, teachers, therapists, and camp counselors, to name a few.

- *What work tasks can I delegate out and to whom can I delegate them?* Consider starting with small, less important tasks and build from there.

· · · · ·

THINK SMALL AND SAVOR

It's possible that the earlier-described strategies to get some rest aren't the perfect fit for you. That's not a problem since you can generate your own detachment practices by tailoring these principles as well as two important S's: Thinking *small* and *savoring*.

Seek out *micro*breaks and then strive to enjoy the heck out of them. Psychologists call this practice "savoring," and the practice involves stretching out positive experiences, whether they are past, present, or future.[33] You can savor a moment by noticing the sensory experiences of the moment (touch, taste, smell, hearing, seeing). Using your senses helps to absorb you more fully and more mindfully inside of an experience and extract the most positivity possible. Savoring can be done privately, of course. But you can also amplify the goodness by sharing a positive experience. That might look like narrating what you appreciate, laughing out loud with your kids (or with your colleagues), or initiating a celebratory event to honor and even ritualize your rest. So whether it's the warmth and solitude of a shower, the moments between finishing the night-time routine with your children and reopening your computer, a new Netflix show, or even taking a slow, centering breath a few times a day, the smallest moments of detachment can count if you approach them with an intention to be mindful and to relish the experience.

PULLING IT TOGETHER

Laurie, a hospital administrator, was profoundly burned out when she began therapy with me. She had two young daughters, ages one and three, and her spouse worked long hours and had a lengthy commute. She was maxed out with both work and parenting, often feeling that she was carrying the load by herself. As we worked together, she began to appreciate how her kids' school settings were supports she could take advantage of with less guilt in tow.

We discussed the general benefits for her and her shy, sensitive kids in receiving the day-care support. A shy temperament, present in about 15 percent of three-year-olds, represents one of the many risk factors for the development of an anxiety disorder. But in one longitudinal study, researchers discovered that those who went to day care in their first two years were more likely to avoid developing an anxiety disorder than those who hadn't attended day care.[34] This finding is a testament to the power of practice. Day care offers shy children opportunities to practice social skills and confidence building. Appreciating the value of day care for herself and her kids helped Laurie's guilt loosen, which in turn helped her to work more mindfully.

The true test came when Laurie hit a particularly stressful work period. One day, she spent hours dealing with frustrated board members and organizing virtual events. She was so consumed by all the things she needed to get done that she was already late for pickups by the time she realized the workday was over. Laurie hurriedly packed her bag and raced over. Panting at the doorway of the preschool, she noticed her mind caught up in all the work still left to do and the guilt over being late. Then, Laurie paused. She took three breaths on the threshold, deliberately bringing herself to the present moment. She carefully set her work worries aside and entered the classroom with arms open. Her daughter ran joyfully into her embrace.

* *

The TL/DR (Too Long, Didn't Read)

CREATE RESTORATIVE BREAKS FROM EACH ROLE

Use the pressure to transition from one role to the other as an opportunity to take a break from the role you are stepping away from.

To accomplish the kind of full role detachment that offers a break:

STEP 1: *Embrace Pressure.* See the advantage of natural pressures in working parenthood. Rather than fighting the pressure, use it to prompt breaks from each role.

STEP 2: *Be present.* Bring yourself, mind and body, to the role you are currently in.

STEP 3: *Return to the present.* Notice when your mind drifts to where you are not (and it *will*, since this is what minds do!) or whether technology or worries are fracturing your time. Then gently bring your attention back to the role at hand.

STEP 4: *Notice Guilty Thoughts.* If guilty thoughts or feelings arise, thank your mind for caring about *all* of your important life roles. Observe those thoughts without judgment, appreciating that your mind is simply trying to help you be a better worker and parent.

STEP 5: *Get Perspective.* Recognize that guilt is often inaccurate in its messaging and counterproductive in its effects. And remember that delegating tasks and taking time away from each role benefits the role (and your kids and job).

STEP 6: *Unhook from Unhelpful.* Guilty thoughts and feelings may not serve you well, but recognizing that isn't going to make them disappear. So rather than fruitlessly attempting to extinguish those thoughts, make space for them. Then gently turn your attention back to your current role and return to step 1.

7

TURN CONSTRAINTS INTO CREATIVITY

> I've been blessed enough to act in movies, TV, and on
> Broadway, but my finest acting moments have been with
> children. Parents of young children are always acting. . . .
> You act excited to read a story for the five-hundredth time.
> ("Yes, that hungry caterpillar is very hungry!") The excite-
> ment I show to some of the children's scribbles should
> get me a Golden Globe nomination.
> —JIM GAFFIGAN

If you attended school before the 2000s, you might have learned
about two different photoreceptors that make vision possible. In
the retina—the layer of tissue at the back of the eye—cones are responsible for daylight vision, while rods are responsible for vision
in low light. But in the 1990s, a third kind of photoreceptor was discovered. This one was photosensitive but did not contribute directly
to visual perception. It wasn't until 2002 that a team of scientists at
Brown University revealed that this photoreceptor's function was to
signal light and set our circadian clock.[1] Felice Dunn, a member of
that three-person team, was an undergraduate student at the time.

As a young girl, Felice's reverence for nature and perception
was captured through artistic expression—mostly oil paints, but
also pen and watercolor. But as an undergraduate, Felice realized

that unlike many in the art department, her passion was not about making social statements but rather "deconstructing how we see the world." So she began to split her time between the neighboring art school and a visual science laboratory. In this split, she found the perfect way to bring her creativity to life.

Felice defines the creative scientific process as "working on a hard problem for years at a time and taking care to study it formally and rigorously, and communicate it in writing and pictorially." It is a labor-intensive, lengthy process. Felice's investments of time paid off in research progress and publications in premier scientific journals. By the time she was in her midthirties, Felice had secured a faculty position at the University of California, San Francisco, a leading research institution, running a well-resourced laboratory funded by grants from the National Institutes of Health and managing talented students and postdoctoral fellows.

Established in her career, Felice felt ready to become a parent and was joyous when she got pregnant. But the transition to parenthood shattered the world she had so carefully built. Everything she thought she knew—her routines, her life goals, and even her strengths—fell apart at the seams. She told me, "I really had an identity crisis when I had him. I didn't know how to gracefully let go of how I was before." No longer could Felice work days in excess of twelve hours, continuing to push on a problem until her energy reserves were completely depleted. Something significant had to change.

Felice didn't want to abandon the work she loves or time with her child. So she sought different pathways to support creativity and productivity. Now Felice takes advantage of different processes, telling me that often "while I'm giggling with my child I realize I've just solved a problem I've been working on for the week—not consciously but *unconsciously*. The balance comes in accepting that things won't happen because I force them to, but they might happen in a nonlinear time frame and in times when I'm not at work as well."

Working parents may be short on time, attention, and energy, but the ways that role conflict disrupts time for creativity can help us when we allow our constraints to *spark* creativity.

GETTING TO KNOW YOUR CREATIVE PROCESS

Creativity has been defined as the ability to produce ideas that are both novel and useful.[2] The creative process begins with knowledge, then takes us beyond what we already know. Remarkably, creative problems can be solved through conscious, attention-heavy, and deliberate approaches *and* through rapid, spontaneous insights.[3] Let's take a closer look at how you store the kind of knowledge used for creative ends to understand why such different pathways can each lead to creative insights.

Consider a typical supermarket. In most supermarkets, you'll find an entire aisle devoted to cereal. You'll also find that all of the dairy, the meats, the vegetables, the soup, the beans, and so on are grouped together by broad category. It's an ideal approach for shopping in an organized, efficient manner. Just like a supermarket, your brain organizes conceptually similar information together in your mental network. This approach to mental structuring allows you to manage a greater quantity of information. It's easier to learn new information, understand it, and recall it when it's associated with what you already know, understand, and can remember. But tidy organization, despite its many advantages, can hinder creativity.

Say you have a recipe for stew that you've grown tired of. You've been making the stew for so long that you're feeling stumped, not inspired, as you attempt to think of ways to invigorate dinner. You are trapped in convergent thinking. Convergent thinking, first described by the psychologist J. P. Guilford in the 1950s, emphasizes speed and logic, relying on what is familiar to help you arrive at a "correct" solution.[4] Convergent thinking is efficient, but it often lacks creativity. Divergent thinking is where the more creative ideas are generated. This kind of thought process is nonlinear, spontaneous, and free-flowing. It's a less efficient but far more creative approach to problem-solving.

Back to your lackluster stew. Your regular weekly trip to the supermarket leaves you with no new ideas, so you consider spending time reflecting on or researching new twists on your old recipe. Tight on time, you also consider shortcuts to activating your creative process. You could seek a different perspective by talking to a friend with a different cultural background and thus a different perspective on flavor. Or this week you could head to a different market altogether, such as the nearby specialty store that stocks vegetables unfamiliar to you. Maybe you could even wander aimlessly about the supermarket you already frequent. Putting the preconceived ideas of stew out of your mind while exploring that familiar store might help you discover the perfect item. Better yet, bring your child to prompt you to see things from a different eye level because, as the twentieth-century French novelist Marcel Proust noted, "The voyage of discovery lies not in finding new landscapes, but in having new eyes." Perhaps your child will help you discover a new item that was there all along. Or else you might just end up with donuts for dinner.

Devotion of time and attention can certainly help you creatively solve complex problems. But it isn't the only pathway available. Nor is it always the most useful one.

CULTIVATING CREATIVITY THROUGH CONSTRAINTS

More time to work can boost creativity. But we can also grow bored (and boring) when we do the same thing all the time. Needing to move between roles limits the time and energy we can devote to any one thing. And at the same time, it can keep us fresh and inspired. As you may recall, the Taoist yin-yang symbol suggests that opposition between forces naturally benefits the whole. A tension between paying attention and *not* paying attention, having constrained time,[5] role conflicts, and general stress each enhances creativity.[6]

Consider the profession of social work, which comprises a host of incompatible demands. Like working parents, social workers regularly face role conflict. Social workers are expected to act in the capacity of both police and social service to help those who may not even want help. Social workers are regularly caught between the needs of clients, community, courts, and other agencies, not to mention their own finite reserves of energy. In a yearlong study of an agency providing mandated social services, social workers described their conflicting demands to be "impossible" yet unavoidable elements of their work.[7] As the social workers were followed through the year, though, it became clear that the challenges of their jobs forced them to rise above what was initially perceived as impossible. By considering multiple points of view, developing flexible approaches that sometimes required a redefined goal, and engaging diverse resources all while serving various stakeholders, their creative problem-solving grew, as did their abilities to meet the needs of their job. Creativity grew out of their constraints.

GOLDILOCKS STRESS

Like many social workers, working parents experience high levels of role conflict, time constraints, and general stress. But like the social workers discovered, stress can stimulate the creative process.[8]

Those who took Psych 101 in college may already be familiar with the idea that stress—that is, physiological and mental arousal—can improve performance.[9] The Yerkes-Dodson law describes an inverted U-shaped curve where a midrange amount of arousal (mapped along the x-axis) results in improved performance. Better performance is more likely when you experience a Goldilocks amount of arousal—not too little, not too much.

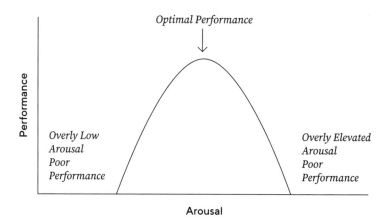

Though this inverted U-shaped curve originated with experiments of Japanese dancing mice being shocked, research conducted since that time shows that having a moderate level of arousal can help you become more creative. In fact, a moderate amount of stress, time pressure, and role conflict can all act to enhance your creativity. [10] What's more, researchers seeking to discover who responded creatively to role conflict at work found that high (versus low) mindfulness heightened workers' creativity. [11]

· · · · ·

Pause to Get Goldilocks–Mindful in Your Stress

You can use mindfulness strategies to *expand* the range of stress that is useful for creativity.

- *Begin by tuning in to your stress.* When you feel physiological or mental arousal, notice what that experience is like. *Where* do you feel the stress? *How* are you experiencing it? What parts of your body does it show up in, and in what way does it occupy your mind space?

- *Use your breath and your values to help you regulate arousal.* Help your body enter a midrange of arousal by using calming or activating strategies, depending on your initial arousal level. If you feel your body entering panic mode, try breathing in for four counts and out for five (a longer out breath helps calm the body). Conversely, if you are feeling bored, reconnect to the reason an activity matters to you. This reason represents the values underlying your efforts, and values can act as an activating agent, propelling you to move toward what matters to you.

- *Notice stories about your stress.* Take particular note of attachment to stories that define discomfort as a problem that needs to be solved. Acknowledge this as "a story" your mind drops into when you feel stress. Perhaps you can experience that story of stress with a touch of distance as you look at it, instead of being absorbed by it.

- *Consider editing "stress stories" in ways that help you remain mindfully present.* Turn toward a story that emphasizes opportunities embedded in stress. For example:

  » A rapidly beating heart or anxious minds signifies that your body is preparing to do something that requires energy.

  » Showing up for a struggle between roles can help you adopt new perspectives.

  » Stress may help you grow more resilient.

  » Time constraints may compel you to seek out greater efficiency.

  » Arousal often points to something that matters deeply to you.

  » Conflict means you are tugged between multiple domains that matter to you.

Each of these stories can help you use the arousal in ways that serve you well. (We'll dive more deeply into strategies to finesse your stress in chapter 10.)

· · · · ·

USE INCOMPATIBLE ROLES TO GET A FRESH PERSPECTIVE

Staying caught up on trendy shows keeps me connected to my girlfriends and my husband. Also, I love mindless screen time. I recently watched the first season of *Emily in Paris*. This show was heavy on fluff, so you wouldn't think it would prompt deep thought. But balancing frivolous screen time with serious reflections on pathways to creative thinking pointed me to a creativity realization: many of my favorite shows, movies, and books have a central plotline of bringing together individuals from entirely different backgrounds or perspectives.

When Emily, played by Lily Collins, arrives in Paris from Chicago, she brings her American perspective on fashion, food, and marketing. The latter is important since she's come to Paris to work at a company recently bought by the American firm where she had been working. Her American perspective is deeply irritating to her French colleagues (cue all the stereotypes). But through lots of trial and error, and all while wearing insanely high heels, Emily proves that intermingling French and American approaches can revitalize the stagnant business.

Relationships between different people, as well as displacements from native environments to unfamiliar ones, are a common entertainment ploy. These plotlines grab our attention like a chemistry experiment where you drop mismatched items into the same pot. "What could happen?" the brain wonders. Might there be a chemical reaction that rearranges the molecular structure of the initial components? If so, we could end up with an entirely new blend, perhaps better than when we started! And what a satisfying ending that would be.

Clichéd as this form of entertainment might be, there is truth at its core. Bringing clashing cultures, individuals, and ideas together often results in a recombination better than what we started with. As the world renowned psychologist Mihaly Csikszentmihalyi wrote, "An idea or product that deserves the label 'creative' arises from the synergy of many sources and not only from the mind of a single person."[12] That is, unless your one brain can hold multiple areas of expertise, like the mind of a polymath. Being able to hold expertise in domains ranging from musical composition to botany or from human anatomy to engineering allows the bringing together of old ideas in new ways.

Expanding out to the cultural level, periods of bountiful creativity, such as the Renaissance, occur because features of those eras (economic prosperity, freedom, patronage) bring a critical mass of brilliant individuals together.[13] Interaction and intellectual exchange of ideas between individuals and the freedom for an individual to reflect on different disciplines lead to creative flourishing.

You don't have to be a genius or live during a period of cultural flourishing to grow creativity. Research shows that moving to a place where people and culture are markedly different from your own[14] or working within teams consisting of diverse people generates greater creativity.[15] For me, shaking up my academic focus with more frivolous fare helped land a fun example of dissimilar ideas bumping into each other. Dislodging from routines—in thought or behavior—pushes you to apply old knowledge in new ways.

Work and parenting, and even hobbies or other diversions outside of work or parenthood, offer just this kind of natural opportunity to regularly refresh your perspective. You can strive to use the regular switches between your roles to see things anew, to dismantle ideas you've long taken for granted, and to get exposed to ideas from one role that you can transplant into the other.

. . . . .

Pause to Activate a Fresh Perspective

Look for fresh perspectives to feed creativity. Try the following:

- *See work from your child's perspective.* This practice is what Buddhists call "beginner's mind." Beginner's mind describes an attitude of curiosity and eagerness that is without preconception. Your child may have little familiarity with the tools you use, the space you sit in, or even the way you interact with people in your work. How might they see you and what you do all day? Use your imagination to step into your child's mind and into a fresh perspective of what you do at work.

- *Consider parenting from a work perspective.* You might also consider your colleagues' different interpersonal approaches to activate your beginner's mind in the parenting sphere. When the boss is immature, how does your savvy colleague respond? When people fight, how does the workplace mediator calm things down? How does the effective boss quell dissent? Step into a work colleague's mind (one whose mind is helpful, that is!) to access a fresh perspective on parenting challenges.

- *Use entertainment as inspiration.* Consider the appeal of the latest Netflix craze your friends are excited about that you never would have gotten exposed to on your own (Bling Empire, anyone?). Ask yourself what a show's appeal—shallow or voyeuristic as it might be—can teach you about the human spirit, what drives us, and what connects us as humans.

- *Stay open.* Above all, remain open to receiving new perspectives in order to reinvigorate your own.

· · · · ·

BEEFING UP PARENTING STEW WITH WORK

The comedian Jim Gaffigan has five kids. I'm envious because I'm pretty certain that the Gaffigan dinnertime is sidesplittingly funny. Having a chef for a parent offers fun, too, with tasty cuisine and much prettier birthday cakes than you'll find in my home. And a fiction-writer parent likely makes for better bedtime stories that diverge from the written page in spellbinding ways each night. My home is missing out on all of that goodness. Luckily, my biomedical engineer husband teaches my boys about concepts like momentum, optics, and even the science of blood, while I regularly engage them in conversations about relationships, values, and emotional health. That counts as inspired parenting. Right?

Okay, sure, my kids might still prefer dinner with Gaffigan (I might, too—his bit on Hot Pockets slays). Still, unfunny parents can make dinner uniquely creative when we use work skills to spice things up. From the arts to science and far beyond, jobs help us hone our specific skill sets. Manufacturing jobs teach about technology, customer service jobs teach about patience and interpersonal skills, science teaches how to ask good questions, skilled labor can offer a leg up on hands-on abilities such as fixing toasters, jumping a car, or making a bookshelf, and so on. We can use our specialized skills in creative ways while parenting. So whatever your job may be, bring your skills home to creatively amplify your parenting.

Creatively Modeling Your Values

Work also offers a creative way to teach children values through your modeling. Rather than lecturing about contributing to society, work ethic, persistence in the face of failure, forgiveness, and navigating complex situations, work offers a way to *show* your children each of these values through your actions. As the author and civil rights activist James Baldwin noted, "Children have never been very good at listening to their elders, but they have never failed to imitate them."[16]

It's easy to lecture our kids about values, but neurological research reveals that our children really are wired to learn by observing us.[17] Your work offers an opportunity to reinforce the importance of your core values, whether it's being empathic, adventurous, amusing, committed, disciplined, health-conscious, friendly, results-oriented, curious, or even creative.

For many women, work outside the home is a way to teach children the value of feminism and that women's roles need not be reduced to the domestic sphere. As my friend and podcast cohost Debbie Sorenson told me, "I stress with my two daughters that my job is really important to me. I want to give them the message that work is important." Natalie, a mother of one who works in Jewish education, similarly described working as providing an important model about careers for women. Growing up, Natalie wished that her own mother had worked because she would have wanted her to have interests outside of the family. She wants her daughter to bear witness to the importance of pursuing nonfamily interests.

Our work can also help us model how we value making contributions to the world outside of our home. As Sara, an executive director at a nonprofit, explained, awareness and action around injustices of equality and opportunity are core values embodied in her work. She told me, "The nature of the work that I do and the values of my organization come out when I'm talking to my son.

'Is that kind? Is that thoughtful? Are you being a caring citizen?' are questions I ask because I'm trying to help him become a good human being." Megan, an obstetric anesthesiologist, has three boys. It's always been important for her that they know the facts about the birds and the bees and that they have empathy for others' pain. Knowing what she does and appreciating the frailty of the human body have given them early lessons in biology and empathy. It might set them up for a caring career, but Megan sees the main contribution of her work to their lives as "growing stronger men that are going to be more adaptable to family situations."

. . . . .

Pause to Reflect on How Work Can Add to Parenting

CREATIVE SKILLS

Jobs require you to get skilled in some area, whether it's counting out change for a cup of coffee, tracking weather changes for agricultural optimization, educating young people, administrating, serving customers, manufacturing equipment, entertaining, and so on. Reflect on what those specialized skills are. Then consider how you can employ them to add creativity to parenting.

MODELING VALUES

Since we teach as much through action as we do through words, work offers an important arena to model what you value. Consider how work helps you show up in the world in ways that matter deeply to you. Find opportunities to have your kids witness your values in action.

. . . . .

Season Work with a Dash of Parenting

My work revolves around relationships. Long before having kids, I dedicated myself to studying and treating romantic relationships. When I entered into working parenthood, though, it occurred to me that relationships don't only exist between people. Relationships also exist between *roles*. Just as a relationship between married partners has layers of complexity we can easily overlook, so does the relationship between work and parenthood. This powerful insight opened up an entirely new professional pathway for me, and you're reading the tangible results now.

I'm not alone in discovering that parenting can open up new ways of thinking about and approaching work. Many individuals find their relationship with work changing in surprising and inspired ways after adding children to the mix. An associate professor of marketing told me about an experience of bringing her daughter to her annual checkup. As she chatted with the pediatrician over her daughter's head, the conversation somehow turned to the topic of how service providers—such as pediatricians—can "fire" the consumer for actions such as refusing vaccinations. The conversation that day spurred a question in her mind about provider-consumer relationships. She located some data to explore the question in depth, activating a new area of inquiry in her research.

Of course, new pathways often don't involve such radical shifts in our jobs. But the less obvious shifts in creative approaches to work inspired by parenting can be extremely powerful, too. Anne, a lawyer, explained, "Being a parent is useful when interacting with employees who have performance issues: Encouraging without judging is useful. That is exactly what you do with your kids." Taking lessons learned from parenting into the workplace, Anne told me, "balances me out and helps me to be a much better corporate citizen." Bring the different perspective you adopt and skills you build as "parent" into your job for a creatively inspired advantage.

. . . . .

Pause to Reflect on How Parenting Can Be Creatively Added to Work

- *Consider how parenting has influenced the trajectory of your work.* Becoming a parent may change not only how many hours you can devote to work but also how you show up (even beyond the spit stains on your shirt-front). Consider ways that being a parent influences your work self. How might your child's passionate interests or interpersonal quirks change your work focus? How might being a parent change—increase or decrease—your drive for promotions? Does having an introverted or extroverted child change how you relate to colleagues from either camp?

- *Consider how parenting has changed who you are and what you value.* Becoming a parent often adds an entirely new element of our personhood. We might become more attentive to relationships, teaching, manners, values, spirituality, meaning-making, or earning a reliable income. And based on our children's needs or interests, we might expand our own passions. Reflect on how parenting has changed you and how you can bring those changes into work in inspired ways.

. . . . .

THE GREAT INCUBATE

According to legend, Archimedes cried "Eureka!" when he had a flash of insight into the principle of buoyancy. Notably, Archimedes was taking a bath, not bearing down at work.

The legend of the Eureka moment might be more fiction than fact, but it endures because it depicts an experience most people have had. Whether you're attempting to solve a complicated work or parenting problem, or striving to remember the name of that 1980s star who disappeared after the Brat Pack era, thinking harder can make that answer you're grasping for more elusive. Miraculously, though, when you turn your attention elsewhere, the answer sometimes magically appears.

Time away from our hardest-driving problems can offer us this same Eureka effect. We can allow the activity in our unconscious mind to take over. Activity in the unconscious sometimes connects the dots that cannot be connected through conscious effort. For this reason, time away from work and time away from parenting can each spur creativity.

The directive to "step away" seems simple enough. But it can be surprisingly hard to follow through with a pause when we live in such a hard-driving world. As the cognitive scientist Sian Beilock explained to me, "We have this tendency or inclination to tough it out, to bang our head against the wall until we get to the answer. But there's a psychological phenomenon called the incubation effect that actually shows when people step away from a difficult task, they're more likely to come back and be able to solve it." You can use your role conflict to impose an incubation period.

Incubation, defined as moving conscious attention *away* from a task, is the second step to creative problem-solving in a model first proposed by Graham Wallas, the social psychologist and founder of the London School of Economics.[18] According to this model, the process of creativity begins with preparation. This is the phase of intense work and conscious, directed effort to clearly identify the problem, think deeply about it, and try to work out a solution. Next is incubation. Here, you step away, allowing your mind to take a break and turn attention elsewhere. It's often during this step away that we bump into the third step—illumination—when a solution appears, sometimes as if out of thin air. You might then return to the problem in the fourth step, called verification, with your new solution in hand to be tested.

Wallas's Four-Step Creativity Process

Wallas's description of the process of having creative insights is one of the most widely accepted models. In it, Wallas outlines four distinct steps:

1. Preparation
2. Incubation
3. Illumination
4. Verification

Wander without Getting Lost

In a rest state where you've turned off conscious problem-solving, an interconnected group of brain structures called the default mode network (DMN) lights up. These DMN structures are associated with creative, outside-of-the-box thinking.[19] That means that when you've stopped focusing on a problem, the unconsciously creative parts of your brain get cracking outside of your awareness.

When we incubate, we engage in a mental process much like aimless wandering around the supermarket. That kind of wandering can lead to creative places. One study comparing groups on a creativity task showed that participants who took a break to engage in a task that allowed their minds to wander were 40 percent more creative than the other three groups who took no break, did a different demanding task, or rested quietly.[20] In other words, engaging in tasks that take the mind *away* from the primary task allows the mind to wander in creative ways. So the lack of intellectual stimulation that you might experience while playing peekaboo or listening to your five-year-old's twenty-minute-long synopsis of his favorite *Paw Patrol* episode can actually provide a boost to your creative thinking.

If you recall, linear problem-solving, or convergent thinking, uses logic, accuracy, and your existing knowledge base. Unlike convergent thinking, divergent thinking leads to ideas that are spontaneous, free flowing, and may even seem bizarre to your conscious mind. As luck would have it, divergent thinking takes place when your DMN is active and your conscious thinking is turned off. Divergent thinking is what happens when your mind wanders about.

But an important condition for enhancing the effects of mind wandering is to do something conceptually different from whatever it is you've been struggling with. For example, one study directed participants to work on a target problem that was either verbal or spatial. This was the "preparation time." After that preparation period, participants were given a different activity to work on (the "incubation period" for the first task). Researchers varied whether the incubation task was verbal or spatial. They discovered that incubation tasks *dissimilar* from the original task led to stronger creativity effects compared to similar incubation tasks.[21] Other studies, too, suggest that when we are trapped in a particularly tedious task, mind-wandering over to content that's more personally interesting can boost our mood, which is also good for creativity.[22] In other words, engaging in different kinds of tasks during an incubation period can help you feel less bored and get more creative.

The divergent nature of work and parenting tasks helps incubation work well. Stepping into roles that require different parts of your brain to be engaged can power up a larger incubation effect. A creative advantage arises *because* work and parenting are so dissimilar in their mental requirements. Even cooler? Being aware of the possibilities inside of forced interruptions can help you all the more. As one study showed, knowing you'll be coming back to a creatively demanding task after that break helps you incubate even more effectively.[23] So power up your working-parent creativity by using tasks at work as an incubation period for parenting dilemmas and parenting as time to incubate your work problems.

· · · · ·

Pause to Incubate

Take advantage of transitions from work to parenthood and from parenthood to work to support incubating problems that need creative solutions.

- *Mindfully turn your attention away from a problem.* This frees your unconscious to engage in divergent thinking.

- *Provide your mind with ample time away—incubation doesn't happen instantaneously!* Assure your boss, your child, and yourself that turning to something different is likely to benefit everyone. Even if that means your active attention will be directed away from something they want from you.

- *Engage in a task different from the domain of your unsolved problem.* A conscious mind absorbed in other tasks will be inhibited from covert attempts at problem-solving. It'll leave your unconscious mind freer to incubate.

These guidelines all provide you—and perhaps your boss and your child—some reassurance that stepping away from work or parenting can serve each of those roles well on the creativity front.[24]

· · · · ·

A CREATIVITY CAPSTONE

Felice Dunn, the creative neuroscientist from the start of this chapter, described to me that her son's "favorite thing to say is 'Whyyy?'" Like his mama, he's a curious and creative kid. Felice told me, "I love being able to say, 'Let's do something together to figure out why.' There's a framework that I get from work in which it's natural for me to answer that, because with a student or postdoc, I'm not going to give them the answer but I can walk them through it. I love being able to apply that to my parenting role because I think he appreciates it. Children are scientists, and they are trying to figure out the world around them. You can either tell it to them or empirically show them."

Being a scientist offers Felice inspiration in guiding her son's developing ideas about the world. She ups her creativity as a parent by bringing her scientist self into the role of parent, teaching her small son the scientific method of answering questions and joining him in his excitement of all that he observes. Her role as a parent gives her the opportunity to incubate solutions for complex problems at work by being forced to step away from problems she is stuck on.

To be sure, Felice continues to experience role conflict, time constraints, and ratcheted-up stress as a result of being both a devoted researcher and parent. Yet those stressors also offer a creative leg up in both spheres.

* *

The TL/DR (Too Long, Didn't Read)

PAUSE WORKING PARENTHOOD TO
BOOST YOUR CREATIVITY

Dedicating massive amounts of time, energy, and attention is just one pathway to creativity. Working parents may not be able to easily access that pathway, but they can take advantage of the creative benefits of stress, role incompatibility, and forced time away from roles.

- *Recognize the upside of constraints.* Stress, role conflict, and time constraints in moderate amounts can help enhance creativity by pressing us to develop new skills, open up to new perspectives, and take time away from each of our roles.

- *Find fresh perspectives.* Inhabiting different kinds of life roles means you have opportunities to refresh your work perspective during parenting and your parenting perspective during work.

- *Grow and share new skills.* Bringing skills that get built in each role back to the other creatively amplifies each role. Improve your work skills with awareness that they serve your parenting. Spend time reflecting on what is particularly unique about your work skills. Find extra motivation to tune up your parenting skills by realizing that those skills can also help you at work.

- *Incubate.* Time away from each role activates your unconscious processes—where creative thinking can occur. By turning off conscious thinking about pressing problems during time away, you can access a creative boost. Just keep a notepad handy in case your wandering mind comes up with answers to pressing problems!

8

REMEMBER TO SUBTRACT

The bedtime routine for my kids is like this Royal
Coronation Jubilee Centennial of rinsing and plaque
and dental appliances and the stuffed animal semi-
circle of emotional support. . . . You know what my
bedtime story was when I was a kid? Darkness!

—JERRY SEINFELD

Leidy Klotz and his six-year-old son, Ezra, love LEGO. The shared
hobby involves fashioning new structures, enlarging existing
ones, and adding yet more LEGO bricks to an already vast collec-
tion. In a podcast interview, Leidy laughingly told me that he had
just recently purchased a six-thousand-piece Harry Potter special
edition set. But though he delightedly buys more LEGO, experiences awe in enormous structures, and has not one but three appointments at the University of Virginia (in engineering, architecture, and business), Leidy's long-standing obsession is with *less*. The
merging of an infatuation with both building and getting to less
culminated in Leidy's thought-provoking book, *Subtract*.[1]

That less holds appeal isn't a novel idea. Taoist philosophers,
for example, came up with the concept of *wu wei*, the power of

nonaction, thousands of years ago. As ancient Chinese philosopher Lao Tzu wrote, "Have little and gain much."[2] In more recent times, minimalist principles and practices have been met with fanfare and chart-topping works from the likes of Marie Kondo (*The Life-Changing Magic of Tidying Up*), Greg McKeown (*Essentialism*), and Cal Newport (*Digital Minimalism*).

I'd hazard a guess that most working parents find the notion of less pretty alluring. We might even fantasize about a day with less— less meetings and chauffeuring and fewer meals that need to be made, emails that need responding to, or transitions between roles. But less can feel like a mirage in the desert. In moments, when the sun is shining just right, we can see what a less overwhelming life might look like. We just can't seem to ever get there.

What's so powerful about Leidy's research is that it not only reveals why it's so hard to see water in the desert but also why traveling to get a closer look—maybe even a thirst-quenching drink—is so stinking hard to accomplish.

An afternoon of LEGO-building with his son offered an epiphany and an inroad to dig into the science of why it's so hard to get to less. When Ezra was just three years old, he and Leidy were working on a LEGO bridge supported by two towers. At one point, the two LEGO support towers under construction sat at different heights. Leidy and little Ezra each saw that they needed to equalize the tower heights to enable a bridge to be built. Leidy turned away to grab some LEGO bricks to add to the shorter of the towers. But by the time turned back to the project, he saw that Ezra had taken a different tack to evening the tower heights. Ezra had *subtracted* a block from the taller of the two towers.

NEGLECTING SUBTRACTION

Most parents wouldn't have made much of a choice to subtract a LEGO block. But Leidy's lifelong preoccupation with why we fill our houses with more stuff (instead of purging), gather more information (rather than refining or condensing what we already know), use more words (instead of deleting the superfluous), focus on increasing income (instead of reducing spending), and add more activities to busy, stressful days (instead of carving out downtime) set the stage for LEGO to offer a powerful aha moment. Leidy recognized immediately that Ezra's choice to subtract was unusual. He began to reflect that even when less is the clearly superior outcome, people often fail to choose the kinds of actions that get them there.

We might desire less as an outcome, yet we rarely choose to subtract.

Leidy and his collaborators set about designing a series of experiments exploring what happens when people are given options to add or subtract in order to improve objects, ideas, or situations. What participants didn't know was that all experiments were designed so that the better choice was subtracting. Whether it was modifying grids, improving theoretical miniature golf holes, revising LEGO structures, or refining soup recipes, experiment after experiment revealed a consistent finding perfectly captured in the title of their paper, published in the premier scientific journal *Nature*: "People Systematically Overlook Subtractive Changes."[3]

What's more, results from this series of experiments revealed that the tendency to overlook subtraction grows even stronger when demands on us are greater. In one of the mini experiments in the larger *Nature* paper, participants were asked to make a grid pattern symmetrical. Again, the better design choice was subtracting. Then an additional task was added. When participants had to simultaneously note a "5" scrolling by, they grew even *less* likely to perceive that better option. In other words, increased cognitive burden made it more difficult to subtract. It's not hard to see that this tendency can easily lead to a cycle of adding to our overwhelm *because* we're overwhelmed.

A classic psychology study from the 1970s offers a great example of how pressure not only causes us to overlook subtracting but also leads to our neglecting opportunities to act in line with our better selves. In the "Good Samaritan" study, Princeton theology students believed they were participating in a study on religious education. After completing some questionnaires, they were asked to go to another building to continue the study. On their route between buildings, a shabbily dressed person (an actor) was slumped in an alley. Interested in what kinds of conditions predicted whether seminary students would help a needy person, researchers varied two elements they thought might have an impact. The first was the topic on which they were to give a talk—either on the biblical parable of the Good Samaritan or a topic unrelated to helping behavior. The second element varied was the amount of urgency to hurry to the next building. The urgency varied from students being told they had a few minutes before the next phase to being told that "they were expecting you a few minutes ago; we'd better get moving." It turned out that the kind of talk given didn't make much of a difference, whereas time pressure mattered a great deal. Most students who thought they had a least a few minutes stopped to help the stranger, whereas fewer than 10 percent of students who were told they were running late did. Being in a hurry caused many of the students to not even *notice* that there was a person slumped in the alley![4]

It's when we most need to subtract because we have too much going on, we feel stressed out, or we're overtired that subtracting is hardest to access. This can cause us to rush around doing activities or buying things we don't care about (hello, rushed Target visit that results in a cartful of things I don't need) while neglecting to do what matters most to us.

PROGRAMMED FOR ADDING

Our tendency to neglect subtracting has an evolutionary basis. Throughout human history, stress signaled deficit. Whether those deficits were in calories, peer connections, or shelter, a stress response that activated adding-oriented action was a good survival strategy in premodern times. Humans thus evolved a wiring for acquiring. That wiring is so powerful that even when we are prompted to consider subtracting items from a to-do list, goods from our homes, or activities in our schedules, we tend to dismiss it.

Subtracting often feels costly. Doing less causes us to feel like we're less capable of shaping our world. And it can cut off our opportunities to exhibit our value to others. Consider that once upon a time, our tribe was more inclined to keep us as a member if we could prove worth through skills and contributions. The desire to show competence motivates more action, not less, because it's harder to show competence if we don't show up, show off, and make a noticeable difference. This tendency to add can emerge more powerfully in roles we care deeply about. For instance, Leidy admitted that for him, subtracting is especially hard in his parenting role where "you feel like you need to do everything" and "if you are not doing something, your kid is missing out and you therefore are an incompetent parent." We are also drawn to adding by a desire not to miss out on experiences that seem important for work or parenting or that seem fun and meaningful.

Action also helps us feel more in control. If I monitor my kids while they are playing or if I call in to a meeting while I'm on vacation, I'm influencing outcomes and I'm showing my commitment in a tangible way. It's reassuring to observe the immediate effect of intervening with my kids' wrestling match or administering a firm consequence when I've discovered my child has snuck the iPad into his bed after I forbade it (totally hypothetical, of course). I can only know whether there is a new development in the office if I am present, virtually or in person, for the meeting. And I can decide whether to participate in the new developments only if I'm present to make that choice.

THE UNCERTAINTY OF LESS

Action, presence, and engagement are empowering. Letting my kids come to their own conclusions and face the natural consequences of playing *Angry Birds* until midnight? Being absent from office politics where alliances are made and battle lines are drawn? Those choices can breed uncertainty and a sense of impotence.

The discomfort of uncertainty is no small thing for most of us. In fact, the stress of uncertain pain outsizes the stress of certain pain. In one surprising study, participants were put into groups in which they either had a fifty-fifty chance of receiving a shock or a 100 percent chance of being shocked (a third group received no shocks). Revealingly, the participants with a 50 percent chance of receiving a shock were *more* stressed than those with a 100 percent chance of receiving a shock.[5] We prefer certainty . . . even when certainty means certain pain! It's no wonder that at work and in parenting, our efforts are often geared toward making outcomes feel more certain through more items in our homes, more research into best practices, and more commitments in our planners.

But doing more in order to avoid incompetence or uncertainty turns out to be an ill-fated practice. That's a general life rule, and one that emphatically applies to roles as complex as parenting and work.

A favorite novel of mine, Laurie Frankel's *This Is How It Always Is*, tells the beautiful story of a loving family whose youngest child, born a genetic male, discovers her identity is female. The parents want to support their daughter and her older siblings by making the kinds of choices that allow each of their five children to thrive. But it's complicated stuff for any parent, let alone parents navigating conditions and situations without socially accepted scripts for the "right" way to proceed. Every decision the parents make fills them with feelings of uncertainty, incompetence, and fear that they have done something that would harm their kids. And, in fact, some of their choices clearly benefit one child and devastate another, while other choices seem wise until it becomes clear they aren't.[6] No matter how hard you try or how much you do, there are always unanticipated consequences in parenting.

This is how it always is at work, too. We can't foretell the consequences of focusing on one client versus another or one project or another, or of staying late to get a job done versus leaving early to get enough sleep for the following day. We can never get enough information to rest assured that we needn't worry about losing our job. The impacts of our behavioral choices matter deeply but there is no crystal ball to determine exactly where any of our life-altering choices will lead. And so we imagine that doing *more* is better than doing *less*.

Except that always adding without ever subtracting leads to exhaustion, overwhelm, and ineffectiveness. Think of it like adding more nutrients to the soil versus pruning an overgrown tree. You might get more out of removing the gnarly, half-dead branches that block sunlight from budding leaves.

We have an alternative to adding, even if it's not the default option wired into our brains. We *can* choose to subtract. At the very least, we can more deliberately consider subtracting as one possible pathway to making our lives better. We can learn to balance the impulse to add with a judicious consideration of subtracting.

THE VALUE ADDED OF SUBTRACTING

In her book *The Gift of Failure: How the Best Parents Learn to Let Go So Their Children Can Succeed*, Jessica Lahey offers the educator's perspective on the dangers of always doing more in parenting, and she highlights the often overlooked benefits of doing less.[7] As a junior high school teacher, Lahey regularly witnessed parents swooping in to save their kids from forgotten lunches, homework, poor grades, and social challenges. She knew the actions stemmed from caring (and freely admitted that she, too, was guilty of the same with her own children). But Lahey was suspicious. She suspected that all of that heavy-duty parental engagement was interfering with an important student activity: learning.

Lahey dove into the social science research and discovered that doing more was causing parents to unwittingly send messages that their kids weren't capable of learning from mistakes or tolerating discomfort. Despite the best of intentions, too much parental action was obstructing opportunities to practice tolerating the embarrassments and failures that accompany growth, gaining independence, and practice in resilience-building. As the subtitle of Lahey's book suggests, to be successful in parenting we need to learn to let go and do less.

The child anthropologist David F. Lancy has studied child development and caregiving across cultures throughout his career, publishing fascinating cross-cultural investigations and the seminal textbook *The Anthropology of Childhood*.[8] Although David proudly admitted to me that he fawns over his baby granddaughter—sending me adorable pictures after we spoke—he strongly believes that parents who are Western, educated, and living in industrialized and democratic nations do too much for their kids.

The solution this world-renowned anthropologist recommends? The same as Leidy Klotz and Jessica Lahey: *subtract*.

As David explained, "If you back off and let the child start making their choices, there may be a bruised knee as a consequence of a bad choice. But that's a great way to learn. That's a much more enduring and lasting way to develop, to learn from the environment instead of always having learning mediated through a parent." David calls this approach to parenting "benign neglect"—subtracting enough of your attention to let your children make choices and learn while still providing ample love, care, and resources for their well-being.

Just as doing less intensive parenting can offer benefit for you and your child, benign neglect of your work can be helpful for your boss, your colleagues, and you. For example, you can set better boundaries that help you sustain effort over time. Saying no to less important projects can help you say a more wholehearted yes to important ones. Doing less at work might even mean reaping more respect. For example, too much head nodding can communicate submissiveness.[9] Accordingly, Olivia Fox Cabane, the author of *The Charisma Myth*, suggests that individuals who reduce how quickly and how often they nod and who pause for a few seconds before they speak will gain an instant boost to their perceived charisma.[10] We can get benign about doing less and neglecting more at work and in parenting.

To get to benign neglect in parenting, though, we have to learn how to interrupt, reduce, or subtract all manner of appliance parenting practices (you know, such as helicopter, lawn mower, and snowplow parenting). "Do more" parenting styles have been shown to hamper children's resilience, independence, academic performance, and mental health, with a 2014 study of college students revealing that having overly controlling parents is associated with higher reported levels of depression and lower life satisfaction.[11] Deliberately doing less in parenting holds the potential of offering kids greater independence and opportunities to develop their own competencies.

But there's no need to give up on aspects of parenting that are important to you, even if they do fall into the "additive" style of parenting. For instance, if you devoured Amy Chua's provocative memoir *Battle Hymn of the Tiger Mother* as I did, you'll know that Chua defended her decision to raise her two daughters "the Chinese way." That is, her parenting explicitly emphasized the importance of parents actively pushing kids—for instance, by requiring and resolutely enforcing instrument practice.[12] While research in parenting generally reveals the benefits of offering children opportunities to find their own passions, we should remember that no study can account for individual differences in families, including differences in family and cultural values, as well as differences in individual temperaments and relationships. Consider what *you* feel comfortable removing. Which subtractions offer you opportunities for sustainability of energetic reserves over time as well as a useful pressure to home in on the activities that matter most? Honor your right to make choices that work best for you, your family, your work, and your general circumstances. And offer the same courtesy to others.

THE HARMONY OF ADD AND SUBTRACT

Of course, subtraction can't exist on its own. We wouldn't have anything to subtract if we never added, for one thing! And let's be clear that while overinvolvement may be harmful, neglect in its more severe forms can be far worse, resulting in great harm to children and lost jobs or broken careers. Subtracting should not be taken to a thoughtless extreme. But we can begin to view it as a natural, beneficial complement of adding and as a viable pathway to better outcomes in work and in parenting (not to mention a less overwhelming working-parent journey).

Being strategic about what we add and intentional about what we remove in parenting and work is where wisdom lives. For instance, the British pediatrician and psychoanalyst D. W. Winnicott wrote about the concept of "good enough" parenting. According to Winnicott, this kind of parenting involves responding to a child's needs and also allowing those needs to be frustrated.[13] In other words, it relies on an ongoing balance of attending to and actively ignoring your kids. That kind of balance between adding and subtracting is what we each can strive for as we consider how to best design our parenting and work activities.

ADD? SUBTRACT? HOLD THE LINE?

Even when you get behind the value of buying and doing less, you'll still be left with a difficult set of questions: How do I sort out what to do and what not to do in my own life? And how can I let go of more without creating problems for those I care about? Because each of our family setups, job demands, individual temperaments, and children's needs differ, we need a decision-making *framework* that guides us to take the steps needed to generate our own best answer in every add-or-subtract opportunity.

A useful decision framework assesses both risk and benefit—and it's important to note that there is always some level of risk. Consider, for example, if you were determined to reduce your risk from traveling, eating unhealthy food, or exposing yourself to allergens. In order to manage that risk, you might stop traveling, eat only salads, and remain indoors. But now you've upped your risk for social isolation, intellectual stagnation, and lack of healthy engagement with nature. You haven't eliminated all risk. You've merely pivoted toward different forms of risk. As another powerful example of the unavoidability of risk, most of us accept that wearing a seat belt reduces risk for car accident fatalities. But while we rarely reflect on it, bruising, organ laceration, and even asphyxiation can occur *because* of seat belts.[14] Yet seat belts save many lives, with evidence that about half of adults and teens who died in crashes in 2018 were not wearing seat belts at the time of car crash.[15] We accept the risk of wearing seat belts because the risk-benefit analysis points to the obvious choice—buckle up!

Adding or subtracting each carries risk. Analysis of your risk-benefit ratio helps you locate the kinds of risk that feel most tolerable for you and the optimal balance for *you* between the highest amount of benefit and the least amount of risk.

You can conduct your own risk-benefit analyses to yield more thoughtful choices about what to subtract from work and parenting. Consider this two-axis graph that displays risk and benefit for subtraction. The horizontal or x-axis charts lowest and highest benefit, whereas the vertical or y-axis charts highest and lowest risk. I've input some of my typical work and parent activities into the graph, placing them in ways that reflect how much risk and benefit I assign to each. Circled are the behaviors associated with the lowest subtraction risk and highest subtraction benefit for my family, my job, and me. These are the activities that, for me, are the low-hanging fruit to subtract.

Your risk-benefit analysis of what to subtract from working parenthood may differ from mine (and from your neighbor's, your sister's, your own parents', or Amy Chua's). The added value of subtracting has considerable subjectivity, which makes this kind of analysis ideal for tailoring to your unique circumstances, priorities, and values.

. . . . .

Pause to Do a Risk-Benefit Analysis of Activities to Subtract

Use this decisional framework as a guide for assessing your own risk and benefit preferences on the next page. Ask yourself where different activities fall along the risk and benefit axes for subtraction? Look for opportunities to subtract at relatively low risk for relatively high benefit.

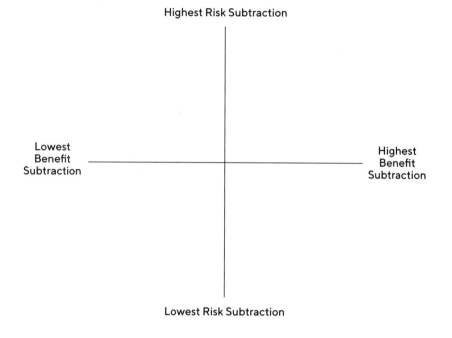

Highest Risk Subtraction

Lowest
Benefit
Subtraction

Highest
Benefit
Subtraction

Lowest Risk Subtraction

· · · · ·

STRATEGIC SUBTRACTION

Subtraction can offer advantage if you seek out the sweet spot between bubble-wrapping children into emotional asphyxia and letting them run free into oncoming traffic. You can locate the sweet spot between burning out and loafing out at work. You'll gain greater access to that sweet spot if you learn to take advantage of natural pressures embedded inside of your working parenthood and complement them with science-backed ways to prompt subtracting.

Cuing Subtraction

If you're like me (and every person who has landed on Marie Kondo's doorstep), you get attached to shoes and jeans that no longer fit despite recognizing that they interfere with your goal of a tidy closet. Activities inside roles we care about can be even more painful to chuck. That's understandable. Saying no to the meeting your boss put on your calendar, the invitation to attend a close friend's birthday party, the volunteer role in your children's school, or the pressure to take on additional hours at work can have real consequences.

Then again, so can saying yes.

Working-parent pressures offer a natural cue to ponder subtraction. You can take advantage of those cues in your personal and family life. You can practice being more deliberate about saying yes to activities you deem to be essential and no to areas that, for you, are unnecessary or unimportant. You can relish removing what is less critical by noticing how it gives you more resources to focus on what matters most.

You can also make the choice to subtract more accessible and habitual by creating routines that prompt subtracting. That might include weekly time set aside to consider what can be removed from your upcoming week. In weekly subtraction time, you can employ what our subtraction expert Leidy Klotz calls a "stop-doing list." This list can even live right beside your to-do list. By bundling the two together, you can take advantage of the natural tendency to add to the to-do list by using it as a prompt to more deliberately refine your stop-doing list.

For me, stop-doing items in the parenting arena have been especially helpful. For instance, before becoming a parent, I had assumed my kids would have bar mitzvahs (a coming-of-age tradition in Judaism). But I didn't anticipate that Hebrew school would be in addition to jobs, school, sports, and a desire for downtime. I also didn't appreciate how much I hate hosting parties of any kind, let alone the huge affairs that typify bar mitzvahs in our town. And I hadn't reflected on why the tradition of bar mitzvahs even mattered to me.

As I began to think more about subtraction, I considered the meaning of Hebrew school and bar mitzvahs for my family. I realized that my core value in this space was building community and connecting to ancient traditions. It struck me that Hebrew school offered neither *because* it was always such a rush job. The desired benefits weren't emerging even though the efforts were inflicting a considerable cost. The knowledge about systematic subtraction neglect gave me the courage to pause Hebrew school. The experience that followed provided evidence of subtractive benefits, with reduced weekly overwhelm and freed-up financial resources and energy—some of which we use to foster spirituality and community in less burdensome ways. Subtraction did, indeed, offer my family more.

. . . . .

Pause to Create Your Stop-Doing List

A stop-doing list can prompt your adding-prone brain to consider subtraction. Subtracting what matters less conserves your attention and energy for the things that matter more to you. To be effective in what matters most, eliminate what matters least. Use your to-do list in combination with your stop-doing list to keep subtracting more easily available.

Commit to stop-doing items in parenting by reflecting on:

- *Which activities matter least to my parenting? Which matter most?*

- *Start small if that's helpful, but be persistent in the quest to subtract activities on the parenting front.*

Commit to stop-doing items at work. Ask yourself:

- *What work matters most for me and my career trajectory?*

- *What can I subtract with benefit to my work or my life more generally?*

. . . . .

Rethinking Your Time

Feeling as if we don't have enough time increases the likelihood of neglecting subtraction as an option. And time poverty also hinders happiness and health.[16] But as Ashley Whillans, a Harvard Business School professor and leading voice in time and happiness research, writes in her recent book *Time Smart,* "Time poverty doesn't necessarily arise from a mismatch between the hours we have and the hours we need. It results from how we *think about* and *value* those hours. It's as much psychological as it is structural."[17] Perceiving a conflict between roles causes us to feel time-constrained and increases our stress and anxiety about our time.[18] But amazingly, without adding any more hours to your day (because that's impossible) or reducing the roles you participate in, you can shift how you feel about the time you have and what you do with what you have.

Adopting a time-in-abundance mindset—particularly for the activities you find most valuable—helps to reduce experiences of time pressure. And dismantling perceptions of time poverty helps subtracting remain a more accessible option. When you feel less pressured, you'll be more likely to take in important cues, enjoy the moments you have, and make small and large life-design choices that better align with your values.

· · · · ·

Pause to Build a Time-in-Abundance Mindset

Building a time-in-abundance mindset begins by getting to know your current mindset, values, and habits. Ask yourself:

- *How often do I feel "I don't have enough time!"?*

- *Where am I devoting time that doesn't feel value aligned?*

- *What do I value that I'm not doing enough of?*

If you find activities consuming portions of your day without offering you value, consider placing those activities on your stop-doing list.

When it comes to activities that you retain in your weekly lineup, consider the following time-in-abundance strategies:

- *Slow down.* Be deliberate about making this possible in your schedule—for example, by scheduling extra time between appointments to make arriving on time less of an urgent matter and so you can really enjoy music during the drive. If you give yourself time to arrive at a Zoom meeting early, consider using that time to enjoy connecting with work colleagues about topics unrelated to work.

- *Be present during nonproductive time.* While commuting, waiting in a long line, or watching *Bridgerton*, show up for the experience. Use the time to breathe, reflect, or savor. Where thinking about the future or past can create a sense of urgency, being connected to the present moment can leave us with a greater sense of time abundance.[19]

- *Transform unpleasant experiences.* Changing how you think about a work or parenting task can shift how you experience it. Finding benefit in hard work or a difficult day with your kid by focusing on learning something new, getting in some physical movement, or learning to tolerate discomfort can transform the way you feel during that time.

· · · · ·

How about the activities you don't value or enjoy but that you aren't able to subtract? This includes chores you hate or work and parenting responsibilities that you have to grit your teeth through. Well, if you can't subtract or minimize, you might consider buying out, if you have the resources to do so. Research Whillans conducted with colleagues has shown that across several countries, people who paid money for services to save their time were happier.[20] Whillans and her research team also followed up with a smaller, Canada-based sample to draw clearer conclusions about the link between how people spent money and their happiness levels. The researchers gave a sample of working adults forty dollars to spend over two different weekends. Participants were randomly assigned to spend the money on a material purchase or something that would save them time. Perhaps by now it will be no surprise that the time-saving expenditures resulted in greater happiness.

Buying out of activities you don't enjoy or care about offers a useful pathway to subtracting. So if you have the means, consider signing up for premade meals, more childcare, rideshares, lawn care, or house cleaning services. If you don't have cash lying around to pay someone else to do activities you detest, consider bartering with friends and neighbors. For example, if you don't like cooking but wouldn't mind driving the car pool, suggest a services exchange. Whatever you do, remember that delegating, exchanging, or buying out of activities can help you conserve your finite time and energy.

Reducing Reactivity

Getting to effortless action can take, well, considerable effort. For instance, in the ancient Taoist martial art of kung fu, students are taught that pushing back against an opponent is instinctive, but that persistent struggle can uselessly sap us of our energy. Kung fu teaches students how to subtract the impulse to push back. They are taught to move *with* (instead of against) resistance in order to throw an opponent off balance and how to redirect incoming force by remaining grounded but relaxed enough to allow the force to move through them. Kung fu masters work their whole lives to gain and refine their skills. Letting go and doing less requires both reflection and exertion.

Nonreactance often involves some discomfort. For one thing, it can mean accepting resistance and even allying with your opposition. This can happen with opposition in the form of a politically offensive client or opposition from your octopus-armed offspring who grabs everything in reach as you exit Target. In one of my working-parent interviews, Jamila, a utility company customer care representative, described how she spends her workdays on the phone with utility customers. They call because they are unhappy, often to the point of fury. Jamila explained that "to do what I do and listen to people complain all day, and even to be yelled at by customers, requires a lot of patience." Jamila viewed herself as highly patient in large part because of her parenting experiences. "As a parent, of course, you need a lot of patience. I'm quite good at that. I will listen and allow them to vent." Jamila offering an outlet and compassionate ear instead of arguing, putting up an emotional wall, or getting defensive helps her customers cool down more quickly. And when they do, Jamila is in an even better position to be helpful to them.

Allowing the forces around you to blow without responding to them is a practice, like any other—it takes effort to build the skill. There's no need to quash whatever feelings and impulses arise. Those internal experiences offer valuable information, including gauging the emotional temperature of those around you. But it's useful to recognize when feelings, thoughts, and impulses to lash out lead to ineffective action. After all, our self-protection impulses are designed to protect ourselves from hungry predators, not cranky customers. Recognizing that nonreactance could offer a more effective strategy helped Jamila begin to practice calmer responses with ultra-ornery customers. So whether it's letting your teenager vent without getting baited into debate or validating a dejected colleague without interrupting, consider the power of reducing your reaction.

. . . . .

Pause to Get Nonreactive

The next time you feel conflict and struggle blowing your way, try this imagery exercise.

Bring forth an image of the Shanghai Tower in China, the second-tallest building in the world. The construction of this 128-story skyscraper required structural engineers and architects to make wind loads a principal design consideration. The result is an awe-inspiring twist-and-turn structure that sheds, rather than resists, gale-force winds. Imagine yourself as that building and consider behavioral choices that would allow you to shed the forceful winds of children, clients, or opinionated colleagues. With this image in mind, you might be more likely to ignore disagreeable behavior and let others' angst and conflicting interpersonal styles flow past. Reducing your reactivity saves your energy. Just consider all the places you can use that energy toward other productive ends.

. . . . .

PRACTICING NOTHING AT ALL

Of course, it's tempting to replace whatever you've subtracted with new activities. But it's worth it to contemplate the value of taking more time and space with what's already present in your life. You might take inspiration from sweet Winnie the Pooh, who said, "Don't underestimate the value of Doing Nothing, of just going along, listening to all the things you can't hear, and not bothering."[21]

But whether you're considering the wisdom of Pooh, *wu wei*, or the Dutch concept of *niksen* (which translates to "not doing anything productive"), doing less or acting without purpose can be challenging to put into action—or, should I say, *non*action. For instance, in a series of studies conducted by Harvard professor Daniel T. Gilbert and his colleagues, college students were left alone in a room for between six and fifteen minutes. They didn't like it much. Accustomed to having access to tools of productivity and distraction, many participants preferred to administer mild electric shocks to themselves rather than be left with nothing but their thoughts![22] The students preferred to experience physical discomfort rather than not have anything to do. Many of us—even we working parents who yearn for time off—feel bored or stressed out during leisure time, as it turns out.[23] As a result, it can take considerable effort to lean in to idleness.

The effort gets easier by practicing. Strange as it may feel, I advise you to practice doing very little—in whatever form that takes. Whether you are sitting quietly observing your breath or your thoughts, praying, stretching your body, or chanting, and even if you are doing it through a short intentional practice, slowing down to engage in slower, quieter forms of activity is a way to practice nondoing. The physical and psychological benefits of doing so range from improving physical health, building the ability to concentrate, developing greater compassion, and hardwiring more happiness into your life.[24] Learning to subtract, then practicing doing less will serve you and each of your important roles well.

· · · · ·

Pause to Idle

Idling doesn't need to take a huge amount of time. A few breaths interspersed throughout your day is a great place to start. Be realistic in finding the pockets of your day where idling is most likely to work out well. And use the science of behavior change to help you out. For instance, cue nondoing by linking it with an activity that's already part of your day.[25]

Consider one of the following ways to bring idling into your schedule:

- A three-breath pause a few times a day, cued by your alarm clock

- A commute without radio (or podcasts or phone calls or snacking)

- A five-minute meditation scheduled after your kids go to school or before you eat lunch

- A walk without music or other nonnature auditory stimulation, scheduled for the lull in the afternoon when you feel least productive at work or during your work break

- A mindful hug with your kids where you really lean in to it, refraining from asking them about their day, checking your phone, or thinking about what you're making for dinner

- A one-minute pause in your car before you head in to work or come into the house after a day at work

- Doing a body scan—noticing each part of your body in turn—as you wait in a long line

Frame these as opportunities to idle, as a chance to build your muscle of sitting more comfortably without stimulation or distraction. And when the discomfort of sitting still or the itch to grab your phone from your pocket arises, note it without judgment, observing "discomfort in idleness" or "desire to engage in scrolling." Then reconnect to the value that led you there in the first place—increasing your effectiveness in the roles you care most about through idling.

*   *   *   *   *

SUBTRACTING FOR THE WIN

There's no question that, at times, we should be adding objects, ideas, and actions to our lives. But let's not forget to prioritize subtracting. Doing less can help us remain effective, healthy, and happy. Choosing to delete certain activities from our lives can help us do better in those we retain by helping us regain and sustain balance, focus, and enthusiasm.

But subtracting isn't easy. Sometimes we struggle to even imagine it as an option. In fact, it was only after Leidy Klotz and I met to discuss subtracting in working parenthood that he—subtraction expert extraordinaire—realized he had been neglecting subtraction in his parenting role. Cue a proud professional moment when Leidy made an email introduction to a colleague, writing, "Yael convinced me to subtract some of my parenting."

Subtracting may not be our default setting. But we can make it available if we remember to subtract. The wisdom and practice of subtracting can help us do less in order to benefit ourselves, our families, and our jobs more.

. . . .

The TL/DR (Too Long, Didn't Read)

USE WORKING PARENTHOOD TO DO LESS
WORK AND PARENTING

Recognize that subtracting isn't the obvious choice for most of us—even when it's the better choice. Be deliberate about considering subtraction, and consider that sometimes less offers much more.

Develop practices of subtracting by finding ways to incorporate the following:

- *Cue subtraction.* Generate a stop-doing list (guided by your risk-benefit analysis) that lives alongside your to-do list.

- *Rethink your time.* Adopt a time-in-abundance mindset in activities you care about and consider buying out of (or bartering away) those you don't.

- *Grow nonreactivity.* Gain skill in nonreactance by practicing responding less to the powerful forces in your life (such as your toddler and boss, for starters).

- *Practice idling.* Develop the muscle for not-doing, recognizing that it will help you improve your health, effectiveness, and happiness.

9

GROW CONNECTION THROUGH THE GOOD, THE BAD, AND THE DOWNRIGHT INFURIATING

Before you marry a person, you should first
make them use a computer with slow internet
service to see who they really are.
—WILL FERRELL

Regardless of your relationship status, working parenthood is rife with interpersonal challenges. Conflicts arise when friends aren't understanding of your challenges, ex-partners refuse to carry their fair share, colleagues have unrealistic expectations, and children, well, act like children. Many readers, too, will be familiar with the statistic that married couples, on average, experience a drop in marital satisfaction after children arrive on the scene.[1] Work, parenting, and relationship roles crash into each other, and a partnership that once offered support is now an additional source of aggravation.

Because relationships are so critical for our well-being, it's an important area to find useful strategies that can work well in working parenthood. I'll largely focus on ideas and strategies to grow connection in committed partnerships, but these strategies can be applied to relationships of any kind.

WHEN YOU HATE THE PERSON YOU'RE SUPPOSED TO LOVE

Jancee Dunn described the final affront in the crumbling of her marital foundation in her hilariously illustrative book with a terrific title: *How Not to Hate Your Husband After Kids.*[2] Dunn is a mom and a successful journalist. A day when her three-year-old daughter was home from preschool due to a fever, Dunn had an interview with the award-winning singer and actress Jennifer Hudson. She and her husband (also a work-from-home parent) had divvied up childcare, with Dunn covering the majority of the day, excepting the interview slot. Then, right in the midst of discussing the addictive dangers of banana pudding with the superstar, Dunn's daughter, in the midst of potty training, appeared beside her. Her daughter said just one word: "Poo." And she kept saying it, even as Dunn mouthed, "Daddy will do it!" and tried to throw a shoe down the stairs to catch his attention. A husband failing to materialize and a kid in dire need of a bathroom buddy, Dunn finally asked Hudson for a quick break. As she rushed her daughter to the toilet, she passed her husband, alight in the glow of online games.

I teach couples to navigate through complex situations for a living, so I know well that many couples struggle with the sometimes-damaging effect that working parenthood can bestow on marriage. I know the science and practices that help couples in sticky situations get unstuck, and I teach them well. But I live inside a real-life marriage—one with two working parents and three small children. Despite my so-called expertise, I, too, sometimes struggle mightily.

The truth is that even healthy, enviable marriages between relationally healthy people encounter periods of deeply unhappy stuckness and high-intensity conflict.[3] The Obamas have famously disclosed that they attend marital therapy when they feel they need it. My favorite celebrity couple, Kristen Bell and Dax Shepard, have shared that they agree on very little, struggled with unhealthy communication habits, and periodically recommit to working on their partnership amid their busy professional and parenting lives. No couple is immune from challenges, least of all those of us with demands pulling at us constantly from every direction. How we respond, our ability to develop new strategies in relationships, and how we ultimately grow from the challenges are what really counts.

FROM GRIDLOCK TO GROWTH

The sex therapist David Schnarch is credited with coining the term "emotional gridlock" to describe what happens when a relationship feels stuck. Your preferences are thwarted by what your partner would rather do (or, for that matter, not do), you feel trapped in an irresolvable conflict, or you feel so distant that you may as well be living on different planets even though you share a bed.

Consider the following common situations: You are in desperate need of a break from parenting so you can get to a work task (and also so you don't blow your top), but your partner feels overwhelmed by work and can't seem to unlock any time for you. Your mind says, "I have needs, why can't he *see* that?" In that same moment, though, he is thinking to himself, "I might get fired if I don't get this work done, how can she *not* see that?"

There are larger, more sustained conflicts, too. One partner wants to work more hours, while the other wants to invest time in taking family vacations. One partner wants to have sex only on weekends, while the other wants to get busy on the odd Tuesday. One partner wants to get pregnant and enlarge the family, but the other would far prefer a feline addition to a human one. In each of these scenarios, it's easy to see the conflict as irresolvable. Gridlock ensues when each person perceives the other's preferences as reigning supreme.

Since the 1970s, the legendary marital researcher John M. Gottman has investigated how couples overcome gridlock. Early in his research, he built a "love lab" where he has brought hundreds of couples in to observe arguments. Gottman and his research team have collected vats of data to determine what leads to successful passage through an impasse versus a relentless stalemate. The results of Gottman's work include a description of communication patterns characterizing happy couples whose relationships stand the test of time and couples whose demise is so predictable that Gottman can famously forecast divorce with 95 percent accuracy from analyzing just one hour of footage.

Among his various fascinating findings, Gottman's work affirms that all couples clash, even those who remain happily married for life. But couples that stay happily married differ from those that divorce in key ways. For one thing, happy couples are likely to be characterized by the couples' version of a growth mindset. Rather than adopting a fixed mindset (one that assumes you can't accept, learn, and grow from differences), happy couples give each other the benefit of the doubt and continue to try to work things out. Adaptation to new circumstances and stressors is a core element of making marriages strong and stable.[4] In other words, it's not individual quirks (read: infuriating qualities or habits) in your partner or life stressors that matter most, it's how you and your partner *respond* to them. Impasses needn't be impassable if you—together *with* your partner—develop ways to cope and grow together.

The key to unlocking your ability to do this kind of work is adopting a mindset that you, together with your partner, can take your relationship to a better place. Take it from Gottman and coauthor Nan Silver, who advise in the bestselling book *The Seven Principles for Making Marriage Work*, "Keep working on your unresolvable conflicts. Couples who are demanding of their marriage are more likely to have deeply satisfying unions than those who lower their expectations."[5]

BUT WHY WON'T YOU *CHANGE*?!

Like many couples entering therapy together, Meg and Jana had been unhappy in their marriage for years. Both described a drop in marital satisfaction that began when their now six-year-old son was born. Meg explained, "My life did a one-eighty after we became moms. I went from ambitious professional to primary parent over-night. I was hustling to pump, keep a store of clean diapers, and nurse on demand to this small infant while still making my hours at the office. But somehow Jana's life didn't seem to change at all!"

In our one-on-one portion of the therapy intake, Meg told me that she was hopeful I could convince Jana to make significant changes. This hope is typical—and understandable. But what marital researchers discovered decades ago is that a partner can't force change. Nor, for that matter, can a therapist!

Back in the 1960s, marriage experts thought otherwise. A treatment called behavioral marital therapy (BMT) taught couples to communicate more skillfully and reinforce each other in more deliberate ways, and evidence showed that it resulted in healthier, happier couples.[6] Yet the data also revealed that a full third of couples treated did not respond to treatment at all. Those who benefited had treatment gains that often faded quickly when treatment ended. By the 1980s and 1990s, two researchers, Neil Jacobson and Andrew Christensen, began to consider approaches that didn't rely so heavily on change. They developed a newer treatment called integrative behavioral couples therapy (or IBCT) that integrated the old behavioral models of learning with acceptance-based skills. Instead emphasizing change—at least at the front end of therapy—IBCT oriented couples toward compassionately tolerating whatever thoughts, emotions, and experiences were present for themselves and for their partners. Individuals were taught to be understanding and soothing toward themselves and their partners *before* attempting behavior change.[7] Longitudinal research comparing the two treatments showed that IBCT helps distressed couples remain more satisfied longer than traditional BMT.[8]

BEFRIENDING RIDERS AND CALMING ELEPHANTS

Getting past an impasse begins with befriending riders and calming elephants. Confused? Allow me to explain. Most of us think that a persuasive argument for why someone should change—especially an argument backed by logic and love—should propel agreement. Nope. Logic, data, and even forceful emotion are ineffective for winning an argument. In fact, trying to convince someone else of your thinking often leads to greater ideological distances.

In his book *The Righteous Mind*, the social psychologist and bestselling author Jonathan Haidt describes the science behind our ineffectiveness in convincing others that our beliefs are correct.[9] According to his work within the field of morality, our reasoning is far more often intuitive than rational. In other words, feelings lead to reasoning—not the other way around, as we might assume. Haidt offers the metaphor of the rider and the elephant to explain. In this metaphor, the rider represents the mind, while the elephant symbolizes emotions and intuition. The rider (mind) isn't as large or as well developed as the emotional, intuitive system because the reasoning system is a more recent evolutionary development.[10]

Picture a rider sitting atop the enormous elephant, enjoying an expansive view that enables well-considered decisions. As the rider and elephant journey through life together, the rider holds the reins to help its buddy, the elephant. The elephant (emotions and intuition) is in the perfect position to take the cues of the rider (reason). But consider this: What if the elephant has seen a mouse? The rider might not find that terrifying, particularly from high up on its perch. Much as the rider might yell, pull hard on the reins, or sweetly cajole the elephant with assertions that it's silly to be afraid of a tiny rodent, the elephant won't cease to be afraid and it won't stop experiencing the fears motivating it to bolt away. Paradoxically, the more frustrated the rider gets, the more threatened the elephant might feel. Regardless of how wise or "right" the rider is, an agitated elephant will overpower any preferences a rider has.

Elephants are better able to receive corrective information when they are calm rather than agitated. I love this line from Daniel B. Wile, the couples therapist and author of *After the Fight*, because it so perfectly captures why communication strategies will fail you in the heat of conflict: "It is impossible to make 'I-statements' when you are in the 'hating-my-partner, wanting revenge, feeling-stung-and-needing-to-sting-back' state of mind. At such a moment you cannot remember what an 'I-statement' is, and frankly, you do not care."[11]

When you feel intensely angry, scared, or even disgusted, your prefrontal cortex—the logical reasoning part of your brain—goes offline. Anger, fear, and disgust reactions evolved to keep you safe, which helps explain why negative emotions can quite literally narrow your visual perception.[12] But these days, the loss of access to our prefrontal cortex rarely saves lives. More often, it makes it impossible to listen thoughtfully, speak compassionately, or perceive anything other than a flashing neon sign proclaiming your partner to be the most odious creature you've ever encountered.

Here's what's important to know: stressful experiences and negative mood shape how you perceive your partner and your relationship and, as a result, how you respond to them. To help you manage the world, as we discussed in chapter 4, your mind creates stories that explain the world outside and inside of you. But with so much happening inside of your body, between you and your partner, not to mention at work and with your kids, your mind can't capture all the information. Consider a situation where you're feeling exhausted, a work deadline is looming, and you have an unhappy toddler who wants all of your attention while the partner who theoretically could help you is nowhere to be found. What kind of story might your mind naturally generate?

Your partner may or may not be the villain. But if you're feeling the way most of us feel under the gun of working parenthood, your mind won't doubt for a moment that your partner is a baddie. Plus, no partner shows up perfectly every time. A human partner in combination with your stress and exhaustion will naturally contribute to a story of partner treachery. One study tracking newlyweds over four years and gathering data every six months showed this effect clearly. Stress over time led to a decrease in relationship happiness, an increase in the perception of specific problems, and an increased likelihood of seeing one's partner as responsible for problems.[13] These results suggest that stress can give rise to more negative perceptions and that stress reduces our ability to process those perceptions in ways that support our ongoing relationship happiness.

Expecting your rider (mind) to generate helpful ideas or to engage with your partner in a calm, rational way simply isn't likely when your elephant (emotions and intuition) is agitated, stressed out, or exhausted. Your most strategic first response in such moments isn't rider management or elephant wrangling. It's soothing the elephant.

Soothing your elephant can be accomplished in a variety of ways. First, recognize that offering yourself validation and compassion can calm your agitated elephant far better than trying to convince yourself that the mouse isn't dangerous. That self-compassion can be expressed through an internal narrative validating that this experience is hard. Anyone in your working-parent position would want to go postal on the boneheaded partner who dropped the ball.

Compassion can get active. You can ask, "What actions could I take that would be soothing in this moment?" Of course, most of us struggle to generate soothing ideas when elephants are agitated. High levels of emotion are exactly what make our riders ineffective. Coming up with ideas for soothing agitated elephants is best done when the elephant and rider are collaborating well.

· · · · ·

Pause to Create a Calm-the-Elephant Plan

Actions That *Calm* Your Elephant	Actions That *Aggravate* Your Elephant
SAMPLE ITEMS:	**SAMPLE ITEMS:**
Take long, slow breaths.	*Scream into an empty coffee can.*
Feel feet on the ground.	*Send your partner an angry email or text.*
Hug yourself.	*Call your partner and leave a screaming voicemail.*
Walk in nature.	*Listen to angry music.*
Listen to calming or joyous music.	*Call a friend who hates your partner.*
Call a wise and validating friend or family member.	*Watch a boring movie.*
Watch a funny movie.	*Read letters from an ex-partner.*
Read a good book.	*Do drugs.*
Take a hot (or cold) shower.	*Drink ALL the wine.*
Meditate.	*Eat ALL the cake.*
Do something creative (write, draw, knit).	*Punch your pillow.*
Write down things you are grateful for.	*Spend too much money.*
Eat one slice of cake.	*Call an ex.*
Allow yourself a good cry.	
Drink a warm beverage mindfully.	
Take a nap.	
Get a massage.	

Now, chart your own!

Actions That *Calm* Your Elephant	Actions That *Aggravate* Your Elephant

. . . . .

Acting to calm your partner's elephant can also be done strategically. Here, empathy, not persuasion, is the name of the game. Psychologists define empathy as an effort to understand what someone else is feeling. When we are empathic, we try to step into the shoes of another to see the situation from their perspective.

But being accurate in your empathy can be hard to do. If you're feeling hurt, angry, or frustrated with your partner, it can feel impossible to understand the situation from their perspective. This is particularly true when your experiences seem incompatible with your partner's. But there is good news—when it comes to empathy, *effort* matters more than accuracy. Shiri Cohen, a researcher at Harvard University, and her colleagues demonstrated this effect in a study that brought couples into the laboratory and videotaped them having conversations about upsetting events. Couples documented the emotions they felt during the conversation, what they believed their partner's emotions were, and how hard they believed their partner was trying to be empathic. For both husbands' and wives' relationship happiness, empathic effort mattered more than empathic accuracy.[14] As Shiri told me, "Partners don't have to be communication superstars or even skilled at reading emotions. What matters more in the process of connection is sensing that your partner is actually *trying*—that they genuinely care about your feelings and want to understand, even if they don't." The reason that effort matters so much, Shiri explained, is that it "can help partners shift out of the toxic 'me-against-you' mindset that often erodes relationships, into more of an attitude of openness and trust."

It isn't just a psychological effect—demonstrating that you care about your partner's emotions has a physiologic effect, too. In fact, empathic concern—both in the giving and the receiving—stimulates oxytocin release.[15] In turn, oxytocin has a calming effect on your nervous system.[16] That's good news since a calmer body will help you manage conflict better. In a study that brought couples into a laboratory to have conflict conversations, half of the couples had intranasal oxytocin administered before having the conversation, whereas the other half received a placebo. Oxytocin increased the duration of positive communication and reduced stress hormones relative to those who didn't receive the oxytocin.[17]

If you're like most people and don't keep intranasal oxytocin handy, you can turn toward attempts to convey empathy or look for evidence of empathic effort from your partner. In a calm moment, you and your partner might even strategize together how to more clearly communicate your effort to understand each other. It's worth trying to be empathic and demonstrate your empathy since for both you and your partner, demonstrations of care (even when you disagree or feel hurt) can calm the agitated elephants. With calmer elephants, you and your partner can each get back to collaborating with each other's riders as well as your own.

And don't worry—the elephants needn't be in a state of nirvana. They just need to be calm enough to stop seeing those flashing neon signs or terrifying little rodents.

A TALE OF TWO STORIES

Even when relationship stories are based on objective facts, our childhood experiences, adult expectations, temperament, unique agendas, and whether we are hungry, tired, or gassy from too much cheesecake color the plotline. It's pretty typical for partners to find themselves experiencing what seem to be entirely different realities. In one study, for example, partners were asked to independently mark behaviors that had occurred during the previous day for twenty-one consecutive days. The list included activities such as having sex, taking a walk together, confiding in each other, or having a conversation about feelings. Shockingly, the average agreement only reached chance levels (47.8 percent agreement).[18] That means that a stranger put to the task of guessing what had happened in your household in the last week would be in agreement about as often as your spouse. And in this study, agreement about events was even worse for less happy couples.

Different stories are natural, but those differences can cause trouble. You and your partner have different histories, different agendas, and entirely different accounts of how an event went down. So it's inevitable that your story will diverge from your partner's to levels that make you feel insane and sometimes insanely furious. You'll feel invalidated regarding your version because your partner sees it so differently. You'll disagree with your partner about not only what happened but also what *should* happen.

Common areas of disagreement such as division of childcare and domestic chores, sorting out whose professional demands should take priority, or how often to let in-laws visit (to name just a few) can feel intractable. They are. You can't solve for the differences that exist between you and your partner because your stories are crafted from different source material.

Much as you long for your partner to see life the way you do, creating a world where no story gaps exist isn't likely. Neither is determining whose story is "right." As the incisive Swiss philosopher and novelist Alain de Botton writes in *The Course of Love*, "By the standards of most love stories, our own, real relationships are almost all damaged and unsatisfactory. No wonder separation and divorce so often appear inevitable." The problem is not our relationship but rather in the approach our mind takes to telling the story. De Botton counsels, "Rather than split up, we may need to tell ourselves more accurate stories—stories that don't dwell so much on the beginning, that don't promise us complete understanding, that strive to normalize our troubles and show us a melancholy yet hopeful path through the course of love."[19]

· · · · ·

Pause to Develop an OURS Story

I'll offer some story-editing tips here specific to relationship stories. The steps center on moving from a my (versus your) story into a story that captures "OURS." They go as follows:

1. *Own your part.* Own your feelings and actions, recognizing that your elephant can get riled up and

hijack a story just as much as your partner's can. For example, turn toward this kind of thought: "I am really angry with you, and I can see that my feelings and actions, too, are a part of our dynamic."

2. *Underscore empathy.* Demonstrate empathic effort. You might say to your partner, "I don't understand why you did what you did, but I do *want* to understand."

3. *Release anger that may come up.* You can do this by actively seeking to give your partner the benefit of the doubt ("I'm sure you had good intentions."), conveying empathic effort ("I'm trying hard to understand why you feel that way."), and focusing on the behavior that's bothersome to you without vilifying the person ("That behavior bothered [horrified!] me, even though I realize it wasn't intended to harm.")

4. *Share a new story.* Invite your partner to join in on the conversation: "Would you be willing to talk it through so we can understand each other better and understand this event from both sides?"

.　.　.　.　.

THE SILVER LININGS OF SAME AND DIFFERENT

Just like gravity, similarities and differences are immutable, unavoidable. Like gravity, they can sometimes feel undesirable (just ask my youngest son, who regularly professes a wish to fly). Hating gravity will not prevent it from keeping my kiddo's feet on the ground, but accepting gravity can help him decide to enjoy the delights of imagining himself a superhero. Down the road, embracing both gravity and a wish to fly might inspire him to pursue studying aerodynamics or ornithology. Just like with gravity, responding to similarities and differences with acceptance can open you to new growth, appreciation, creativity, joy, and fortitude.

You might assume, for instance, that couples in which both partners work are worse off since that similarity breeds higher levels of stress. Yet shared experiences—even stressful ones—can enhance relationship satisfaction. Connecting around shared experiences helps us feel allied as we journey through important pieces of life. As one study of infertility-related stress showed, partners who undergo a stressful event and perceive it similarly are more likely to experience higher levels of marital satisfaction.[20] Finding ways to connect around stressful experiences by sharing daily struggles with each other can be an important point of empathic connection.

Sharing stressors of work, parenting, and working parenthood can help you use stressful experiences as a bridge to connection. But let's not forget the fun and connectivity of shared positive experiences. As working-parent Anne described, she and her husband "both find the kids hilarious. We have a lot of moments at home catching each other's eye and laughing." Sharing positive experiences boosts your own and your partner's mood—humor elevates most relationships, after all. Sharing fun experiences strengthens your relationship by helping it grow more connected, loving, intimate, and full of shared joy. In fact, sharing positive events with your partner increases positive feelings (beyond the positive events themselves), and responding in active ways to the sharing of positive events increases that effect even more.[21] In other words, find small and large ways to celebrate good things together!

There's a huge variety of what you can enjoy, since working parenthood involves such a diversity of experiences. Variety really is the spice of relationship life, helping our long-term relationships remain fun and interesting over time. In one study, for instance, couples were randomly assigned to participate in tasks that were either mundane or silly and novel. The silly, novel task involved partners being velcroed together and carrying a cylindrical pillow around an obstacle course on hands and knees, whereas the mundane task had partners slowly roll a ball to each other. Couples who participated in the novel task experienced an increase in their relationship happiness compared to the mundane task or no-activity control group.[22] Doing novel, silly, or simply different activities keeps things interesting—and interest helps your relationship remain fun.

As a working parent, you have access to the novel, peculiar, and silly. Share it with your partner. Giggle together when your child becomes a method actor who stays in character as a dog . . . all day long. Get fascinated by the strange, sometimes disturbing work experiences you each have. Celebrate each other's professional victories even (and especially) when it brings change. The variety that comes with a full life offers huge benefit in keeping things interesting in a long-term relationship.

Locating similarities—both difficult and enjoyable—is just a start. You can also find ways to transform differences from incompatibilities into fodder for relationship connection and satisfaction. Consider looking for ways that your differences offer benefit. For example, my podcast colleague, Diana, has a partner who prefers to vacuum. She favors food prep. Their different domestic chore preferences support a natural division of responsibilities, no arbitration required.

Differences can also help create healthy balance where similarities can lead to unhealthy extremes. For example, I often see couples in therapy in which one feels strongly about strictness, while the other is passionate about parenting warmth. But parenting experts recommend against either extreme.[23] A parenting style that accentuates discipline can lead to overly harsh parenting (called authoritarian parenting), whereas overly kind parents can be too lenient (called permissive parenting). A *combination* of love and limits, one in which you consistently and firmly set limits but do so with high levels of warmth, is optimal parenting. Psychologists call this style of parenting "authoritative," or "wise parenting." You can capitalize on major differences, such as parenting style, in any domain where you and your partner starkly differ. Seek out ways to understand how your differences help you balance each other out.

Surprisingly, too, even intensely painful differences offer opportunities, sometimes by way of growth. Communication stuck points can incentivize you to experiment with different approaches, leading to the kind of learning that helps in your relationship and in parenting or work. Difficulty tolerating arguments can push you to locate more strategies to bear emotional discomfort and recover from relationship fractures. And much as this might seem like naive sunny-siding, the intense emotions that come with disagreement often offer valuable information about what's important to you and to your partner. Transform intense conflict by practicing viewing conflict over differences as an opportunity to learn about each other and about yourself. This perspective will undoubtedly help you during the years of parenting a teenager, whose developmental responsibilities include learning how they differ from you while finding your buttons and pushing them as hard and as often as they can.

. . . . .

Pause to Transform Incompatibilities

Appreciating the silver linings of our differences can be tough. I recommend you begin by taking your internal temperature. If you're running hot (or just generally less than willing), start by soothing elephants or connecting to a value of building a life with less strife.

Next, spend some time reflecting on the following tips:

- *Turn incompatibilities into synergies.* Reframe differences by asking: In what ways might our differences provide complementary benefit? For example, in what ways do our differences help us achieve greater harmony *because* we are pressed to find a middle ground?

- *Learn about yourself and your partner.* Ask yourself, "In what ways can our differences help me learn more about what's important to me? How can they help me understand my partner in new ways?"

- *Use discomfort to prompt growth.* Ask yourself, "How do uncomfortable differences help me grow in ways I otherwise wouldn't?" Some couples, for instance, find that differences push them to engage in life in ways they don't feel comfortable doing, either by traveling more (or less), spending more money (or less), or considering different political opinions, parenting styles, or approaches to working.

- *Teach your children well.* Ask yourself, "How can we use our difficult differences to teach our kids to more skillfully manage disagreements/divergent perspectives?" Offering a model for how to compassionately, respectfully, and even assertively navigate differences is an important lesson to impart, even to young children.

. . . . .

BAD HABITS FORM EASILY BUT DIE HARD

Once you've begun to develop greater acceptance of your and your partner's elephants and riders and have practiced building a shared story that (when possible) recognizes the worth of both similarities and differences, it may be time to turn attention to tweaking relationship habits. The biggest challenge here is a reality most working parents face: *time*—that is, the lack of it. What working parent has time to work on their relationship?

Many working parents rationalize that next week, after the holidays, when the kids' sports season is done, once the toddler can wipe their own bottom or the teenager can help prepare dinner and drive their siblings to practice, *then* work on a relationship can begin. The trouble is, all the while you don't make time to nurture the relationship, your habits of not discussing, not practicing skillful listening, not enjoying time together, and not holding hands, hugging, or having sex progressively calcify. By the time you realize how much your relationship has deteriorated, you can't even imagine having a lighthearted conversation, let alone wanting to touch your partner (or have them touch you).

Two general ideas can lighten the lift of starting now, before bad habits become more fully entrenched. The first has to do with tiny habits. Start where you are and start small. Small habits involve practices that can easily fit into the life you are already living but which grow you and your life in value-aligned ways. The best kinds of habits have self-reinforcing features, meaning that while they take effort to initiate, the effort is inherently rewarding.[24] The second idea is to catch bad habits early and often. Habits like, say, hours of nightly crappy television (instead of talking with your partner), drinking alone (instead of having a glass of wine together), or eating the *whole* tray of brownies (instead of offering one to your partner) can quietly sneak back in. Remain on the lookout for habits you engage in that could be changed out for ones that nourish your relationship. You might begin by considering specific habits from the following domains.

HABITS TO NOURISH YOUR RELATIONSHIP

A small habit I've long struggled with is remembering to water my indoor plants. I like greenery, but I'm always forgetting my poor plants—they're much quieter than my three boys. My sad plants remind me that while some vegetation can withstand a drought or a chilly winter or a negligent gardener, all plants require some tending. For black-thumb gardeners like me, small habits are the difference between a plant that thrives (or survives!) and a withering eyesore. Relationships are the same, only the ingredients they require aren't water, sunlight, carbon dioxide, and minerals. The ingredients your relationship requires come in the form of your (and your partner's) attention, time, and energy.

Be Optimalistic

Begin by considering where in your week you can send resources toward your relationship. Make an agreement with your partner about what kind of a commitment you can each make given your constraints. Perfection isn't the goal here. *Optimalism* is. Tal Ben-Shahar, a psychologist and the author of *Happier*[25] and *Being Happy*,[26] defines optimalism as good enough given the constraints of your reality. And as he told me, "Good enough really is good enough." You can start small relationship-nurturing habits by considering ideas such as the following:

- A phone call during commute time to check in with each other

- Finding something you can express appreciation for

- Spending a few minutes together cuddling before you fall asleep at night or before you get the kids going in the morning

- Setting aside a half hour per week to focus on each other (park kids in front of a screen or do it while they are at school, in an activity, or sleeping)

- Committing to a monthly date night where you book an actual babysitter or do a date-night exchange with

a friend (as in, take turns with a friend—one of you
watches kids and the other gets a night out)

Attaching new habits to something you already do (such as commuting) makes it all the more likely that the new habit will stick.
The author James Clear highlights the power of attaching a new
behavior with a habit that's already well ingrained in *Atomic Habits*,
his guide for behavior change.[27] You can even go the extra mile by
making an explicit commitment to having fun together. This fits
in with a concept called "temptation bundling," developed by the
University of Pennsylvania professor Katy Milkman and discussed
in her book *How to Change*.[28] By attaching a naturally gratifying
behavior with a "should" behavior, you make it more likely that the
new habit will stick. In other words, you're more likely to dedicate
yourself to going on a brisk walk if you attach it to time spent listening to your favorite pop culture podcast. You feel good about getting
your walk in and less guilty about enjoying the gossip.

Use the principles of habit stacking and temptation bundling to
build relationship-nourishing habits. Consider, for instance, the
following:

- Send a sweet (or sexy) text *in addition* to that question
  about whether your partner can pick up dinner tonight.

- When you make dinner, include a dessert you both love
  and that is associated with a positive memory.

- When you pick up your next leisure book, invite your
  partner to read it as a couples' book group.

- When you put on your moisturizer at night, offer to
  give your partner a hand massage (and ask for one,
  in return, too!).

• Invite your partner to join your next Netflix binge (sit on the *same* couch, perhaps even cuddling while you take in the mindless fun).

You'll notice that many of these positive exchanges require little time, money, or energy (though they do require remembering to do them until the new habit is established). But those small actions can have positive ripple effects. Particularly when you respond in kind. So make sure that when your partner reaches out, you attempt to respond favorably. John M. Gottman and his team call this making a bid for connection and responding to a bid for connection.[29] That doesn't mean you must drop everything to connect or respond to your partner's reaching out. Instead, strive to acknowledge and appreciate each other's efforts to connect as often as you can. And remember that declining an invitation for a walk with an "I'd love to but today is nuts. How about tomorrow?" is far more helpful than a stony silence or an eye roll.

Work Your Ratio

It's helpful to know, too, that upping enjoyable interactions makes it easier to weather the snippy ones most of us mortals can't avoid. As one branch of Gottman's research reveals, couples who maintain ratios of at least five positive interactions to one negative interaction are happier and more stable (the least happy couples are closer to a one-to-one ratio).[30] So give yourself a break when you're too grumpy to be kind and caring. Then take responsibility for upping the positive exchanges when you are able.

Remember, too, that heaven for one person can be hell for the other. For example, one partner may find check-ins cathartic and connecting, while the other finds them aversive—an unpleasant opportunity for one partner to vent about dissatisfaction. Be aware of how each person experiences behaviors intended to be nurturing.

Strive to achieve a ratio of more pleasant experiences than unpleasant ones—for both of you.

Set Flexible Goals

Still, life will upend even your best-laid plans. Work deadlines, sick kids (currently typing this while sitting beside one of those!), and sometimes grumpiness can make it feel impossible to engage lovingly with your partner. Here is where flexibility comes in handy. Set a realistic bar for your commitment. Put time together on the calendar once a week, but consider two weeks out of the four a success. This form of flexible goal-setting allows you to achieve success within the realistic constraints of working-parent life.

Practice Better Communication

ONE LISTENER, ONE SPEAKER

Communication—the blessing and the curse of most relationships, at work and at home. Communication is the problem that couples most often highlight when they first come into the couples therapy room, so we'll focus on family communication here, but these strategies apply in other contexts as well.

One of the primary challenges of communication is a conversation with two speakers and no listeners. It seems obvious that being and feeling heard can only happen if someone is listening while someone else speaks, but it's a mistake that happens more often than most of us realize. Successful conversation involves skillful listening and speaking, and a good amount of turn-taking between the two roles. Pay attention to who is in which role. If it gets confusing, consider the following tips:

- Set a timer for fifteen minutes. Designate who is the listener and who is the speaker for that fifteen minutes, then reset the timer and switch roles.

- Designate a night for each of you to have airtime. (As in, take turns on who holds the speaker role on a given night. The partner who isn't speaker that night will be the listener, and then you'll switch roles the following night.)

- Take turns writing and responding to letters or emails.

If you find you are repeating the same conversation over and over again, that might be a clue that one (or both) of you feel that the other person hasn't really absorbed or isn't fully tracking the message. Consider upping listener effort. If your partner keeps bringing up the same topic, ask what they think you don't yet understand. Really get curious about the message your partner is trying to convey. You might even paraphrase what has been said to demonstrate where the understanding already exists and where it needs more work.

KNOW YOUR TYPE (OF COMMUNICATION)

Conversations can generally be distilled into two different categories—discussions and problem-solving—each with a unique goal.

- The goal of a discussion is to share feelings, perspective, or experiences.

- The goal of problem-solving is to generate a solution to an identified problem.

A common communication kink is that partners engage in problem-solving and discussion . . . at the same time! You may well think you're talking about the same thing—a rough day, a child's behavior problem, or a complication in the workplace. But because your conversation goals diverge, you end up talking right past each other and miss out on an opportunity to support, understand, and connect. You'll both feel incredibly annoyed (or downright livid) that the other person so insensitively held up their end of the conversation.

Take the example of my patients Akil and Jada. Akil often came home from work frustrated by a boss who liked to tease but ended up undercutting him in front of other colleagues. Jada would listen and nod with as much empathy as she could muster. But after venting for a while, Akil would grow frustrated with Jada. He couldn't understand why she just sat there, nodding away, instead of helping him figure out what to do. For her part, Jada couldn't figure out why her efforts to be compassionate would anger Akil. She eventually became resentful about how unappreciative Akil was of her sincere efforts to listen.

Unlike Akil, Jada worked from home. She also took on the majority of the childcare for their child. She struggled with balancing her professional aspirations with the caregiving responsibilities. When Jada shared her woes with Akil, he would troubleshoot, suggesting she drop some of the items on her to-do list. He figured Jada would be less frustrated if she stopped worrying so much. As Akil made suggestions, Jada would become furious with Akil's suggestions to simply "do less" instead of his making an offer to take some of the items that needed doing off her plate. The lack of empathy in addition to his assumption that it didn't matter if the clothes were clean, the dishes done, or the birthday presents purchased led her to calling him an insensitive and unsupportive partner. Akil grew angry with Jada for dismissing his perspective, seeing it as yet one more way she slighted him and made him feel incompetent and inadequate as a partner and parent.

Over time, Jada and Akil found themselves having these same arguments over and over again. They started believing that they were a terrible fit for each other, and it became increasingly hard for them to recall ever having felt supported and appreciated in their relationship.

Undoing this kind of damage takes time and patience. But a simple and powerful first step for couples can be clarifying the conversation type they want to have. Like Jada and Akil, many partners naturally default into different conversation types. Akil felt more comfortable problem-solving, while Jada preferred spending time connecting through sharing thoughts and feelings. By recognizing and appreciating different default tendencies or unique conversation agendas, you and your partner can set a clear agenda at the outset. You can also use this tool mid-conversation, when you notice the intensity rising and the frustration growing. You or your partner can call a brief pause and request a moment to get curious together about what kind of conversation makes sense to have.

· · · · ·

Pause to Communicate More Skillfully

Communication is complicated, and there is no single magic pill to get it working perfectly. But by understanding (1) the roles of speaker and listener, and (2) differences in types of conversations and unique partner communication preferences, you can get more effective in feeling heard and in hearing your partner.

It's helpful to know your own communication preferences as well as your partner's. You can gain insight by asking yourself:

- *Who is speaker and who is listener? Who needs a turn in each role?*

- *What kind of communication do I most naturally fall into? What kind of communication does my partner naturally fall into?*

You can then practice acting on this information. You can do so by trying out some of the following:

- Clearly and explicitly establish your communication goal at the start of the conversation. For example, you can say, "I had a hard day and I need to vent. What I really want is for someone to just hear me out." Or, alternatively, "I had a hard day and I need help problem-solving how to handle it. I'm really looking for some help figuring out how to deal with this issue."

- When you notice conversations going off track or getting heated, take the opportunity to pause and ask your partner, "Are you wanting to be in speaker role? Can I have a turn at speaking in ten minutes?" Or, "What kind of conversation were you looking to have, a problem-solving conversation or a sharing conversation?"

. . . . .

IN THE THERAPY ROOM

Coming back to the therapy room where I was treating Jana and Meg, I learned that Jana, too, had been unhappy with the transition to dual working parenthood. Jana shared that she had felt brushed aside as a partner immediately after her and Meg's son was born. She often felt like a third wheel in her own home, wondering if Meg and their son would be happier without her. In other words, both Jana and Meg were dismayed with the distance that had grown. Each yearned to reconnect.

Together we slowed down their conversation to ensure understanding of different perspectives. For example, we explored their individual preferences around parenting and work. Jana pointed out that they had jointly planned for Meg to carry their child and Meg had been enthusiastic about nursing their child. Jana had assumed that her role would be to stay on the professional fast track in order to better support their family's financial needs. While Jana admitted that she didn't want to pull back on work, she did want to play a bigger parenting role and to feel greater connection to Meg. They began to appreciate that differences between them allowed each one to prioritize a different role (work or parenting) while still allowing both of them to participate in the role that wasn't the top priority.

In viewing their differences in priorities with a more positive bent, they grew more willing to come to the negotiation table with greater benefit of the doubt. This more charitable stance helped them take a more effective team-based approach to renegotiating some of the domestic responsibilities and support for work time. It helped them, too, to prioritize making time to connect and enjoy each other in their busy family setup. Managing what was hard more skillfully and building habits to connect and nurture their relationship in an ongoing way helped them improve their working-parent marriage.

. . . .

The TL/DR (Too Long, Didn't Read)

USE WORKING PARENTHOOD TO STRENGTHEN YOUR RELATIONSHIPS

Set the Stage for Relationship Health

Get rid of the image of your partner as "villain" by recognizing that each person in a relationship struggles, that miscommunication and stress are inevitable, and that impasses happen to everyone. Work together to create a shared understanding of what's difficult and what you can be grateful for inside of your relationship.

Cultivate Healthier Relationship Habits

Happy, stable relationships are characterized by good habits, including expending resources to nourish your relationship, having more positive exchanges than negative ones, and practicing productive communication. Imperfect as you'll be, strive to build a habit of direct energy, time, and attention to your relationship.

PART THREE

FROM THE HEART

*How to Working-Parent
Happier*

My mission in life is not merely to survive, but
to thrive; and to do so with some passion, some
compassion, some humor, and some style.
—MAYA ANGELOU

10

FINESSE YOUR STRESS

I had to go back to work. NBC has me under contract.
The baby and I only have a verbal agreement.
—TINA FEY

In the classic 1989 comedy *Parenthood*, Steve Martin plays stressed-out sales executive and dad Gil Buckman. Gil does not have it easy. He gets called out by his colleagues for leaving business meetings early to attend his son's baseball practice, and then he's passed up for a promotion because another colleague "dazzled" the bosses (ahem, by not bringing the whiff of family into the office). Even as Gil is feeling the pressure at work, the stress at home ratchets up, too. Gil's oldest son is struggling with crippling anxiety and his daughter has developed an affinity for kissing classmates, his cherubic-looking toddler for headbutting. When his wife shares her desire to have a fourth child, Gil freaks out, growing increasingly bad-tempered and, in the characteristic styling of Steve Martin, eccentrically twitchy.

Toward the end of the movie, Gil attends his daughter's school play with his wife and toddler son. Gil's unhappy face is cinematically contrasted to his wife's loving amusement as they watch *Snow White and the Seven Dwarves*, the elementary school edition. When Gil's daughter receives a scripted onstage push, his toddler son concludes that his sister has been hurt. He takes rapid heroic action by rushing the stage, ducking the adults who try to restrain him, and biting the offender who pushed his sister. The mayhem grows as the teacher tries to catch the toddler, the young actors begin hitting one another, sets topple, and parents and grandparents loudly laugh or scream angrily. It's all too much for Gil. He begins to hyperventilate, burying his face in his hands, and we can hear the tidal waves of stress crash down on him.

But then, a Hollywood moment of revelation. Gil drops his hands as his eyes land on his daughter and son sitting at the side of the stage. Despite the chaos around them, the kids are giggling together as Gil's daughter puts her fake dwarf beard on her brother. Gil's eyes fill with tears. He, too, begins to smile, the tenderness evident as he turns to include his wife in an adoring gaze.

It's a scene that reeks of platitudes. That's partly why I love it! But I also love that this corny scene depicts something true. As a long line of stress research has shown, stress isn't what kills us; our reaction to it does.[1] Until the revelatory movie moment, Gil had been caught in a worry spiral, convinced that the stress was an indication of his failure as a father, professional, and spouse, certain he couldn't handle the stressors of working-parent life.

Neither Gil's worries, nor the worries of any working parent, are unfounded. In fact, the experience of being stressed-out makes good sense given the often cavernous gaps between the high demands we face and the resources we have to meet them. Still, there are more (and less) effective ways to respond to stress. There are also ways to use the inevitable working-parent stress to your advantage.

THE STRESS PARADOX

Unlike Gil Buckman, Shifali didn't need a Hollywood moment of revelation to appreciate her love of parenting or her love of work. Shifali always wanted to be a mother. She even had the foresight to use her experiences as a child to pen a handbook for herself of "what not to do as a parent." Written as a young girl frustrated with her own parents, her guide helps her to remember what kids truly want—an attentive, loving parent. Except professional life, which also sits at the core of Shifali's identity, regularly pulls attention away from parenting. Shifali mostly appreciates participation in both roles, since "raising good kids is important. But I also want to contribute outside of that." As a public relations manager, Shifali makes her valuable contributions by using her background in journalism, TV, and radio to help clients place work in national media outlets.

Shifali is upbeat about each of her roles, but she's also human. So she gets stressed-out. Part of the stress is the typical stuff of working parenthood—too much to do and not enough time to do it. But Shifali bears an added element of stress resulting from the protracted, contentious divorce and custody battle she went through a few years ago. Shifali now operates as a single working parent. The feeling that she's falling short in all the life roles that matter most to her is constant. She told me that as a single working parent, "You almost set yourself up for failure because you can't show up everywhere."

As the renowned stress researcher Richard Lazarus wrote, "Stress arises when individuals perceive that they cannot adequately cope with the demands being made on them or with threats to their well-being."[2] Yet there's a paradox embedded in the seemingly impossible challenge of doing so much. As Shifali explained it, her "divided passions" and desire to meet the challenges of each stress her out to the nth degree. But they also prompt her to improve her parenting and work skill sets, her psychological health, her ability to locate the silver linings, and her resilience.

Stress both worsens Shifali's working-parent experience *and* enriches it. It reminds me of my favorite Homer-ism (Homer as in *The Simpsons*, not *The Odyssey*) where he notes that beer is both the cause of and solution to all of his life's problems. This is the paradox of stress, too. Stress can deplete us even as it can fill us up. It can diminish our performance even while it propels excellence. It can make us feel alone even as it simultaneously connects us to others and to our larger purpose. Stress has downsides *and* upsides that go hand in hand. To take more advantage of those upsides, we can learn how to manage our stress response.[3]

Recognizing the complex nature of stress helps us take better advantage of the "antifragility" of being human. The concept of antifragility was developed by Nassim Nicholas Taleb, a mathematician and the author of *Antifragile*.[4] Unlike a glass that shatters when it is dropped on the floor, many complex systems grow stronger after getting batted about. Antifragility applies to what can happen after we experience stress. Factors such as our mindset about stress, our interpretation of stressful experiences, and our behavioral responses shape the trajectory following stressful events.

THE STRESS RESPONSE

By definition, stress rattles you. No matter how Zen you are, the death of a loved one, illness or injury, a child's health issues, financial problems, facing discrimination or harassment, loss of a job, starting a new job, or interpersonal conflict will tax your body and your mind. Then there's the impact of daily hassles. The never-ending to-do list, the pressure of trying to keep up with the fabled Joneses, the constant advice from experts and books to add to the things you are "supposed" to do such as exercise, bubble baths, meditation, and naps. In this chapter, I'll offer some science-backed advice for managing stress (including the stress I may be inducing by offering so much advice!).

First, a bit about the stress response. When you perceive stress, your body prepares for action. The well-known "fight-flight-freeze" response can save your life, your baby's life, and your professional life, too. When you interpret a threat, that automatic fight-fight-freeze response gets triggered. Your vision narrows, as do your cognitive resources and the available energy sources in your muscles.[5] Your body releases glucose and fatty acids to energize a response and shuts down your digestive, immune, and restorative functions (to conserve resources for the emergency response).

But such an intense and rapid stress response has certain drawbacks. For one, the likelihood goes up that you'll respond quickly but based on limited information. And remaining in that state (or returning there too often) depletes your mental and physical resources. No bueno. It's no wonder that we want to avoid major life stressors and daily hassles. It makes perfect sense that highly stressful events or more enduring low-level stress increase our vulnerability for physical and mental illness.[6] Copious research even confirms that those who endure more stress are at higher risk for cardiovascular problems,[7] insomnia,[8] and premature death.[9] Stress can even make us more susceptible to the common cold![10] Ergo, the ubiquitous message that stress is the enemy of your health and happiness.

But something critical gets lost in this widely disseminated, broad-strokes summary of the relationship between stress and illness. For one thing, the majority of individuals subjected to stressful events—including traumatic ones and chronic stressors—don't become ill.[11] Most people who get exposed to the cold virus don't develop runny noses or any other illness symptoms,[12] and even horrific events such as losing a child or spouse don't lead most individuals into developing clinically diagnosable depression.[13] Stress doesn't foretell physical and mental illness. In fact, the opposite is more often the case. Which is curious, isn't it?

ADVANTAGE, STRESS

The story of stress is far more nuanced than most of us imagine. In fact, our stress response offers adaptive functions that help us not only survive but also perform well, socially connect, learn, and grow. Getting stressed-out is the body's natural way of managing change and challenge. As Benjamin Franklin noted, "Change is the only constant in life. One's ability to adapt to those changes will determine your success in life." The stress response facilitates adaptation to new and changing demands.

Stress, by virtue of it being uncomfortable, helped humans thrive in early human times by motivating action that saved our own butts or the butts of our kin when danger arose. Stress prompted moves to environments with more food and encouraged social alliance building that kept individuals safely surrounded by a tribe. It should therefore be no surprise that the evolution of the human body has yielded a variety of cool presets for reacting to stress. Our immune response, for example, exists to respond to novel illnesses. When our body isn't successful in eradicating a dodgy foreign element through its immune response, stress then prompts our brain to innovate in medicine. When innovation doesn't do the trick, stress might motivate us to reach out for social support to meet the challenges with deliveries of chicken soup. If social support doesn't help us overcome it, then we might instead use our relationships to help us heal from the disappointment or loss. The relationship between stressors and our inherited stress responses induces each of these processes to help us survive, beat the odds, then grow from the challenge in ways that strengthen us.

On a daily basis in modern working-parent life, too, low-level stress can provide a valuable assist, though we may not initially experience it this way. For example, healthy kids constantly grow. You might stress about keeping them clothed and fed. That stress prompts you to locate funding for new pants and remember to prepare larger dinner portions. Their growing brains and constantly evolving social and emotional needs create stress. This prompts you to check in with their teachers, read new books, and engage more thoughtfully with them to discover how you can grow as a parent to better meet needs. Stress about a lack of progress at work might prompt more initiative-taking, while the stress of too-rapid progress could prompt you to ask for help, delegate, reassess growth goals, or take time off.

In many stressful situations, the narrowing of focus and hyper-arousal of your body offer more of a blessing than a curse. That's particularly true when the stress response happens and is followed by a recovery period. Using your stress response helps you to focus on this *one* problem in *this* moment in time with *all* the energy to help you get the job done and done well. This benefit explains why stress at work prompts initiative-taking and proactive problem-solving and activates your brain to process information more quickly. Even memory consolidation and performance on tasks are boosted when the tasks are more stressful.[14]

As the psychologist Kelly McGonigal describes in her transformative book *The Upside of Stress*, the wiring of the stress response facilitates success in achieving goals, motivation to connect to loved ones or to seek help, growth of resilience, and even the fostering of happiness.[15] By shifting how we think about stress, we can use its natural functions more advantageously.

BUILDING A BRIDGE TO GET OVER (AND THROUGH)

The advantages of stress grow when you cultivate a very particular kind of relationship between yourself and your environment, the demands, and your resources. Psychiatrist Viktor Frankl has often been quoted as saying, "Between stimulus and response there is a space. In that space is our power to choose our response. In our response lies our growth and freedom." Stressors may be unavoidable. That's true for working parents—some far more than others. It's no surprise, for example, that factors such as living in a neighborhood with higher crime[16] or experiences of racism[17] produce more acute and chronic stress in individuals. There's no question that some working parents face far more than their fair share of massive systemic stressors. You may not be able to control the stressors of life. But some of elements of the stress response? Those, you can influence.

In the 1960s, Richard Lazarus described what occurs in that space between the stressful stimulus and response. Lazarus's theory pointed out that stress responses differ between people because of how they interpret what is happening to them and what coping options they believe to be available to them.

Let's return to Gil Buckman from *Parenthood*. He believed that there was no good to be found in the stress of his life for much of the movie—and he was miserable. That misery seemed to contribute to the progressive deterioration of his parenting attitude, the quality of his work, and relationships with colleagues, his kids, and his wife. But when he was able to view his circumstances with a different frame, to appreciate the joy amid the stress, and to connect to the love he had for his family, he opened up new coping options for himself.

Taking the lessons from Gil Buckman to heart, you'll see that you don't need to change your stressors or undo stress arousal per se. Instead, you can learn how to use the arousal in response to stressful situations to benefit your psychological, biological, and performance outcomes. How we accomplish this feat has little to do with abolishing or even reducing stressful experiences or the arousal that happens in stressful situations. It has everything to do with changing how we *relate* to the stressful experience.

To begin, social scientists draw an important distinction between interpreting a *threat* versus a *challenge*. A threat is a stressful situation that literally puts your life at risk. In our modern lives, few situations actually call for this designation. But our brain, with its outdated wiring, often fails to recognize this, so we err on interpreting things as being more dangerous than they really are. But if you recall, unhooking from unhelpful interpretations can have huge benefits for you, your kids, and your work. You can strive to more thoughtfully distinguish imminent threat from uncomfortable challenge by recognizing that the vast majority of modern stressors fall into the "challenge, not threat" category. And of course, if a stressor truly is life-threatening, then it's wise to interpret it as such!

Techniques of reappraisal come in handy in distinguishing between actual threats and the more common challenges. You can, for example, practice prompting your brain to more deliberately tease out threats from challenges by asking yourself, "Am I truly under threat or is this a challenge I can rise to meet?"

After determining what kind of stressor you're encountering, the next area of reappraisal involves determining the optimal coping response. Here, it's useful to ask yourself, "What can I *do*?" There are two general categories to answer this question:

- Problem-solving
- Emotion-focused coping

If you can do something to change your stressful circumstances, then your optimal response would be to *problem-solve*. Problem-solving might include activities such as:

- Getting organized
- Tweaking your time management strategies
- Learning and practicing assertive communication
- Reaching out for tangible forms of support

However, it's folly to say that something can always be done. Sometimes you're too tired, your boss too sinister, your kids struggling too much, just as you find your support systems disintegrating all around you. In this case, even the most stellar problem-solving won't undo the impact of the stressors coming at you. Here, the best option is *emotion-focused coping*. This category of coping includes activities such as:

- Distracting yourself with pleasant activities
- Talking to someone you trust
- Mindful breathing or other relaxation practices
- Self-compassion, and allowing for discomfort without judgment

Knowing what kind of stress you're experiencing guides you toward the most workable coping strategies. Often the wisest approach incorporates both of these responses.

To design a wise coping strategy, you can ask yourself, "What parts of this situation can be problem-solved? What parts can't be changed and require emotion-focused coping tools?" Or, more simply, "What's in my control and what is not?" This internal coaching helps you to be flexible in your coping response. Flexible coping sets you up for responses that leave you better adjusted, in a position to take advantage of the useful elements of stress, and better able to rebound from the less helpful aspects of stress more efficiently.[18]

Let me go deeper into my working-parent friend Shifali's history before I explain how she pulled from both forms of coping strategies. Shifali's single-working-parent status came about as a result of the many painful stressors she endured being married. She told me, "I was paralyzed with fear for ten years. I would have left a lot earlier, but I was scared. It got to the point where it was impacting the kids, and I said, 'I have to do something because I don't want them to think it's okay to talk abusively to a woman. I don't want them to think it's okay to be an aggressive bully.'" At first, Shifali believed that she should simply cope, that change was not possible. Then she very deliberately changed her appraisal. She determined that the danger of staying outweighed the danger of leaving. But even as relieved as Shifali was to be free of her ex-husband, she admitted that there were new challenges: "I don't have someone helping me do breakfast and making sure backpacks are packed and making sure that we get to school on time. So that's where it's like—crap. It's all on you."

Shifali used problem-solving coping to get out of her abusive marriage, and she now regularly employs emotion-focused coping. For example, Shifali inevitably drops balls at work and gets called out because she simply has too much on her plate. She loses patience and yells at her kids when she wishes she had stayed calm. She loses her keys, her shoes, and sometimes her confidence that she can get it under control. As a single working parent, she doesn't always have good options to problem-solve and do it all better. In these moments, she very skillfully applies emotion-focused coping techniques. For instance, as she explained, "I've chosen to say to myself, 'I'm human. It's okay to be human.' And you teach your kids that it's okay to be human." Those, too, are pretty useful lessons to impart.

STRESS MINDSET MATTERS

Join me in considering a hypothetical scenario. Imagine that you're a professional singer readying yourself for a live solo performance. You've completed your vocal exercises and you're dressed to the nines. Your head to center stage and gaze out to a dimmed, packed theater. Your ears fill with the rustles of audience anticipation. You feel the thrumming of your pounding heart, the heat rising in your face, the clamminess of your hands, and the buzzing of your mind on high alert.

How do you interpret your stress cues?

One possible interpretation is that your body and mind are determinedly communicating that you're in terrible danger. The fact of your body preparing for fight, flight, or freeze indicates that you're not ready for a prime-time stage with all eyes and ears locked on you and your negative-thought spiral is trying to save you from embarrassment and the high likelihood that you're about to end your singing career before you've even started.

But there's an alternative explanation. You might instead conclude that your body is preparing to do something that requires intense energy and heightened awareness. Your stress response reveals just how important this performance is to you as well as how ready and willing your body is to nail it. Your keyed-up body has high energy and a focused mind ideally suited for dynamic performance. Your mind and body are ready to sing.

You're not alone if you naturally default to a more threat-based interpretation of your body's stress response. That default setting is aided by our wiring and from the consistent demonizing of stress. But our mindsets around stress are malleable. A study led by Alia Crum, a Stanford University professor of psychology, showed that mindsets could be shifted. In one study, participants were separated into two groups to watch videos. In one set of videos, a message of stress-as-debilitating was hammered home. In the other, a message of stress-as-enhancing was provided. Amazingly, these brief educational videos significantly shifted stress beliefs.[19] An even more impressive finding? Folks in the stress-as-enhancing group reported improvements in their health and work performance. Stress mindsets can be changed, and those changes impact how you feel and how well you perform.

Crum and her colleagues then got curious about how different stress mindsets influence behavioral and physiological responses to stressful tasks. So they recruited undergraduates to complete a stress-induction task. In this classic social-stress task, called the Trier social stress test, participants are asked to deliver a speech and perform mental arithmetic in front of evaluators. But here's the devious truth about the task: the evaluators are not really there to evaluate—they're there to stress the participants out! As participants perform, evaluators disapprovingly furrow their brows, frown, and cross their arms in snooty judgment. Regardless of your mindset, this set of tasks and harsh evaluation is bound to stress you out. But study participants with a stress-as-enhancing mindset were better at using stress to their advantage: they were more interested in receiving the optional feedback offered after the task than those who saw stress as debilitating.[20] Asking for feedback, of course, is one of the ways we can grow as a result of difficult experiences. Participants in the stress-as-enhancing group were also more likely to have midrange cortisol levels that indicate adaptive levels of the stress response. In other words, a stress-as-enhancing mindset was more useful than a stress-as-debilitating mindset.

A mindset that assumes stress to be problematic and unbearable overlooks many of stress's benefits. It can aggravate the negative impacts of stress and interfere with the positive ones. Yes, stress can be uncomfortable, even deeply painful. But it's also unavoidable. The belief that stress is bad for us is what really puts the nail in the coffin—literally. One study attempting to disentangle the effects of stressors and beliefs about how stress affects health found that neither stressful events nor a stress-as-debilitating mindset was independently associated with premature death.[21] In fact, people who experienced high levels of stress but didn't view stress as harmful had lower risk of death, lower even than those with low stress. But here's the kicker: having *both* higher levels of stress *and* beliefs that stress affects health negatively increased risk of premature death by 43 percent.

We can't always control, change, or exit from the stress in our lives. But we can be deliberate about our stress mindsets. Or as the pioneering stress researcher Hans Selye said, "Adopting the right attitude can convert a negative stress into a positive one." Whether you're heading onstage for a performance or moving through your complicated working-parent life, consider the benefits of cultivating a stress-as-enhancing mindset.

Because so much of thinking is language based, part of cultivating a stress-as-enhancing mindset comes down to building new habits around your stress labels and story. Just as moving from labeling "pain" as "discomfort" can shift how you think about and respond within uncomfortable experiences,[22] so can changing your language around stress. For example, Jeremy Jamieson, a professor of psychology, and his research team at the University of Rochester investigate how interpretations of stressful events can lead to different kinds of responses. During an interview, Jeremy shared that his early insights into how labeling stress responses can change what happens in your body and mind came through sports. He told me that as a kid, he played a lot of sports and that "one thing I noticed is people with different contexts, like your teammates before a football game, would be amped up and excited ready to play." But, he said, "If they had an exam, they'd be kind of nervous. There'd be a lot of freaking out." Athletics and academics were both leading to stress reactions. But those reactions seemed wholly different depending on the context.

Jeremy took his observations and interest in science to the laboratory to investigate people's appraisals and physiologic responses to stress, investigating what happened for folks who labeled experiences of the social-stress test as a "threat" versus as a "challenge." When Jeremy and his colleagues had participants go through the Trier social stress test, described earlier, of doing a talk and mental arithmetic in front of hypercritical evaluators, they found that participants coached to think about stress responses as functional, adaptive, and likely to aid in performance did better. Both groups had stress responses characterized by arousal of the sympathetic nervous system, but those who thought of stress as a challenge were better able to perceive their available resources, experience more adaptive cardiovascular responses, and had a diminished bias toward threat-related words.[23]

These days, Jeremy continues to conduct stress research, and he applies these ideas in his parenting. He tries to teach his son and daughter, ages seven and four, that "you don't have control sometimes over what happens to you, but you have control over how you respond." And he applies these ideas to his own appraisal of the stress he experiences within parenting, telling me that "engaging with difficult challenges and using stress to power through can be exhausting but rewarding. For instance, when our children were small, my wife and I would feel drained at the end of a day but satisfied that we accomplished something difficult: chasing toddlers."

Importantly, though, Jeremy emphasized that there are times when stress really does indicate a threat. As he told me, if you need to wrestle a bear, thinking about it as a challenge and not as a threat isn't likely to be of much help to you. But working carefully with your appraisals of stress can help you discern challenge from threat. This approach to your labels truly can optimize your stress response inside of working parenthood.

· · · · ·

Pause to Practice Stressing Skillfully

To cultivate a helpful stress mindset, consider the following options:

- Unless it truly is an imminent threat, label the stressor as a "challenge."

- Get curious about how you can rise to the challenge.

- Look for the silver linings of the stressful experience.

To get strategic in your coping, get curious:

- *Is it useful to prioritize problem-solving coping?*
  If yes, consider brainstorming ideas for organizing your time, accessing more help, gaining new skills, and/or setting stronger boundaries.

- *Is it useful to prioritize emotion-focused coping skills?*
  If yes, consider giving yourself a break and finding a pleasant activity to distract yourself, getting emotional support, doing deep breathing or meditation, getting out into nature, and/or practicing self-compassion.

We can learn to see aspects of stress as enhancing. We can gain skills in coping with the elements of stress that don't feel helpful. Through these strategies, we can exploit our stress responses by turning attention toward participating in experiences that support growth, healing, meaning-making, connection, and even opportunities to creatively cultivate happiness.

· · · · ·

DON'T SUFFER. BUFFER.

When asked how he managed the stress of being president, President Barack Obama credited temperament and his exercise routine, but noted that the "most important" way was "spending time with family." He went on: "When you have dinner with your daughters—particularly teenage daughters—they'll keep you in your place and they'll teach you something about perspective."[24]

Like President Obama, you can shift your relationship to stress by using your different life roles. This may seem counterintuitive at first, but if you consider your week, you might find evidence for a stress-buffering experience of your own.

Consider the following:

- When you're engaged in your work, it's often easier to forget how painfully sleep-deprived you are compared to when you're around your infant.

- The self-worth impact of critical feedback from your colleague can get diminished when your toddler tells you you're his favorite person in the world.

- The space in your brain occupied by your teenager's unwillingness to abide by curfew sometimes recedes while you're treating patients at the office or engaging with customers at the store.

- The anxiety about an upcoming meeting can fade while you're watching your kid play baseball or listening to them jam out to the radio during a car ride.

Work life can prevent you from getting caught up in the stressors of parenting life, and parenting life can prevent you from getting hooked by the worries of work. This kind of stress mitigation can occur even in extreme circumstances. A colleague of mine whose son was diagnosed with pediatric cancer at the age of three remained working throughout his son's multiple years of treatment. I'll note here that it would be simplistic, even offensive, to suggest that work was an unadulterated "good" for my colleague while his son fought to live. Yet he acknowledges that work, while adding to his overwhelm, simultaneously provided a place where he could momentarily recenter himself. The demands of work required that he think about something other than cancer, even if for a brief period.

Work and parenthood offer better perspective in both directions. Our children naturally offer us a reminder of "what really matters." And work helps us to worry less about our children, which can be sanity saving, too. Or as Alma, a child psychology professor, told me, "If my kids are acting up today, I can say my class went well. If things went badly at work, I can go home and get a hug."

Positive or neutral experiences in one domain of your life can neutralize (at least to some extent) negative experiences in the other. Having multiple life roles gives you more access to experiences that can buffer your stress.

CONNECTING TO CALM

Having more roles gives greater access to social connection, and social connection is a hugely influential predictor of how well we tolerate stress. There's evolutionary and biological science to back this up.[25] Meeting a threat in premodern times was more likely to be successful if you had allies backing you up. A group was more likely than an individual to be able to take down a predator, to locate a food source, and to ensure the survival of the young. It helps in modern life, too, with evidence that social support diminishes how painful we assess an uncomfortable experience to be.[26]

Social connection also helps you to engage allies. Whether that means talking with friends, hiring a babysitter so you can work, or asking your partner or neighbor to do a drop-off so you can take a nap, social support helps you manage your parenting stressors. The same goes for work where collaborating with colleagues helps you cover all bases of skill that are required, helps you find solace when you've failed to achieve a work objective, and provides encouragement when you've all but given up.

Connection also helps us feel better about the challenges we perceive. In one fascinating demonstration of this effect, researchers recruited individuals passing by the base of a hill who were either alone (lower social support) or with a friend (higher social support). The participants were then asked to judge the steepness of the hill. Those accompanied by a friend, particularly a close friend they had known for some time, judged the hill as less steep than those who were alone. In a second phase of this study, participants who were asked to imagine a supportive friend also saw the hill as less steep than participants who thought about someone they disliked or had neutral feelings for.[27] Studies like this one reveal that even when social connection doesn't diminish the magnitude of a challenge, feeling supported helps us experience it in less burdensome ways. And of course, social support can quite literally help to lighten our loads, such as when a friend brings you a coffee during an exhausting workweek, offers to watch your kid while you get a mammogram, or helps you carry the heavy backpack up a hill. More connections—be they to friends, family, or work colleagues— means more opportunities to access the benefits provided by social connection.

Social connection also helps you recover more quickly from a stressful event at a physiological level.[28] It helps you tolerate discomfort with greater ease. For example, in one study, married women were faced with the threat of an electric shock. The researchers varied whether the women were holding the hand of a spouse, an experimenter, or no hand at all and found that someone's hand (a spouse or a stranger) lessened the stress response at a neurological level. What's more, holding a spouse's hand was even more powerful than holding a stranger's, especially when marital satisfaction was high.[29] Connection with someone we care about helps us manage stressful experiences better.

Hormones, too, play an integral role in our stress response. Among the many hormones that get released when we encounter stress is the hormone oxytocin. Though better known for its role in social bonding, oxytocin serves an important role in stressful circumstances. It prompts connection. Yep, stress can make you more social.[30] And social engagement has stress-alleviating effects. Hormonal and brain research shows that stress decreases when we connect in positive ways with our kids.[31] Parent-child connections even quiet activity in brain regions associated with negative feelings and thoughts. Mothers shown pictures of their infants, who hold them or smell them or think about them, experience a diminished threat response.[32] That means oxytocin can motivate connection as well as bolster your courage. Oxytocin release is naturally prompted for new mothers,[33] offering distinct stress benefits. For instance, mothers who breastfeed show a decreased neuroendocrine response to stress and a reduced negative mood (of course, this is a statistical finding that doesn't negate the fact that some mothers find nursing highly stressful!).[34] Notably, oxytocin is also associated with bonding between foster mothers and infants,[35] as well as fathers and their children,[36] offering caregivers of all kinds the attachment and stress benefits associated with oxytocin.

These connections help our kids with their emotional regulation, too. Feeling understood and supported by the people in our life helps calm the threat response for humans of all shapes and sizes, making it worthwhile to connect with family or with work colleagues during stressful times.[37] Taking time to feel gratitude, and even to express it to the people we connect with, can enhance the stress alleviation effect all the more.

BE OF SERVICE

When researchers attempted to parse out the unique ways that social engagement reduces stress, they found something very surprising: forms of social connection are not created equal when it comes to buffering our stress responses. In a study looking at mortality risk among older adults, researchers examined the effect of stressful events, health, receipt of social support, and helping others. Individuals who did not report being of service to others and who were exposed to stressful life events had a 30 percent increase in death risk.[38] In other words, not being helpful was, on average, deadlier. This makes sense when you consider that one of the main ways we transform unavoidable stress into an asset is by making meaning in it. By seeing stress as a pathway to making a difference for others, we benefit, too.

You can thank your working parenthood, with its cornucopia of options for being helpful to others, for reducing your mortality risk. And use that piece of science to really shore up your stress-as-enhancing mindset! Attempt to embrace the stress-buffering potential of teaching your kid to tie their shoes, offering your clients and colleagues professional support, or giving your tired working-parent partner a back massage. As much as these activities tax your resources, they simultaneously provide opportunities to be of service. Others will benefit and so will you.

PUT YOUR EXISTENTIAL EGGS INTO DIFFERENT BASKETS

"What's the point of it all, anyways? What's the meaning of my life?" These kinds of thorny questions can sink people into a deep hole of existential fear. But children, meaningful work, and relationships of various kinds independently and jointly offer avenues of meaning-making. Working parenthood thus supports us in tackling these daunting questions.

Let's admit, first, that parenting and professional roles each have inherent limitations in allowing us to make meaning in life, leave a unique legacy, and dive deeply into joyful experiences. Parents, for example, may feel a sense of loss when their legacy eventually chooses to live an independent life after eighteen (or, say, thirty-five) years. And many jobs feel pretty devoid of meaning. But by diving into both parenting and professional roles, we can ease the loss of children leaving us to make their own way in the world by appreciating the meaning we can make through our work. And we can inject purpose into tedious, meaningless work by considering its benefit for our children and our family.

Having two roles in which you can make meaning can ease the pressure you place on either. As Shifali explained to me, in Indian culture (as in many sectors of American society), children are often seen as extensions of parents and a tangible means of demonstrating success. That's hard on children and parents alike. Working parenthood offers an antidote to this problem by creating opportunity to achieve success outside of parenthood, thereby reducing the pressure placed on kids. As a computer scientist expressed to me during an interview, "My anxiety has gone down so much since having a child. Before having a kid, I felt like my work needed to justify my life. Now I feel like I can be merely good enough at my job. It takes the pressure off of each domain and makes the stakes much lower for both of them."

STRESS ON TRIAL

A few years ago, on the day of her custody hearing, Shifali felt crippled with anxiety as her vision tunneled on her children's future. But the pressure to keep her job afloat forced her vision to widen outside of her parenting role. As she did, she found support from her boss, a distraction in her clients, and a sense that she was doing all right despite the stress. As she told me, "You know, when everything else is shit, work offers another place where you can have something positive come in, another avenue to have goodness come into your world." Working parenthood can, indeed, help you to stress less.

. . . .

The TL/DR (Too Long, Didn't Read)

FIND HIDDEN BENEFITS IN WORKING-PARENT STRESS

- *Consider the benefits of developing a stress-as-enhancing mindset.* Practice appraising your stress by getting curious about what is a true threat and what is a challenge. Next, consider what kind of coping response will serve you best. Then reflect on the ways that stress has enhanced your resilience, growth, skill set, and social connection.

- *Connect to calm.* You can use mindful engagement with your children to cool your stress or savor opportunities to bond with people at work. Pause and fully immerse yourself in the experience of being together, taking note of the impact connections have on your stress response.

- *Gain perspective.* Use each role to help you gain perspective. Reflect on how the balance of roles in working parenthood helps you understand what "really matters."

- *Spread your meaning.* Consider how having a foot in each role reduces the existential pressure you experience in each. Reflect on how your ability to make your days matter gets expanded through the impact you have on your children (and that they have on you) and through your work (whether that's by making a difference in the world or making an income through your effort).

11

TEND TO YOUR
HAPPINESS NEEDS

I didn't think it was going to be this fun. But every-
thing just gets heightened when you have a baby.
The volume gets turned up on life.
—JIMMY FALLON

My dad had a happy childhood in Israel. But his primary caretakers weren't his parents, though they were alive and well
and lived in the same community. My dad was raised on a kibbutz,
a small, agricultural society in Israel organized according to Zionist
and socialist ideology. From the time his parents brought him home
from the hospital, my dad lived not with them but in a "children's
house" with his same-aged peers. While he saw his parents daily,
the majority of his caretaking was done by kibbutz members whose
official role was "caretaker," rather than his own parents.

Kibbutzim (the plural of *kibbutz*) were very deliberately designed to reconstruct the family unit and redefine work and family
divisions. They were intended to be utopian, collective societies
emphasizing perfect equality between the sexes. The fact of kids

being raised communally was meant to permit adults, regardless of gender, to work and to have warm relationships with their children. It may seem strange to those who weren't raised this way, and evidence suggests this model didn't work for some children, but my dad thrived. He developed deep connections with peers, treasured his independence, worshipped his parents, and cultivated a lifelong passion for hard work and relationships from early in his childhood.

When he hit adulthood, though, my dad decided that the kibbutz was too professionally limiting. What need was there for an ambitious young engineer on an agricultural commune? So after my parents met, my dad proposed to my mom with an invitation to pursue the American dream together. They married and booked one-way tickets to the United States. When it came time to raise a family, they jointly decided to return to a more traditional family structure. They figured with modern thinking, American resources, and intentionality, they could vastly improve on the traditional roles that the kibbutz model had rejected.

For my mom, though, the full-time parenting role turned out to be less than ideal. For all of my parents' modernity, resources, and flexibility, my mom felt bound to the domestic sphere in ways that strongly interfered with her happiness needs.

BASIC HAPPINESS NEEDS

Like plants, which need water, minerals, carbon dioxide, and sunshine, human happiness has been shown to have critical basic psychological needs. Across roles, age, and culture, fulfilling these needs increases the likelihood of thriving[1] and reduces the likelihood of happiness withering.[2] The three core psychological needs include:

1. *Competence*—the ability to bring about outcomes you desire
2. *Connectedness*—a sense of closeness or relatedness to others
3. *Autonomy*—self-determining activities or goals

Decades of social science research suggest that getting core needs met is critical for happiness and that when needs don't get met, our well-being suffers.[3] For my mom, need fulfillment was thwarted.

In the competence realm, it rankled her that she had so little control in parenting. We three kids regularly foiled the execution of her desired aims by doing what *we* wanted rather than what she thought was best (my karma on this front is already catching up with me). When it came to connectedness, though she was usually physically near us, she often felt lonely. She yearned for connection to people who could really see and appreciate who she was, not just the services she offered. Finally, in the autonomy realm, my mom felt a marked lack of agency in determining the structure of her days. Instead, she felt at the mercy of the needs and schedules of her family members and pressed to neglect her own. And although my dad viewed their money and other material property as being shared, my mom felt financially dependent.

To be clear, many stay-at-home parents experience life satisfaction as a result of their parenting role. In no small part, that's because it's entirely possible to access the experiences of competence, connectedness, and autonomy that nurture enduring happiness. For instance, we certainly can feel competency in parenthood or in other activities we participate in while having kids. And there's no reason that a stay-at-home parent can't find connection in family or with friends and other communities such as religious communities. And many parents influence the structure of a day and have agency in choosing or declining participation in hobbies, health and wellness, and spiritual engagement. Ultimately, whether working, parenting, both, or neither, each of us can grow skill in getting basic psychological needs met.

Yet for some people—perhaps particularly for immigrants like my parents and others whose lives are naturally more constrained—stay-at-home parenting makes the varied experiences that naturally feed happiness harder to come by. As a young girl, I heard my mom chronicle this reality regularly. As a study in contrasts, my father seemed mostly cheerful. He awoke with an eagerness for the day ahead, relishing his role as an entrepreneur, feeling pride in supporting his family, and enjoying whatever time he spent with us in combination with the time he had connecting with colleagues. Although my dad wasn't an outwardly reflective person, I interpreted his sunniness to mean he thoroughly enjoyed working-parent life.

I absorbed messages about my dad's childhood on the kibbutz, witnessed my dad's happiness, and noted my mom's frequent frustration. I concluded that working parenthood made the most sense for a happy adult life. But, of course, as I shared in the introduction, becoming a working parent revealed how much more complicated it was to build toward happiness as a working parent than I had anticipated. My dad surely had it easier than I do in many respects by having my mom as a partner who was a stay-at-home parent! The overwhelm I sometimes feel naturally leads me to thoughts that life would be easier if I were to make the same choice my mom did and give up on working. Or perhaps finding someone to be my own stay-at-home partner. My days would surely be less taxing. I might even drink less coffee, meditate for longer than three minutes at a time, and do some sit-ups.

But I always return to a conviction that began forming during my childhood: for me and for many others, working parenthood offers an advantage in fostering happiness. That advantage comes *as a direct result* of the many burdens and daily hassles of working-parent life.

Consider these potential happiness benefits:

- In working parenthood, we've got to learn how to parent *and* we've got to stay current in our jobs. While that can mean more opportunity to feel incompetent, it simultaneously creates more pressure to cultivate skills and more opportunities to have a place where we really are skillful and able to influence desired outcomes. *Having more roles presses us to build a greater number of competencies.*

- Working parents often have a daily structure that requires lots of interaction with lots of different people—we must interact with our kids, colleagues, clients, and the magical barista who keeps us caffeinated. *More interactions mean more opportunities to feel connected.*

- More places we need to be and more ways we need to show up also mean more opportunities to make choices in what we do and how we do it. *Access to diverse experiences increases likelihood of autonomous choices.*

In short, working parenthood can offer access to diverse experiences that foster happiness.

THE FULL LIFE

The political science professor Elizabeth Corey, whom we met in chapter 2, adores her three children and her professor husband. She has managed to be an involved parent, even homeschooling her eldest daughter for several years while climbing the academic ranks at Baylor University. She is deeply involved in both work and parenting, with demands intense in both spheres. So much so that she admitted the thought of "putting my career on hold comes into my mind once a week. Or maybe once a day!" She confessed to me that just that morning, "I was chasing the dog, my youngest needed to be wiped, I needed to get dressed, and I had the thought, 'Why am I doing all this? I am trying to do too much.'" But then she imagined what life would be like if she gave up on her professional ambitions. She concluded, "I would be sorry. I would feel like I hadn't actualized the talents that I have."

It can seem as if fewer roles and fewer demands would be a recipe for greater happiness. For some people it may well be. Yet a life with more demands and more roles can offer us a greater chance to self-actualize. It can give us more access to the kinds of experiences that breed happiness, including opportunities for pleasant experiences, connection to others, and creating meaning.[4] The cognitive scientist Sian Beilock, whom we met earlier, described it during our podcast interview: "So I'm a college president of Barnard College at Columbia, which is the premier institution focused on women's intellectual leadership in the country. But I'm also a cognitive scientist studying performance under stress. And I'm a mom and friend. And the idea is that we have better and worse days in each of these areas of our lives. And being able to come home and hug one of my kids when I've had a bad day at work can be mentally beneficial for me."

Assorted experiences nourish greater happiness because happiness itself isn't one-dimensional or monochrome. The word *happiness* captures all sorts of positive emotional experiences including joy, gratitude, serenity, interest, hope, pride, amusement, inspiration, awe, and love.[5] We can increase the likelihood of having various desirable emotions by having varied life experiences. For instance, you might want some tranquility in the space of your week, but tranquility can get boring after a while. Even if you're an adrenaline junkie, from time to time you might yearn for a quiet day at home with your books. Happiness relies on wide-ranging experiences that set the stage for varied positive emotions.

THE PURPOSE OF POSITIVITY

By now, you well know the function of negative emotions—they are wired into our brain and body to help us survive when our physical or our social safety is under threat. While the function of emotions such as anger, anxiety, and disgust have been well understood for decades, it's taken researchers a bit longer to reveal the evolutionary function of positive emotions. In fact, before the 1990s, few researchers studied the role of positive emotions and human thriving.

In 1998, the renowned psychologist Martin Seligman, then president of the American Psychological Association, began an initiative to promote positive psychology as an independent field of study. Since that time, research on flourishing has, well, flourished. We know now that positive emotions are just as instrumental for survival as the negative ones. As a growing body of research shows, fostering pleasant feelings does, indeed, support happier and more successful living.[6]

According to the renowned happiness researcher Barbara Fredrickson's broaden-and-build theory,[7] negative emotions narrow our attention to manage threat, and happier emotions broaden our attention. In so doing, positive emotions motivate us to build up critical physical, psychological, and social resources. For instance, positive emotions can prompt us to learn new skills, improve our health, reach out to friends, nourish intimate relationships, pursue interests, think more inclusively or creatively, see challenges with optimism, and grow resilience.[8] Those actions all line up with safety, health, and community. Positivity even triggers enduring healthy changes at the neurological level.[9] And positivity buffers the effect of negativity. That's especially useful when our natural negativity biases interrupt our ability to flourish inside of work and parenthood. Positive emotions can disrupt a downward spiral and initiate more positive ones.

Negative experiences are inevitable. But the good news is that a combination of negative and positive experiences sets the stage for optimal functioning. Remarkably, we've even come to understand that there is an optimal ratio for positive to negative experiences. Work from Fredrickson and her colleagues reveals that a ratio of three positive experiences to one negative one offers a kind of gateway to flourishing.[10] When your positivity ratio drops too low, you can deliberately move toward engaging in whichever role will help you get your ratio back to where you'd like it to be, with a focus on autonomy, competence, and connectedness.

A RECIPE FOR HAPPIER

Say you were having a rough go of it and I told you, "Go do something that makes you feel happy!" You might have no clue where to begin and feel overwhelmed, even paralyzed. That's the experience of people struggling with depressed mood when they are told to seek out positivity. A more specific recipe can offer a structure that makes it easier to get started or redirect when things go off-kilter. This is where Fredrickson's ratio of three positive experiences to one negative experience and the awareness of the three basic psychological needs can provide helpful guidance.

Good recipes executed in complicated circumstances, however, require flexibility. For instance, you might want to bake some bread and have all the ingredients in the pantry. But if you're used to baking bread at altitude in a place like Boulder, Colorado, moving to Boston, a city at sea level, is going to require some pivots in your approach. If you are baking from your usual altitude but your spouse used up the yeast in the house (or if you're like me and dump oil on top of nine cups of flour before realizing you are out of yeast), you'd be wise to have some alternative plans for rising agents. When the bread is a bust because baking soda isn't a great replacement for yeast, you might want to have backup ideas for the dinnertime starch. Like bread baking, remaining flexible in happiness baking will help you to find and take advantage of the ingredients you need.

．．．．．

Pause to Practice a Positivity Recipe

By actively turning toward daily experiences of competence, autonomy, and connectedness, you create some clear objectives and flexible structure for building positivity, and you make it easier to achieve a ratio of three positive experiences to one negative experience. Consider examples provided below:

EXPERIENCES OF COMPETENCE

- *Calmed the toddler*
- *Made headway into email backlog*
- *Practiced tolerating discomfort (of melt-downs and overwhelm) more stoically*
- *Refined skill in calming an unhappy client*
- *Activated the power of a twenty-minute nap*

STRESSFUL EXPERIENCES

- *Toddler committed themself to an hours-long tantrum*
- *Project at work went belly-up*
- *A fight with your partner*
- *Not enough sleep*

EXPERIENCES OF CONNECTEDNESS

- *Hugged toddler extra tightly at day-care pickup*
- *Vented with colleague about challenges of the project*
- *Asked partner out on a date*
- *Got coffee with a colleague*
- *Mindfully read stories with the kids before heading to bed early*

EXPERIENCES OF AUTONOMY

- *Left unhappy toddler with caregiver and stopped to get a coffee before going to work*
- *Took ownership of picking the Friday family movie*
- *Told boss I want to seek additional training in an area of relative weakness*
- *Told partner I needed an hour to myself in the evening*

· · · · ·

THREE-TO-ONE RATIOS IN ACTION

I've interviewed a lot of busy people, but Angela Duckworth has to be the busiest. She's the recipient of a MacArthur Fellowship (often referred to as a "genius grant") and a bestselling author;[11] she runs a nonprofit whose mission is to advance science that can help kids thrive; she advises CEOs of Fortune 500 companies and NBA and NFL teams; she collaborates with many other scientists on research studies and teaches at the University of Pennsylvania, where she is a professor; and she is a mother to two girls. Busy as she is, she's one of the most delightful people to be around. She's infectiously happy.

Her status as a busy social scientist and a supremely happy person is not coincidental. She's known for studying grit, but she was trained in the science of happiness in Martin Seligman's laboratory. Angela very deliberately feeds her positivity through what she has gleaned from her own and her colleagues' research. She offered an example from the week prior to our meeting to illustrate how she does it:

> It was the Tuesday that [author of *How to Change*, Katy Milkman's] book came out. And I remember looking at my schedule and figuring out that if I speedwalked, I could go to the florist, pick up the flowers that would match her book cover just when the florist opened, drop them off, turn tail, and speedwalk home before my Zoom call. And as I was rushing home, I remember thinking consciously, "This is great. I'm doing what I *want* to do." I wanted to express some affection for my academic BFF, I really like walking, I feel like I'm doing what my mother always taught me to do, which is what I always think anytime I do anything vaguely kind. I'm like, that's because I'm my mother's daughter and that's a kind of alignment. I mean, that's happiness, right?

We want to do the things we want to do. When the activities we want to do embody elements of autonomy, competence, and connectedness, we find happiness growing. Being deliberate about accessing the various nutrients that we need on a daily basis and savoring them ensures our own thriving.

BUT WHAT ABOUT ALL THE OBSTACLES?

It's well and good to be in Angela Duckworth's shoes, but some individuals don't have sufficient autonomy available inside of their days to go for a brisk walk. How many of us can say we've won grants attesting to our genius, thus offering us reassurance of professional competence? How about those of us who don't have accessible BFFs to connect with regularly, or whose jobs are isolating? Amid the pressures of working parenthood, who can claim carefree choice in how we accomplish our daily task log?

It's a fair point that autonomy at work may be an impossibility. And in the parenting sphere, connectedness is far from a given. For each of us—sometimes temporarily and sometimes more enduringly—work and parenting roles create obstacles to getting basic happiness needs met. This is where access to multiple realms of experiences and roles can help.

Zooming out from an imperfect working-parent day offers a view of many smaller, multifaceted experiences. The absence of important elements from one role can almost certainly be replenished in another.[12] When my children, for instance, were engaging in dictatorial sleep torture, choosing when to refill my coffee cup at work felt liberating. When I feel socially isolated in my private practice work, the moments of connection with my children provide me with vitality. While feeling totally inadequate teaching my three-, seven-, and ten-year-old kids during the COVID-19 quarantine, I treasured my competence doing therapy. Like plants who can get their needs for water met through rain, a sprinkler system, or a good old watering can, we can take advantage of a multitude of ways to get psychological needs met.

. . . . .

Pause to Consider When, Where, and How to Get Needs Met

Remain attuned to which needs have been met and which have been frustrated. Once you recognize which areas are wanting, you can take deliberate advantage of your many life roles and daily experiences to fulfill your daily dose of autonomy, competence, and connectedness.

Ask yourself:

- *Which role—work or parenting—is most likely to satisfy an unmet need for autonomy, competence, and connectedness?*

- *How can I use that role to provide that kind of experience today?*

Then turn toward that role to meet it with deliberate intention.

. . . . .

EXPERIENCES OF COMPETENCE

As a young girl, Leslie Forde was a creative kid as well as a productive and practical one. She became fascinated by how products came into being and became commercially viable. She told me that as "a Black woman whose parents are immigrants," it became clear that it was "important to work really hard, and to work harder than others." Leslie adopted a style of working that built competencies quickly: "I kind of dove in and relished in the intensity of being able to contribute and feel that rush associated with getting things done."

These days, Leslie is a mother of two who does product management and strategy for an educational publishing company. She's also the founder of Mom's Hierarchy of Needs, an organization whose mission is to help moms manage stress and embrace self-care. And she's still a person for whom competency reigns supreme as a goal. So it's no surprise that for Leslie, "the biggest challenge is the desire for excellence in both [parenting and professional] roles." Her desire can't be met in the same way she used to meet it because Leslie can no longer be the one into the office earliest and out latest—at least, not if she wants to be the kind of parent that she values.

The consequences of feeling incompetent have long been of interest to psychologists. In the 1960s and 1970s, Albert Bandura, one of the most celebrated psychologists in history, came across a surprising finding about competence while studying the processes by which different phobias could be alleviated. He found that the likelihood of improvement after treatment of a snake phobia depended on the beliefs individuals held about their ability to cope. In other words, recovery depended on patients' perceptions of their own competence.[13]

In the decades since, the importance of feeling effective and capable in areas we care about has become increasingly clear. In the parenting realm, for example, believing you are a competent parent fuels greater competency in parenting. A comprehensive review of over one hundred studies showed that believing you can parent in a manner that promotes your children's health and success has been shown to be associated with a whole host of positive outcomes including better relationships, better parental mental health, and better outcomes for kids in behavior, mental health, academic outcome, and sleep and eating habits.[14]

But let's face it. When our time, attention, and energy are divided, competence can take a hit. So it can be useful to rethink what it means to you to be competent inside of working-parent life. That's just what Leslie did.

Before becoming a parent, Leslie defined competence as dedicating herself wholeheartedly to cultivating excellence at work. Now she focuses on a competence that comes from double-dipping into her roles. She strives to develop skills in each role that can be usefully applied to the other. For example, she's become a master of problem-solving, empathy, and being present for whatever the role requires in that particular moment in time. That's helped keep her at the top of her game at work, even as it's helped her excel in the realm of parenting.

When I asked Leslie what other kinds of on-the-ground strategies she employs, she, true to form, had a truly competent answer: "Some of it is very tactical, like being ruthless about my time, looking at every form of productivity improvement I could possibly get my hands on and trying them." And, she added, "part of it is psychological. I'm firmly aware at all times that both things—both the parent me and the work me—they're things I've chosen and they're both important to my identity." So she regularly asks herself, "Are there adjustments that allow me to do better? I question that, at some level, probably all the time, but especially as things newly evolve."

· · · · ·

Pause to Craft Competence

A sense of mastery isn't always available, but you can pull the levers to increase its chances of showing up. Consider trying the following steps:

- Use skills you feel confident about in one domain of your life to show competence in the other.

- Read books, listen to podcasts, seek advice in areas you want to strengthen your skills (check out the resources section at the back of the book).

- Remind yourself of the skills and strengths you feel most proud of because trusting in your areas of competence helps you to shine more brightly in them.

- When you have an experience of competence, allow yourself to fully attend to it, noticing how it feels and allowing its effects to permeate.

. . . . .

CONNECTEDNESS

In one classic study, sweetly titled "Very Happy People," the happiness researchers Ed Diener and Martin Seligman investigated a wide range of "keys" that might unlock happiness by following 222 undergraduates over a period of fifty-one days. Data was collected on happiness, as well as dozens of variables thought to be associated with happiness including GPA, exercise, personality, mental health, religiosity, television watching, sleeping, use of substances, and objective physical attractiveness. They then compared the happiest 10 percent to the least happy 10 percent. Among all the characteristics assessed, the one that most stood out was the nature of social relationships. Very happy people had fulfilling social relationships and spent less time alone than people with lower levels of happiness.[15]

One of the longest studies ever run shows similar findings: The Harvard Study of Adult Development has followed 724 men over eighty years, and their main findings suggest that close relationships sustain both happiness and health.[16] As the psychiatrist George Vaillant, who directed the study for over thirty years, summarized, "The most important contributor to joy and success in adult life is love."[17] And it isn't just our closest relationships with friends and family that foster happiness. Having more daily interactions, even with people on the periphery of your social network, is associated with better social and emotional well-being.[18]

Much of the research on well-being focuses on White, college-educated individuals from wealthy countries. But cross-cultural research, too, reveals that social connection is strongly connected to positive feelings, even more than monetary wealth.[19] That doesn't mean money isn't important in our happiness but rather that social connections tend to matter even more. Social connection doesn't exclusively predict happiness, but a trove of research suggests that attachments to others is a fundamental human motivation, rooted in survival and growth.[20]

Barbara Fredrickson, who identified the three-to-one positivity ratio, describes love as the most important of the positive emotions—the *supreme* emotion. But the love she describes isn't that which only exists between parent and child or even the feeling we idealize between romantic partners. She's referring to a feeling of human connectedness. In her book *Love 2.0*, Fredrickson writes that the experience of that kind of powerful connection results from three interlocked events:

1. A shared positive emotion
2. Synchrony between your and another's behavior and physiology
3. A motivation to invest in one another's well-being[21]

Love in this form offers us the experience of being known, being connected, and having access to real care. You can access this form of love in your closest relationships, but you can also access connection experiences with work colleagues, your boss, the elderly man who returned your credit card after you dropped it, parent friends, your child's teacher, and so on.

Having more places to go, more people to interact with, and more roles to participate in offers greater prospects to accessing happiness-fueling connections.[22] Isolation at work need not prevent you from feeling connected, seen, and cared about if you can find those experiences at home. A contentious relationship with your teenager won't prevent you from connecting if you can grab lunch with a friend at the office. Some forms of connection don't even require actual interaction with others—they rely instead on using imagery and meditation as a pathway to connection, as illustrated in the following suggestions.

. . . . .

Pause to Cultivate Connection

Fredrickson and her colleagues have identified various practices that help you lock down experiences of connectedness.[23] These brief practices have been shown to enhance how connected people feel. You can try them out for yourself.

- *Make eye contact and engage touch.* These kinds of tangible, on-the-ground experiences create a felt sense of connection. So make eye contact with a colleague, hug your partner, or hold hands with your child.

- *Loving-kindness meditation.* Drawn from Buddhism and increasingly popular in modern psychology, loving-kindness meditation can offer a sense of connection even in the absence of actual human contact. It can also induce more positive feelings (and less negative ones), enhance empathy, and reduce interpersonal stress.[24] Loving-kindness meditation involves sending a mantra of love and kindness in five different directions: to yourself, to someone dear to you, to someone for whom you have neutral feelings, to someone you have a difficult relationship with, and finally to all beings. You can use a mantra such as "May you be happy, may you be free from suffering, may you be safe, and may you live with ease." Set aside fifteen minutes to go through the mantra for each of these five entities. Then observe whether you, like many, find a sense of connectedness growing.[25]

- *Reflect on your most meaningful interaction of the day.* Whether it was with your boss, your infant, or the smiling jogger who cheered you on as you pushed your kiddo in the stroller, reflecting on your most meaningful interactions of the day can strengthen the feelings of connectedness and well-being. Ask yourself what was the most meaningful connection that you had today and take a moment to marinate in any positive feelings that arise.

. . . . .

AUTONOMY

Having choice, willingness, and personal endorsement of one's own actions and goals defines experiences of autonomy. Autonomy, in other words, is having the ability to make self-directed choices. When done well, autonomy even enhances connection. It's not hard to see why when we consider the power of autonomy-supportive parenting. In this style of parenting, we deliberately offer children agency in age-appropriate ways. That might look like providing choices, giving guidelines instead of rules, and when we do establish a firm rule, offering a clear rationale for it.

Kids—like adults—enjoy and appreciate experiencing autonomy. Love grows in that space. Autonomy not only feeds connection but also fosters competence. As my preschooler insists on doing more for himself—dressing himself, picking out his own snacks, toileting alone—he grows skill.

In the couples therapy room, I regularly advise partners to shift away from attempts to gain control over each other's choices and beliefs and to instead move toward efforts to actively offer autonomy. Paradoxically, giving up control increases your chances of having greater influence. Consider what happens for you when a loved one respects your opinion (even when they see it differently), supports your choices (even if they would make different ones), and allows for you to be your unique self (even as they want to remain emotionally close). How do you feel toward that person compared to how you'd feel if they tried to dominate your choices? If you're like most of the people I work with, you're likely to want to genuinely consider the views of and build more intimacy with the person who offers you more respect and a sense of agency.

Surprisingly, too, giving autonomy to our kids fulfills our own needs for autonomy. In a study following parents and children during the COVID-19 pandemic shutdown, parents who provided autonomy support to their children were more likely to feel fulfilled in their own needs for autonomy, competence, and connectedness the next day. In other words, there's a reciprocal relationship between supporting your kids' autonomy and getting your own psychological needs met. Supporting your kids' agency thus helps you feel more agency, competence, and connectedness, which is good for your own and your children's well-being.[26] Similar findings emerge in workplace studies, where feeling that your manager supports your agency is associated with feeling more competent, autonomous, and cared about. In turn, those needs contribute to higher motivation and well-being.[27] How's that for a virtuous cycle?

But what if your boss micromanages you or your work conditions simply don't leave you with opportunity to make autonomous decisions? What if your kids don't give you much autonomy? (Or, as my youngest likes to tell me, "Mommy, wherever you go, there I am!") You aren't powerless to gain autonomy in these situations, either. You might be familiar with the notion that people tend to get more joy from giving gifts than receiving them.[28] The same is true about gifts of autonomy. In one study looking at both the benefits of giving and receiving autonomy support in close friendships, researchers showed that both the giving and the receiving of autonomy support have a positive effect on well-being.[29] But when the giving and receiving were pitted against each other in predicting well-being, giving autonomy support was the statistical winner. Offering autonomy to colleagues, children, your partner, or a friend is always an avenue available to fulfill your autonomy needs and attempt to trigger that positively reinforcing cycle.

Offering yourself autonomy is within your purview, too. My favorite quotable individual, Viktor Frankl, discussed autonomy in the concentration camps in *Man's Search for Meaning*. Of course, being interned in a concentration camp meant that virtually all autonomy was taken away. Yet Frankl noted that "everything can be taken away from a [person] but one thing: the last of the human freedoms—to choose one's attitude in any given set of circumstances, to choose one's own way."[30] We can always choose something, whether it's asking for greater autonomy, giving it to others, or recognizing the choice we always have in our attitude.

• • • • •

Pause to Advance Autonomy

When it comes to autonomy, we can always find some area of relative freedom. Seek out an area where you can exert some deliberate choice.

Consider the following:

- Say no to requests (including those from your children and boss).

- Say yes to self-care.

- Choose to pause once a day to marinate in a good feeling, including the fact that you're making the choice to do so.

- Choose an activity that is pleasant, productive, or meaningful. Be deliberate and mindful, attending to the fact of your autonomy in doing this activity (even if it's for a short period of time!).

. . . . .

SPOTLIGHT THE STARS

As the Rolling Stones famously belt out, we can't always get what we want. Unfortunately, the difference between what we want and what we have can contribute to our quality of life: the larger the discrepancy, the less happy we feel. There are a few ways to deal with this discrepancy. One is to lower our expectations. That seems a little depressing, but it doesn't have to be. Embracing a more realistic view of what is possible and seeing it as "enough" can truly help us cultivate contentment in life. We can also decrease that difference by improving what we have.

But a different approach to dealing with the discrepancy between "want" and "have" involves attention shifting. When we move attention away from where life isn't what we want and toward areas more in line with our ideals, we control the spotlight of our attention. This approach doesn't change your standards. Instead, it modifies your importance hierarchy. According to one study, by emphasizing life domains that have a smaller discrepancy between what you want and what you have (and de-emphasizing those with a larger difference), you can improve your happiness.[31] So, if basic needs are getting met at work, spotlight those. If parenting is going smoothly, shine your light there. If you managed to text an old friend, put some laundry away, or go to the bathroom without a companion, illuminate those accomplishments.

VIRTUOUS CYCLES

Plants both take from and give back to the environment in a way that can offer inspiration. Plants uptake carbon dioxide, a waste product from animals. Then, through the process of photosynthesis, they release oxygen into the atmosphere. The oxygen sustains animals, the oceans, and the atmosphere. Plants also uptake minerals from the soil. Using these nutrients, they create more vegetation, such as the fruits and vegetables that feed birds, insects, and mammals. Even a plant's demise is a gift. Plant lives end as decomposing vegetation, feeding nutrients back to the soil through their decaying process. Not to put too fine a point on it, but it's evident that when plants get what they need, they become energy-fueled and able to give back in abundance.

Nourishment → Thriving → Giving Back to the World

You, like a plant, can offer much more to the world, to your work, and to your family when you get what you need. Ensuring that your needs get met results in your higher levels of energy, inspired creativity, longer-lasting patience, authentic friendliness, and sustained strength.[32] In fact, being happier leads to marital happiness, income, work performance, and health as much as it reflects these happy circumstances.[33]

Meeting your psychological needs leads to thriving in line with what happens for plants. Just like plants, having needs thwarted leads to *less* giving back and *less* effectiveness in our core life roles. In one proof of concept study, researchers in Belgium showed this among parents of teenagers. Ah, teenagers, our quintessential need-thwarters. Sure enough, many teenagers managed to kick their parents' needs to the curb. But when parents were able to outsmart their teens and get their needs for autonomy, competence, and connectedness met, parenting went much better. More specifically, parents with satisfied psychological needs engaged in healthier, more autonomy-supportive parenting. In contrast, on days where parental needs couldn't get met, parents were more likely to engage in psychologically controlling forms of parenting.[34] For many of us (ahem, that would be me), this can sum up the link between nightly sleep allotment and daily parenting style. Getting basic needs met helps us parent more effectively.

This example underscores a larger point: Getting your basic needs met helps nourish you, energizes you, and puts you in a position to do your best in the roles you care about. It's a reason to prioritize getting your needs met at that optimal three-to-one ratio of positive to negative experiences.

A MOTHER'S REFLECTIONS

When I asked my mom about whether she thinks she'd have been happier as a working parent, she responded, "Yes, I would have had more places to get validation and self-worth." She recognizes now that she placed too much weight on the role of parenting to fulfill all her happiness needs. She believes that working parenthood could have offered her more places to capitalize on the kinds of opportunities that would have led to more flourishing. These include financial independence, publicly acknowledged status, opportunities to build and apply skills in competent ways, and access to more forms of social connectedness.[35] My mom admits that she envies my choice to both work and parent, even as she recognizes I have a lot on my plate.

I maintain that no matter how many or how few roles you inhabit, virtually anyone can seek out the experiences of competence, connectedness, and autonomy. Regardless of circumstance, you can practice getting closer to a ratio of three positive experiences to one negative experience, savor positive experiences, reduce the discrepancy between what you want and what you have, and spotlight what's going well. I also believe that participating in more roles can offer greater access to meeting your basic happiness needs. In this way, you can see your working-parent life offering a distinct happiness advantage.

. . . .

The TL/DR (Too Long, Didn't Read)

USE WORKING PARENTHOOD TO MEET
YOUR HAPPINESS NEEDS

Consider your basic needs. In rough patches of your day, ask yourself which of your basic needs have gone unmet. Remember that you're looking to have experiences in each of the following categories:

- Opportunities to feel skillful, capable, or masterful

- Connection to people or causes you care about

- Freedom to choose your own actions

Aim to have experiences in each of the domains listed above, seeking to achieve a three-to-one ratio of positive to negative. When you experience competence, connectedness, or autonomy, pause, acknowledge, and relish that moment. Spotlight what's going well! This practice of savoring will increase and extend experiences of happiness.

12

BALANCE YOUR PLEASURE
AND MEANING

When you're a working mother, you have to
pretend you feel guilty all day long.
—AMY POEHLER

Fridays are my longest workday. I'm often switching between seeing a couple and trying to make progress on writing during breaks between patients. Accomplishing this kind of workday while having three young children requires a highly compressed schedule and elaborate coordination that includes partner negotiations, schedule alignment at multiple childcare facilities, and too many peanut butter and jelly sandwiches. It also involves dealing with whining from my kids about the length of their Friday and tolerating guilt knowing that they, like me, are exhausted long before the day is done.

I easily count Fridays as being "meaningful," but it's only when I pause to reflect that I see the many moments of pleasure. Sure, there are pressures, guilt, and a prevailing sense of not being able to get enough done. But there's also the couple who learned something new, the money I earned for providing therapy, a tricky paragraph I reworked, the delightful reprieve from hearing the whining of my small people, and the sweet excitement (thanks to temporary amnesia about that whining) of returning home realizing just how much I've missed my boys.

THE BATTLE OF PLEASURE AND MEANING

From ancient philosophers to modern science, humans have long struggled with how to achieve the happy life and how to even define what "happiness" means. The *Epic of Gilgamesh*, a Babylonian story recorded soon after the invention of written language, provides one of the earliest examples of philosophizing on happiness with a recommendation to "let days be full of joy."[1] Emotional experiences or physical sensations that feel *good* represent a core feature of happiness. Just as in ancient Babylon, positive feelings remain associated with the sensory and emotional pleasures we most commonly equate to happiness today.

The trouble is that pleasures can feel hard to come by inside of working parenthood. That difficulty tends to get magnified by a pervasive messaging about how hard working parenthood truly is. There is truth in these portrayals. In fact, a well-known study of Texas-based working mothers from 2004, led by the Nobel prize-winning economist Daniel Kahneman, suggested that parenting was a daily driver of unhappiness.[2] I love my kids more than words can capture, but I admit that this finding makes intuitive sense to me. The days can feel relentless, pressures forever increasing in magnitude, the unhappy feedback from disappointed small people unavoidable. Yet this widely cited finding is misleading. Its focus on happiness was quite narrow, using an average positive emotion score and rank-ordering for a combined sample of parents and non-parents on daily activities, which included taking care of children.

But in a subsequent study, Sonja Lyubomirsky, the happiness researcher we first met in chapter 2, went a step further in defining happiness. She and her colleagues examined both the experience of positive emotions (happiness, warmth, and enjoyment) *and* experiences of having meaning and purpose in life. In their study, data on happiness for daily activities was categorized into "childcare" or "non-childcare" (versus simply rank-ordering activities) and happiness of parents and nonparents was compared on various activities. Unlike the earlier findings in the Texas-based study, this study showed that parents had higher levels of life satisfaction, positive emotion, and more thoughts about meaningfulness than nonparents.[3] In a follow-up study, this same research team showed that happiness benefits of parenting can fade when we encounter more stressors (financial, sleep debt, marital conflict). But they can become magnified when we experience more meaning inside of our lives, have our basic psychological needs satisfied, and find opportunities to savor positive emotions.[4] In other words, parental happiness can depend a lot on your situation or how you define happiness. And, of course, is also depends on your capacity to manage stressors and capitalize on opportunities for happiness in its varied forms.

Here's one challenge, though: moving through our days at the breakneck speed required by working parenthood can easily cause us to overlook the many small, sweet, funny, proud, loving, interesting, awe-inspiring moments. Consider whether you stopped to really attend to the feeling of your toddler grabbing your face with pudgy hands and positioning you to receive a sloppy kiss. If you did, you might have noticed your heart momentarily filled with love so intense that you felt the urge to consume them. Or when your teenager told you an off-color joke that caused you to laugh so hard you cried? Did you notice the fleeting sense of wonder in having participated in creating this hilarious human being? And at the end of a long, exhausting day, you might have felt a sense of pride in your parenting, contentment to be home safe. Did you pause to relish the ecstasy of putting up those tired old dogs before dozing off?

For most of us, work can be filled with pleasurable delights, too. Receiving gratitude from a client, customer, or colleague; earning a bonus after a productive year; discovering that your work efforts made someone else's life better; or completing a project that has plagued you for months can each bring a sense of gratification. You might feel deep pride in being able to support your family or splurge on extras such as a fancy meal or a trip you hadn't thought would be possible. And there are daily sensory delights, such as sounds that don't involve crying children, the scent of cleaning supplies (rather than the diaper pail), the warmth of a mug of afternoon coffee, and the sight of adults whom you didn't need to help dress. Pleasures lie in wait if you can turn your attention toward their discovery.

But pleasure—emotional and otherwise—is not the only form of happiness. The Greek ideal of eudaemonia has been translated as the flourishing that is achieved when one works to develop their virtues and live a life oriented toward areas of skill and making valued contributions. This form of happiness propels us to work hard, love altruistically, and advance our creativity, resilience, and deeper purpose. When we focus on purpose as the pathway to happiness, the virtues and skills we foster in each sphere feed on the other, creating a positive cycle of growth, even in the absence of laidback sunbaths, brainless movies, or chocolate indulgences.

I had you until I exposed the absence of crappy movies and chocolate gluttony, didn't I?

In fact, defining "happiness" in this way can seem incomplete, even paradoxical. How can we call it "happiness" if we are constantly striving to perfect our virtues, shunning experiences of pleasure? Then again, pleasure has its own paradoxes. We experience delights, but, too soon, the pleasure passes. Like my youngest son after his cookie is gone, the post-pleasure crash can leave us feeling worse off than we felt before.

Just like any complex system, harmonious happiness relies on balance. If we just had fun in working parenthood, we would have few opportunities to grow. If we only sought virtues and excellences, life would be a tiresome uphill battle. Like the yin and yang in Taoist philosophy, pleasure and meaning each offer unique gifts and each has important up- and downsides.

Neither meaning nor pleasure on its own can win the happiness battle. But meaning and pleasure aren't adversaries. They are *allies*. Victory lies in their combined capacity to counterbalance one another, alleviating each other's drawbacks and making it easier to foster a more enduring happiness.

PITFALLS OF PLEASURE

The experience of pleasurable feelings is a critical pathway toward happiness. There may be no sweeter feeling than your toddler wanting your arm around them or feeling their insistent hand on your chin directing your attention to something important they want to tell you. Just like the feeling we get from being hugged tightly by someone we love, the experience of being in the flow of work, or the sensations of eating ice cream housed in a fresh waffle cone, pleasures create joy and vitality in life. But despite the pleasures of pleasure and the skill we might build in having more of these kinds of experiences, there are downsides to be on the lookout for.

First and foremost, no matter how hard we try to make it last longer and fulfill us, pleasure tends to fall short of our desires and be too short-lived. These shortcomings of relying on pleasure for our happiness arise from two human tendencies:

- Rising expectations
- Habituation to emotional states

Our minds tend to overestimate our ability to sustain emotion (not to mention the consequences of trying to hold on to something that can't be detained). As it is written in the Tao Te Ching, "To seize it is to lose it."[5] Whether you enjoy the feel of the sun on your skin during a vacation in Tahiti or delight in a delicious cocktail on a date with your partner, grasping tightly onto feelings of pleasure invariably leads to misfortune (as in crispy skin and hangovers). Or, as Sonja told me, "Human beings are remarkably good at getting used to changes in their lives, both positive and negative—but especially positive—changes."

As an added pitfall of pleasure, when we experience positive feelings, we naturally find expectations for positivity intensifying. For instance, I might feel pride at the end of a day where I finally circulate a new research manuscript to colleagues and still make it home in time to get dinner on the table for my family. I've kicked butt in working parenthood, I'm a superstar! But—largely outside of my awareness—my expectations for daily success naturally rise. I begin to expect that subsequent days should and will recur. The next day, when I discover that the manuscript I had sent around to colleagues had a glaring omission, that my oldest child forgot his homework, and that there is no food in the fridge for dinner that night, my good feelings flatten. My raised expectations lead to greater deflation in the face of my working-parent reality.

It isn't just elevated expectations that make it hard to extend pleasure. The shortcomings of relying on pleasure and gratification for our happiness also arise from a natural tendency to get used to emotional and physical states of satisfaction. Evolution has, in fact, hardwired humans to habituate to feelings of happiness. For instance, in premodern times it was highly adaptive for a good meal only to satisfy for a short period of time before you felt an urgency to find more food. And it was adaptive that the happy high from connecting with a partner would be transformed to irritation as they got comfortable enough to stop bothering to mask the smell of their stinky feet. This happiness habituation mechanism offered survival benefits in keeping humans motivated to seek out calories, attend to dangers, and seek out and sustain helpful social connections.

That wiring endures even though the dangers are far less common or acute these days.

In a classic psychology experiment from the 1970s, researchers from Northwestern University and the University of Massachusetts interviewed recent lottery winners and recent victims of accidents who became paraplegic or quadriplegic about how they experienced happiness. In the interviews, individuals were asked to rate the amount of pleasure they experienced in mundane daily activities—events such as chatting with friends, hearing a joke, or receiving a compliment. Compared to individuals who had neither won the lottery nor been in a catastrophic accident, people who had won the lottery were not happier. Even more startling, lottery winners found ordinary activities significantly *less* pleasurable than participants in the control group. Their expectations of pleasure had risen, causing normal activities to be less gratifying.[6]

In the decades since this study, researchers have continued to inquire into the human ability to adapt to new, sometimes tragically difficult circumstances. There is now a consensus that negative circumstances do have an impact. Yet life satisfaction often returns to satisfying levels, even for individuals with sudden onset of paraplegia or other major disabilities. We overestimate our ability to sustain emotion. We underestimate the impact of our expectations on our emotional well-being.[7]

Still, recognizing the dangers of urges for pleasure cannot purge a longing to experience it. This longing is as human as our habituation to those very pleasures. Working-parent lives full of challenges and stressors can make our yearning for those positive physical and emotional experiences all the more powerful.

GROWING GOOD FEELINGS

If working parenthood interferes with pleasurable experiences, it can also enhance them. Let's consider one surprising way that working parenthood helps you grow good feelings: the necessity of so much switching between roles.

Role switching can be costly in terms of energy and attention, and it can disrupt a fun workflow or a rocking dance party with your kids. On the one hand, that's a total bummer for a happy high. On the other hand? As discussed earlier, role switching has benefits for recharging, enhancing creativity, even fostering flexibility and independence in your kids. Most surprisingly, those irritating interruptions can increase your pleasure. They can stop the fun before the fun has devolved into something far less gratifying and more boring, conflict-ridden (especially if siblings are involved), or annoying (if anyone you've spent too much time with is involved). Interruptions can save the day by keeping the fun *fun* and by prompting you to savor the joy more because the joy is so time-limited.

Interruptions can make pleasant experiences even more pleasant. For example, interruptions while getting a massage or listening to music and even having a television-watching experience interrupted by commercials are associated with greater enjoyment than not having interruptions.[8] The same case can be made for the value of having interruptions to our pleasurable experiences in close relationships with our children and our colleagues.[9] Interruptions thwart our tendency to get used to the fun (which makes the fun less enjoyable). Or as Sonja summarized for me, "Interrupting positive experience is actually good because it kind of resets your adaptation point." That means you can find comfort knowing that interruptions to your pleasure help you sustain joy over the weeks and months where unrestrained engagement might not.

Working parenthood can help us get the most out of our pleasures when it confronts us with our constraints. After all, we can't *actually* work like we don't have families because we *do* have families. And we can't parent as if we don't work because we *do* work. Acknowledging that we simply cannot be all in to either parenthood or work when we are actively engaged in both can help us set (and then regularly reset) realistic expectations. And, as we've explored, making ourselves unavailable to work and to parenting turns out to be a healthy and productive practice for all of our life roles.

· · · · ·

Pause for Pleasure

When it comes to pleasure, we can expect the positive experiences to come and go. But by using our constraints wisely, we can enhance and extend them in surprising ways.

- Enjoy how role constraints keep activities enjoyable over time through natural variety in activities and regular interruptions.

- Use your natural working-parent limitations as a method to keep your expectations realistic.

Consider the following pleasure-activating activities that have been tested and shown to help folks extend pleasurable experiences:

- Journal about the blessings/gifts of balancing work and parenting roles.

- Deliberately engage in acts of kindness at work and in parenting.

- Be mindful during enjoyable activities by tuning in to your sensory experiences and bringing yourself back to them when your mind wanders away.

- Replay positive activities from your past and/or visualize future ones.

- During an enjoyable activity, pause to focus on and savor the metaphorical or literal sweetness.[10]

. . . . .

FIND YOUR FLOW

One of the most joyous experiences of life is getting fully absorbed in a task that we find interesting and challenging but not too challenging. When we do, we feel full of energy and enjoyment as our sense of self and time fall away. The prolific psychologist Mihaly Csikszentmihalyi called this kind of experience "flow."[11] We achieve this level of absorption when the challenges are high but not too high and when growth opportunities for our skill sets exist.

It's easy enough to come up with all the times you were decidely not in flow—I'm sure they are plentiful! But let's take a moment to reflect on a time when you might have accessed some elements of flow.

For most of us, being in a state of flow is a wonderful experience. An hour feels like a few minutes, and we experience a sense of vitality and engagement of the kind that defines our best life moments. Experiences of flow represent the most dynamic kind of living. Csikszentmihalyi suggested it is the "optimal experience" because when we are in flow, we achieve elevated gratification in whatever we are doing.

We can access flow in both work and parenting, but when we remain too long in one role, whatever we're doing can begin to feel like watching paint dry. Anyone who has parented a toddler knows this feeling well. As delightful as these creatures are, they tend to ask the same questions, read the same books, tell the same jokes, and want to play the same games again and again . . . and again. The same goes for work where tasks often become tedious and predictable. For instance, I love doing therapy, but after I've seen six or more patients in a row, I'll find myself checking the clock and finding time moving more slowly than I expected.

Stepping away from one role and into another and having the challenge of limited time can help a boring or repetitive task feel more stimulating. You need to stack up enough consecutive minutes to achieve flow—not easy if you're working from home with children present! But if you can get your kids (or partner or other caregiver) or colleagues and clients on board to give you a chunk of time, you can increase your opportunities for flow in each role. For example, Lori Mihalich-Levin, the founder of the website Mindful Return, used twenty-minute chunks of time to develop her e-course on returning to work after having a child. This was during the period of time when she had a toddler and an infant and worked full-time. She explained to me that doing it wasn't easy, but like the famed Pomodoro Technique recommends,[12] breaking large tasks into smaller ones and using short chunks of dedicated, focused time helped her get the job done in what little time she had available. That effort yielded an award-winning educational and social connection tool that has changed the lives of many working parents.

. . . . .

Pause to Practice Flow

Csikszentmihalyi's research on flow points to the joys we can access when we enter into this state. Here are some tips, adapted from Csikszentmihalyi and colleagues' work, to set the stage for flow:

- Create conditions where you can concentrate on one task. Remove all distractions (or put them in front of a screen with headphones). Then set a timer so you can allow your attention to fully be immersed in what you are doing.

- Set a specific goal for that chunk of time.

- When you become bored, increase the challenge either by reducing the time you allow yourself or by adding new complexity to the task.

- When you become anxious, break the task down into smaller parts either by reducing your goal of what to accomplish or by doing a smaller part of a larger task.

· · · · ·

PURPOSE

Unlike pleasure, the pursuit of purpose and fulfillment need not be attached to positive emotional or physical experiences. In fact, according to Aristotle and modern social science researchers, a life lived with meaning and a sense of purpose—even when it doesn't feel good in the moment—is actually where greater happiness lies. That doesn't mean that garbage collectors with a greater sense of purpose like trash more. Instead, it means that focusing on a self-transcendent purpose in work helps us find fulfillment—even if we are engaged in less desirable activities. In other words, a garbage collector who sees their role as making the world a cleaner, more pleasant place will feel a greater sense of purpose in work than one who simply does it for the paycheck.

Connecting to a sense of purpose makes it easier to bear difficult, distasteful, or boring work. For example, the University of Texas developmental psychologist David Yeager and his colleagues had students complete a "self-transcendent purpose for learning" exercise. Part of this exercise involved writing testimonials for other students that explained how learning might help them grow as a person or make a greater positive impact on the world. Students who had the opportunity to deliberately tap into their learning purpose went on to earn higher math and science grades compared to students who didn't do the exercise. This effect bore out even more strongly for lower-performing students.[13] Pain tolerance is helped by purpose, too. In a study investigating adults' habituation to painful stimuli (pain from exposure to heat and cold), having a higher purpose in life predicted better adjustment.[14] A sense of purpose keeps us motivated, even when we're in pain or when we'd prefer to do something more gratifying.

For all my fellow burrito lovers out there, you could also think of it this way: If you find meaning in living a healthy life, then you might choose a salad over a poodle-sized burrito. Let's face it: that burrito would give you more pleasure in the moment. The salad? Much less immediately gratifying. But if you zoom out from pleasure and tap into your value of healthy living, you might connect to a sense of purpose available in choosing the salad. You might feel proud of yourself for prioritizing your health, even as you recognize your meal doesn't taste quite as good or feel as filling. Let's also add that you might enjoy your evening more because you aren't so bloated. Taking it to the work sphere, maybe you find meaning in sharing your work with others—like, say, through podcasting or writing. By sharing publicly, you're opening yourself up to criticism that comes with putting yourself and your work out in the world. You know the trolls will have things to say and part of you thinks maybe you'd be wise to just stay quiet and in the background. But a sense of purpose can keep you moving toward what matters most to you. Ultimately that feels pretty darn good, too.

In the balance of life as a working parent, you might take a similar approach. The days might feel exhausting, the pain of falling short pervasive. But tolerating the exhaustion and sense of not-enoughness can be easier when you have clarity in the values of your journey. For instance, if you are clear that working parenthood offers a means of loving deeply and contributing meaningfully, then maintaining a foothold in both roles can contribute to your happiness—even when it doesn't feel pleasant in the moment.

In the various interviews I've done with working parents, I am regularly reminded of how working parenthood allows us to cleverly spread out our meaning-making resources. Alyssa, an intensive care unit nurse, explained to me that she feels an "inherent need to better the whole world, not just my little world." The balance of engaging with her family at home and making her contributions outside of the home provides her with an overarching and reliable sense of fulfillment that feeds her soul. Joshua, a father, clinical psychologist, and university training clinic director, similarly explained, "As much as I love my daughter, just [parenting] being my life would be hard. I love being with her, but the part of me that wants to be more generative and teaching and part of larger professional conversations, that would be hard to do without. And I am a better parent for being able to be fulfilled that way."

Seeking purpose in your roles as parent and worker—even when the balance becomes challenging—helps you sustain a sense of satisfaction. You can feel happy even in moments when you don't feel pleasure.

That doesn't mean you don't acknowledge the frustration, exhaustion, and even failure. That doesn't mean you need to love your work or maintain angelic patience and appreciation for your offspring. But recognizing that life can be unpleasant or painful need not prevent you from enjoying the richness that comes from being able to inhabit both worlds. Shifting your narrative to one that emphasizes meaning and enrichment offers an important pathway toward growing happiness.

· · · · ·

Try This: Pause to Find (or Reconnect to) Your Meaning

Meaningful living can bring a sense of satisfaction—even when it's accompanied by moment-to-moment discomfort! Consider, first, that many working parents have motives that include making money, having freedom, and doing enough to make sure needs are met. And, in addition to a desire to maintain a balance that is enjoyable and competent enough, many working parents also want to make a positive impact.

Take a moment to reflect on the kind of impact you'd like to have. Consider asking yourself the following kinds of questions:

- *What kind of working parent do I want to be in order to have an impact on the people around me and on society in general?*

- *What do I want my work, my parenthood, or my working parenthood to stand for?*

· · · · ·

THE HIGHEST HOW OF WORKING-PARENT HAPPINESS

Ultimately, most of us are not creatures who can thrive on meaning alone. And pleasure is insufficient (and too doggone fleeting!). But recognizing that the pressure to engage in two demanding roles offers greater access to a balance of pleasurable and meaningful experiences helps us enjoy both the pleasures and the meaning more.

Each of us can work toward greater enjoyment of our lives—even during the tougher moments of our life's journey. And the work of locating the joy can even be, well, enjoyable, when we focus on both meaning and pleasure.

Let me offer a trivial example of the human capacity to find happiness, even in unpleasant, seemingly meaningless tasks. When I complained to a friend about my disdain for vacuuming the debris that regularly finds a home in the carpet despite the fact that I like having a clean home, she expressed surprise. "I *love* vacuuming," she told me. She continued: "I find it so satisfying to hear the dirt get sucked up into the vacuum," and then she mimicked the sound of dirt getting sucked away.

I contemplated what she was saying. Actually, vacuuming didn't sound so bad in the way she described it. I didn't exactly rush home to vacuum, but the next time I pulled out the machine, I paused to consider whether I could turn my intentions toward experiencing the kind of satisfaction she had described. I decided to pay close attention to the sound and the feeling of the dirt moving out of the carpet and up into the nozzle. To my surprise, as I pushed the vacuum around the floor I could see what my friend meant—it *was* kind of satisfying. Locating some pleasure in vacuuming has noticeably shifted my obstacles to vacuuming, making it easier to keep the carpet clean (okay, clean*er*). That shift in my vacuuming mindset helped me connect more firmly to my value of keeping my home space tidy and getting my boys to participate in the effort. Part of teaching my boys about housekeeping is skills-based: how to scrub the toilet and run the vacuum. But the more important lesson is learning how to find both pleasure and meaning in tasks of life that aren't inherently fun but which matter to the kinds of lives we care to build.

The truth is that happiness doesn't appear magically. At least not most of the time. Working parenthood, by nature of being resource intense and high-pressured, can limit pleasures, wear us out, and cause us to feel uncomfortable feelings, have negative thoughts, and engage in ways we aren't entirely proud of.

Still, we can take advantage of various pathways through which working parenthood helps us optimize happiness. We can use the pressures, constraints, and challenges of working parenthood to boost happiness. We can intentionally set the stage for and pause to appreciate the pleasures. We can be deliberate about making meaning from the challenges—for example, by using each role to make meaning in the other. We can learn to value our obligations because they connect us to people and activities we care about as well as the larger world around us. We can savor the feeling of accomplishment from doing hard things. And we can open our eyes to the various ways that working parenthood provides opportunities to meet our basic happiness needs, even during times when life feels hard. True happiness can emerge when we show up fully, to connect to meaning and to experiences of pleasure.

· ·

The TL/DR (Too Long, Didn't Read)

FORTIFY YOUR HAPPINESS

- *Enjoy the pleasure.* Find daily opportunities to experience pleasure, whether in the successes at work or the sweet connections had in parenting life.

- *Make meaning.* Look for daily opportunities to cherish meaningful activities that give your life purpose. That may include the mission of your work or the recognition that your work helps provide for your family. It might also include the meaning of raising your small people or being the kind of parent you value.

- *Appreciate constraints.* Rather than bemoan interruptions to pleasurable experiences, appreciate how they keep pleasures enjoyable over time because the constraints help prevent happiness stagnation.

- *Combine happinesses.* Recognize that a combination of meaning and pleasure helps us achieve persistent happiness. In tougher moments, look for ways to reconnect to the meaning of your work and parenting. In more gratifying moments, savor the experience of pleasure.

LOVE DEEPLY,
CONTRIBUTE MEANINGFULLY

My most pleasurable Friday moments are after I am done with my workday. Long ago, my husband and I realized that neither of us is up for the task of cooking a Friday meal. I look forward to my Friday burritos more than I should admit. Friday is not a salad night, my friend, it is poodle-sized burrito night (though I generally appreciate the value of a healthy salad). Of course, my kids despise burritos. And since Friday night needs some pleasure, we give them a picnic-style dinner meal of fruit and cheese. This, too, is their favorite meal of the week.

I'll drive home from my therapy office, eager for my too-big dinner and filled with excitement for the love awaiting me. After I get home and drop my bags, my boys and I gather on the couch. My youngest will be sitting in my lap with his messy blond hair tickling my nose, my middle son (who has large adenoids) mouth-breathing into my left ear, my eldest cuddle-leaning his sharp shoulder into my rib cage while playing with his Rubik's Cube, and my husband splayed out beside us. My kids will be talking over one another, with my little one saying, "Mommy, I'm telling you something!" as my big guys, too, vie for airtime.

In that chaotic, sweet, and exhausted moment, I take a deep breath in and let it out slowly. I savor the acute pleasure of feeling those small, squirmy bodies against mine. I immerse myself in a blissed-out delight of these comical creatures that I'm so dang lucky are mine. And I reflect back on a week that involved working hard to use my skills and energy to make a difference. Mostly, though, I feel a deep gratitude in having a life that allows me to love deeply and contribute meaningfully.

Working parenthood isn't always fun, and it's rarely easy. But thanks to what I've learned about balancing pleasure and meaning, I've discovered that working parenthood can be profoundly happy.

ACKNOWLEDGMENTS

Working parenthood, when done well, requires an active cadre of allies. Writing a book is no different—done well is not done alone. Any shortcomings belong to me, but whatever strengths exist in this book are a credit to the team of allies that collaborated in bringing this brainchild into the world.

My agent, Katherine Flynn, took a chance on an academic who wanted to write a book about working parenthood, going above and beyond her job description and guiding me from being a scientifically trained writer to a writer who communicates to audiences outside of academia. I also lucked out in landing at Shambhala Publications. Thank you to KJ Grow and Sara Bercholz for making a home for me as an author at Shambhala. The biggest win of being a Shambhala author was working with my editors. First, in addition to considerable editing talent, Sarah Stanton is infinitely patient, thoughtful, compassionate, and attentive to the diversity of struggles working parents encounter. She worked tirelessly (mostly after her own child went to sleep) to help me shape the book into one in which working parents of all kinds could find wisdom and guidance. And I was lucky enough to work with Sami Ripley, whose boundless energy and eagerness in the work belies the fact that she doesn't drink caffeine. Thank you also to Emily Wichland, whose copyediting talents are the reason this book will cause fewer headaches.

I certainly could not have written this book without the many individuals who dedicate their lives to studying work, parenting, relationships, stress, mindfulness, evolution, cognitive science, and happiness. Many of my favorite researchers and writers generously gave their time, practical advice, and active assists, and many even entrusted me with their personal working-parent stories. I'd like to give special thanks to Sian Beilock, Tal Ben-Shahar, Elizabeth Corey, KJ Dell'Antonia, Daphne de Marneffe, Angela Duckworth, Felice Dunn, Jeffrey Greenhaus, Rick Hanson, Jeremy Jamieson, Leidy Klotz, Jessica Lahey, David F. Lancy, Lori Mihalich-Levin, Sonja Lyubomirsky, Emily Oster, Susan Pollak, Barry Schwartz, Steve Stewart-Williams. Thank you also to the many individuals who agreed to be interviewed for this project and to my working-parent patients. Research only goes so far—it's *your* stories that bring the science to life and are the vehicles for teaching the most important lessons about how to work, parent, and thrive.

I'm grateful, too, to have a position at Brown University, an academic institution that has supported me throughout my professional twists and turns as a working parent. Thank you to my mentors and colleagues who taught me to think deeply, to ask interesting questions, to write carefully, and to collaborate on projects exploring big ideas: Mark Whisman, Emily Richardson, Alisha Brosse, Greg Stuart, David Strong, Michael Stein, Jennifer Johnson, Christine Timko, Terrie Fox Wetle, and Beth McQuaid. And, of course, writers need ways to get the word out about their ideas. I am indebted to the *New York Times* and Honor Jones, who were the first to take a chance on my ideas about working parenthood. Thank you also to Gary Rosen at the *Wall Street Journal*, Evan Nesterak at *Behavioral Scientist*, and Jeremy Smith at *Greater Good Science*

Center for opportunities to share the science of working parenthood with the public.

I am exceptionally grateful for my team at the *Psychologists Off the Clock* podcast, a podcast whose mission is to share science-backed ideas from psychology, for supporting my writing and giving me a place to talk through ideas. To my cohosts Diana Hill, Debbie Sorensen, and Jill Stoddard, and our team Michael Herold, Katy Rothsfelde, and Melissa Miller: you all make the world of psychology more thought-provoking, deeply meaningful, and most importantly, full of laughter.

Writing support has come in other forms, too. I hit the jackpot when I reached out to Alex Soojung-Kim Pang to invite him to be my very first interview on our podcast. He must have sensed how starstruck I was, but he was kind, funny, and generous from the first moment of our meeting. Lucky for me, he's continued to be extraordinarily generous, offering me various assists that made this book possible. Thank you also to Jill Stoddard and Emily Edlynn. I am beyond grateful to have you both as my writing partners in crime.

Of course, a working parent can't write a book without a whole lot of help in the childcare department. Let me begin with my mother-in-law, Michelle Fredson, who breaks every stereotype in the books about mothers-in-law. Her love for her grandsons and support of me provided the large chunks of time required to do the deep work of writing. But because Michelle lives a flight away, I've also needed to rely on an assortment of professional childcare providers. Jeannie Lothrop and Moza Mustafa made their family day cares a home away from home for my kids and made me feel like a part of their families, too. Thank you also to Emily Wynn, Tiffany Williams, and Inna Govorov-Chernysh, teachers at Auburndale Community Nursery School, Williams Elementary School, and to Terese Walkeapaa. And to my neighbors and dear friends Sarah

Henry, Joanna Glennon, and Sondra Watson—my boys and I are so fortunate to have you in our village!

Many beloved friends and family members supported me by reading early pieces of writing, compassionately listening when I was in worry mode, and cheering my every step of this journey. My dear friend Megan Kurth talked through nascent ideas, read early drafts, and combed through hundreds of pages of interview transcripts with me all while keeping me in stitches with her brilliant wit. Thank you Melanie Wang, Erica Speier, Bob Poelstra, Karyn Clarke, San Huynh, Susan Juroe, and Alee Miller for always supporting me. And to my father-in-law Michael Schonbrun, my dad would have been happy to know that I had a father figure to turn to in his absence—especially one as kind and smart as you. Thank you to my Chatav family: my sister, Maya, was the first to teach me the joy of falling in love with books, and my brother, Eitan, introduced me to Taoism and thoughtfully read early sections of this book. And to my mom and dad, who came to America with a dream to work hard and build a loving family. They succeeded.

Finally, to my family at home. Thank you, Ethan Schonbrun, for being my teammate in life. You quietly inspire me with your humility, creativity, and thoughtfulness, supporting me in ways I often fail to recognize at the time. (I'm working on that!) And last but definitely not least, I wouldn't know the many challenges and the many more profound gifts of working parenthood without my children. To my passionate hobbyist, my earnest daydreamer, and my mischievous superhero, you help me grow wisdom and find meaning while filling my days with love and laughter. Thank you, sweet boys, for being mine.

NOTES

INTRODUCTION

1. Pew Research Center, "The Rise in Dual Income Households," press release, June 18, 2015, https://www.pewresearch.org/ft_dual-income -households-1960-2012-2/.

2. U.S. Bureau of Labor Statistics, "Employment Characteristics of Families—2020," press release, April 21, 2021, https://www.bls.gov/news.re lease/famee.htm.

3. Gretchen Livingston, "The Changing Profile of Unmarried Parents," Pew Research Center, April 25, 2018, https://www.pewresearch.org/social -trends/2018/04/25/the-changing-profile-of-unmarried-parents/.

4. Steven C. Hayes, Kirk D. Strosahl, and Kelly G. Wilson, *Acceptance and Commitment Therapy: An Experiential Approach to Behavior Change* (New York: Guilford Press, 1999).

5. Steven C. Hayes, Jason B. Luoma, Frank W. Bond, Akihiko Masuda, and Jason Lillis, "Acceptance and Commitment Therapy: Model, Processes and Outcomes," *Behaviour Research and Therapy* 44, no. 1 (2006): 1–25.

6. Jeffrey Greenhaus and Gary N. Powell, "When Work and Family Are Allies: A Theory of Work-Family Enrichment," *Academy of Management Review* 3, no. 1 (2006): 72–92.

7. Thich Nhat Hanh, *No Mud, No Lotus: The Art of Transforming Suffering* (Berkeley, CA: Parallax Press, 2014).

CHAPTER 1. WHEN YOU'RE LOST, LET VALUES BE YOUR GUIDE

1. Henry Louis Mencken, *Prejudices: Second Series* (New York: Alfred A. Knopf, 1920), 155.

2. Irene Padavic, Robin J. Ely, and Erin M. Reid, "Explaining the Persistence of Gender Inequality: The Work-Family Narrative as a Social Defense against the 24/7 Work Culture," *Administrative Science Quarterly* 65, no. 1 (2020): 1–51.

3. Jay Belsky, Deborah Lowe Vandell, Margaret Burchinal, Alison Clarke-Stewart, Kathleen McCartney, and Margaret Tresch Owen, "Are There Long-Term Effects of Early Child Care?" *Child Development* 78, no. 2 (2007): 681–701; Pedro Carneiro, Katrine Løken, and Kjell G. Salvanes, "A Flying Start? Maternity Leave Benefits and Long-Run Outcomes of Children," *Journal of Political Economy* 123, no. 2 (2015): 365–412; Maya Rossin-Slater, "Maternity and Family Leave Policy" (working paper, National Bureau of Economic Research, January 2017); Deborah Lowe Vandell, Jay Belsky, Margaret Burchinal, and Laurence Steinberg, "Do Effects of Early Child Care Extend to Age 15 Years? Results from the NICHD Study of Early Child Care and Youth Development," *Child Development* 81, no. 3 (2010): 737–56.

4. Rachel G. Lucas-Thompson, Wendy A. Goldberg, and JoAnn Prause, "Maternal Work Early in the Lives of Children and Its Distal Associations with Achievement and Behavior Problems: A Meta-Analysis," *Psychological Bulletin* 136, no. 6 (2010): 915–42.

5. Emily Oster, *Cribsheet: A Data-Driven Guide to Better, More Relaxed Parenting, from Birth to Preschool* (New York: Penguin Press, 2019).

6. Lonnie Golden, "The Effects of Working Time on Productivity and Firm Performance" (research synthesis paper, International Labor Organization, Geneva, Switzerland, September 2012).

7. Margaret Deery and Leo Jago, "Revisiting Talent Management, Work-Life Balance, and Retention Strategies," *International Journal of Contemporary Hospitality Management* 27, no. 3 (2015): 453–72.

8. M. Joseph Sirgy and Dong-Jin Lee, "Work-Life Balance: An Integrative Review," *Applied Research in Quality of Life* 13, no. 2 (2017), https://doi.org/10.1007/s11482-017-9509-8.

9. Francisco J. Ruiz and Carmen Luciano, "Improving International-Level Chess Players' Performance with an Acceptance-Based Protocol: Preliminary Findings," *Psychological Record* 62, no. 3 (2012): 447–62.

10. Steven C. Hayes and Michael E. Levin, eds., *Mindfulness and Acceptance for Addictive Behaviors: Applying Contextual CBT to Substance Abuse and Behavioral Addictions*, Context Press Mindfulness and Acceptance Practica Series (Oakland, CA: New Harbinger, 2012).

11. Laura Campbell-Sills, David Barlow, Timothy A. Brown, and Stefan G. Hofmann, "Effects of Suppression and Acceptance on Emotional Responses of Individuals with Anxiety and Mood Disorders," *Behavior Research and Therapy* 44, no. 9 (2006): 1251–63.

12. Steve Stewart-Williams, *The Ape That Understood the Universe: How the Mind and Culture Evolve* (New York: Cambridge University Press, 2018), 173.

13. Steven C. Hayes, *A Liberated Mind: How to Pivot Towards What Matters* (New York: Avery, 2019), 116.

CHAPTER 2. CHANGE YOUR WORKING-PARENT MINDSET

1. Teri Kanefield, *Free to Be Ruth Bader Ginsburg: The Story of Women and Law* (San Francisco: Armon Books, 2016).

2. Stephanie Francis Ward, "Family Ties," *ABA Journal*, October 1, 2010, https://www.abajournal.com/magazine/article/family_ties1.

3. Ruth Bader Ginsburg, "Ruth Bader Ginsburg's Advice for Living," *New York Times*, October 1, 2016.

4. Daniel Lombroso, Jackie Lay, and Ryan Park, "Ruth Bader Ginsburg on the Perspective That Comes with Motherhood," *The Atlantic*, February 6, 2017.

5. Yael Chatav Schonbrun, "A Mother's Ambitions," *New York Times*, July 30, 2014.

6. Heather Antecol, Kelly Bedard, and Jenna Stearns, "Equal but Inequitable: Who Benefits from Gender-Neutral Tenure Clock Stopping Policies?" *American Economic Review* 108, no. 9 (2018): 2420–41; Laura M. Giurge, Ashley V. Whillans, and Ayse Yemiscigil, "A Multicountry Perspective on Gender Differences in Time Use during COVID-19," *Proceedings of the National Academy of Sciences* 118, no. 2 (March 23, 2021); Shruti Jolly, Kent A. Griffith, Rochelle DeCastro, Abigail Stewart, Peter Ubel, and Reshma Jagsi, "Gender Differences in Time Spent on Parenting and Domestic Responsibilities by High-Achieving Young Physician-Researchers," *Annals of Internal Medicine* 160, no. 5 (2014): 344–53.

7. Lisa A. Neff and Elizabeth F. Broady, "Stress Resilience in Early Marriage: Can Practice Make Perfect?" *Journal of Personality and Social Psychology* 101, no. 5 (2011): 1050; Mark D. Seery, E. Alison Holman, and Roxanne Cohen Silver, "Whatever Does Not Kill Us: Cumulative Lifetime Adversity, Vulnerability, and Resilience," *Journal of Personality and Social Psychology* 99, no. 6 (2010): 1025–41.

8. Stephen R. Marks, "Multiple Roles and Role Strain: Some Notes on Human Energy, Time and Commitment," *American Sociological Review* 42, no. 6 (1977): 921–36; Sam D. Sieber, "Toward a Theory of Role Accumulation," *American Sociological Review* 39, no. 4 (1974): 567–78.

9. Nan Zhou and Cheryl Buehler, "Family, Employment, and Individual Resource-Based Antecedents of Maternal Work–Family Enrichment from Infancy through Middle Childhood," *Journal of Occupational Health Psychology* 21, no. 3 (2016): 309–21.

10. Grace K. Baruch and Rosalind C. Barnett, "Role Quality, Multiple Role Involvement, and Psychological Well-Being in Midlife Women," *Journal of Personality and Social Psychology* 51, no. 3 (1986): 578–85; Stephen R. Marks and Shelley M. MacDermid, "Multiple Roles and the Self: A Theory of Role Balance," *Journal of Marriage and the Family* 58, no. 2 (1996): 417–32; Francesco Montani, Ilaria Setti, Valentina Sommovigo, Francois

Courcy, and Gabriele Giorgi, "Who Responds Creatively to Role Conflict? Evidence for a Curvilinear Relationship Mediated by Cognitive Adjustment at Work and Moderated by Mindfulness," *Journal of Business and Psychology* 35, no. 4 (2019), https://doi.org/10.1007/s10869-019-09644-9; Lois M. Verbrugge, "Role Burdens and Physical Health of Women and Men," *Women & Health* 11, no. 1 (1986): 47–77.

11. Jeffrey Greenhaus and Gary N. Powell, "When Work and Family Are Allies: A Theory of Work-Family Enrichment," *Academy of Management Review* 3, no. 1 (2006): 72–92.

12. Greenhaus and Powell, "When Work and Family Are Allies," 72–92.

13. Carol S. Dweck, *Mindset: The New Psychology of Success* (New York: Random House, 2006).

14. Alia J. Crum, William R. Corbin, Kelly D. Brownell, and Peter Salovey, "Mind over Milkshakes: Mindsets, Not Just Nutrients, Determine Ghrelin Response," *Health Psychology* 30, no. 4 (2011): 424; Alia J. Crum and Ellen J. Langer, "Mind-Set Matters: Exercise and the Placebo Effect," *Psychological Science* 18, no. 2 (2007): 165–71; David S. Yeager and Carol S. Dweck, "Mindsets That Promote Resilience: When Students Believe That Personal Characteristics Can Be Developed," *Educational Psychologist* 47, no. 4 (2012): 302–14; Lauren C. Howe, Kari A. Leibowitz, Margaret A. Perry, Julie M. Bitler, Whitney M. Black, Ted J. Kaptchuk, Kari Nadeau, and Alia J. Crum, "Changing Patient Mindsets about Non–Life-Threatening Symptoms during Oral Immunotherapy: A Randomized Clinical Trial," *Journal of Allergy and Clinical Immunology: In Practice* 7, no. 5 (2019): 1550–59; Daryl R. Van Tongeren and Jeni L. Burnette, "Do You Believe Happiness Can Change? An Investigation of the Relationship between Happiness Mindsets, Well-Being, and Satisfaction," *Journal of Positive Psychology* 13, no. 2 (2018): 101–9.

15. Carol S. Dweck, "Mindsets and Human Nature: Promoting Change in the Middle East, the Schoolyard, the Racial Divide, and Willpower," *American Psychologist* 67, no. 8 (2012): 614.

16. Young Eun Chang, "The Relation between Mothers' Attitudes toward Maternal Employment and Social Competence of 36-Month-Olds: The Roles of Maternal Psychological Well-Being and Sensitivity," *Journal of Child and Family Studies* 22, no. 7 (2013): 987–99.

17. Michael Broda, John Yun, Barbara Lynn Schneider, David S. Yeager, Gregory M. Walton, and Matthew A. Diemer, "Reducing Inequality in Academic Success for Incoming College Students: A Randomized Trial of Growth Mindset and Belonging Interventions," *Journal of Research on Educational Effectiveness* 11, no. 3 (2018): 317–38.

18. Eran Halperin, Alexandra G. Russell, Kali H. Trzesniewski, James J. Gross, and Carol S. Dweck, "Promoting the Middle East Peace Process by Changing Beliefs About Group Malleability," *Science* 333, no. 6050 (2011): 1767–69; Dweck, "Mindsets and Human Nature," 614–22.

19. Alan Watts with Al Chung-liang Huang, *Tao: The Watercourse Way* (New York: Pantheon Books, 1975).
20. Ursula Le Guin, *Lao Tzu: Tao Te Ching: A Book About the Way and the Power of the Way* (Boston: Shambhala, 1997), 4.
21. Greenhaus and Powell, "When Work and Family Are Allies," 72–92.
22. Rosalind C. Barnett and Janet Shibley Hyde, "Women, Men, Work, and Family: An Expansionist Theory," *American Psychologist* 56, no. 10 (2001): 781–96.
23. Daniel J. Siegel and Tina Payne Bryson, *The Whole-Brain Child: 12 Revolutionary Strategies to Nurture Your Child's Developing Mind* (New York: Bantam, 2012), 12
24. Emile Durkheim, *Suicide: A Study in Sociology,* trans. John A. Spaulding and George Simpson (New York: The Free Press, 1951).
25. Robin Romm, ed., *Double Bind: Women on Ambition* (New York: Liveright Publishing, 2017).
26. Sonja Lyubomirsky, Kennon M. Sheldon, and David Schkade, "Pursuing Happiness: The Architecture of Sustainable Change," *Review of General Psychology* 9, no. 2 (2005): 111–31.
27. Kennon M. Sheldon and Sonja Lyubomirsky, "Revisiting the Sustainable Happiness Model and Pie Chart: Can Happiness Be Successfully Pursued?" *Journal of Positive Psychology* 16, no. 2 (2021): 145–54.
28. Daniel T. Gilbert, Elizabeth C. Pinel, Timothy D. Wilson, Stephen J. Blumberg, and Thalia Parker Wheatley, "Immune Neglect: A Source of Durability Bias in Affective Forecasting," *Journal of Personality and Social Psychology* 75, no. 3 (1998): 617; Timothy D. Wilson and D. T. Gilbert, "Affective Forecasting: Knowing What to Want," *Current Directions in Psychological Science* 14, no. 3 (2005): 131–34.

CHAPTER 3. UNHOOK FROM UNHELPFUL LABELS

1. Jill A. Stoddard, *Be Mighty: A Woman's Guide to Liberation from Anxiety, Worry, and Stress Using Mindfulness and Acceptance* (Oakland, CA: New Harbinger Publications, 2020).
2. Joseph Ciarrochi, Ann Bailey, and Russ Harris, *The Weight Escape: How to Stop Dieting and Start Living* (Boston: Shambhala, 2014).
3. Sabiha K. Barot, Yasuhiro Kyono, Emily W. Clark, and Ilene L. Bernstein, "Visualizing Stimulus Convergence in Amygdala Neurons During Associative Learning," *Proceedings of the National Academy of Sciences* 105, no. 52 (2008): 20959–63; Carol A. Seger and Earl K. Miller, "Category Learning in the Brain," *Annual Review of Neuroscience* 33 (2010): 203–19.
4. Sian Beilock, *Choke: What the Secrets of the Brain Reveal About Getting It Right When You Have To* (New York: Free Press, 2010).
5. Tim P. Moran, "Anxiety and Working Memory Capacity: A Meta-Analysis and Narrative Review," *Psychological Bulletin* 142, no. 8 (2016): 831–64.

6. Hannah-Hanh D. Nguyen and Ann Marie Ryan, "Does Stereotype Threat Affect Test Performance of Minorities and Women? A Meta-Analysis of Experimental Evidence," *Journal of Applied Psychology* 93, no. 6 (2008): 1314–34.

7. Anne C. Krendl, Jennifer A. Richeson, William M. Kelley, and Todd F. Heatherton, "The Negative Consequences of Threat: A Functional Magnetic Resonance Imaging Investigation of the Neural Mechanisms Underlying Women's Underperformance in Math," *Psychological Science* 19, no. 2 (2008): 168–75.

8. Steven C. Hayes, Kirk D. Strosahl, and Kelly G. Wilson, *Acceptance and Commitment Therapy: The Process and Practice of Mindful Change*, 2nd ed. (New York: Guilford Press, 2012); Steven C. Hayes and Kelly G. Wilson, "Acceptance and Commitment Therapy: Altering the Verbal Support for Experiential Avoidance," in *Mindfulness: Clinical Applications of Mindfulness and Acceptance: Specific Interventions for Psychiatric, Behavioural, and Physical Health Conditions,* vol. 3, ed. Brandon Gaudiano BA (New York: Routledge, 2017), 3–25.

9. Michele S. Hirsch and Robert M. Liebert, "The Physical and Psychological Experience of Pain: The Effects of Labeling and Cold Pressor Temperature on Three Pain Measures in College Women," *Pain* 77, no. 1 (1998): 41–48.

10. Ben Colagiuri, Lieven A. Schenk, Michael D. Kessler, Susan G. Dorsey, and Luanna Colloca, "The Placebo Effect: From Concepts to Genes," *Neuroscience* 307 (2015): 171–90.

11. Tor D. Wager, James K. Rilling, Edward E. Smith, Alex Sokolik, Kenneth Casey, Richard J. Davidson, Stephen M. Kosslyn, Robert M. Rose, and Jonathan D. Cohen, "Placebo-Induced Changes in fMRI in the Anticipation and Experience of Pain," in *The Placebo: A Reader*, ed. Franklin G. Miller, Luanna Colloca, Robert A. Crouch, and Ted J. Kaptchuk (Baltimore: Johns Hopkins University Press, 2013), 158–65.

12. Kristin D. Neff and Roos Vonk, "Self-Compassion versus Global Self-Esteem: Two Different Ways of Relating to Oneself," *Journal of Personality* 77, no. 1 (2009): 23–50.

13. Alan Watts with Al Chung-liang Huang, *Tao: The Watercourse Way* (New York: Pantheon Books, 1975).

CHAPTER 4. SPIN YOUR STORY

1. Shel Silverstein, *The Missing Piece.* (New York: Harper & Row, 1976).

2. Kennon M. Sheldon and Sonja Lyubomirsky, "Achieving Sustainable Gains in Happiness: Change Your Actions, Not Your Circumstances," *Journal of Happiness Studies* 7, no. 1 (2006): 55–86.

3. Yuval Noah Harari, *Sapiens: A Brief History of Humankind* (New York: Harper, 2015).

4. Jonathan M. Adler, "Living into the Story: Agency and Coherence in a Longitudinal Study of Narrative Identity Development and Mental

Health Over the Course of Psychotherapy," *Journal of Personality and Social Psychology* 102, no. 2 (2012): 367.

5. Jonathan M. Adler, Jennifer Lodi-Smith, Frederick L. Philippe, and Iliane Houle, "The Incremental Validity of Narrative Identity in Predicting Well-Being: A Review of the Field and Recommendations for the Future," *Personality and Social Psychology Review* 20, no. 2 (2016): 142–75.

6. Ashley E. Mason et al., "Stress Resilience: Narrative Identity May Buffer the Longitudinal Effects of Chronic Caregiving Stress on Mental Health and Telomere Shortening," *Brain, Behavior, and Immunity* 77 (2019): 101–9.

7. Allison S. Troy, Frank H. Wilhelm, Amanda J. Shallcross, and Iris B. Mauss, "Seeing the Silver Lining: Cognitive Reappraisal Ability Moderates the Relationship between Stress and Depressive Symptoms," *Emotion* 10, no. 6 (2010): 783–95.

8. Viktor Frankl, *Man's Search for Meaning* (Boston: Beacon Press, 1959).

9. Jennifer E. Graham-Engeland, Marci Lobel, Peter Glass, and Irina Lokshina, "Effects of Written Anger Expression in Chronic Pain Patients: Making Meaning from Pain," *Journal of Behavioral Medicine* 31, no. 3 (2008): 201–12.

10. Erica B. Slotter and Deborah E. Ward, "Finding the Silver Lining: The Relative Roles of Redemptive Narratives and Cognitive Reappraisal in Individuals' Emotional Distress after the End of a Romantic Relationship," *Journal of Social and Personal Relationships* 32, no. 6 (2015): 737–56.

11. Marlene Matos, Anita Santos, Miguel M. Gonçalves, and Carla Martins, "Innovative Moments and Change in Narrative Therapy," *Psychotherapy Research* 19, no. 1 (2009): 68–80.

12. James Pennebaker and Joshua M. Smyth, *Opening Up by Writing It Down: How Expressive Writing Improves Health and Eases Emotional Pain* (New York: Guilford Press, 2016).

13. Karen A. Baikie and Kay A. Wilhelm, "Emotional and Physical Health Benefits of Expressive Writing," *Advances in Psychiatric Treatment* 11, no. 5 (2005): 338–46; James W. Pennebaker, "Writing about Emotional Experiences as a Therapeutic Process," *Psychological Science* 8, no. 3 (1997): 162–66.

14. Steven C. Hayes, Kirk D. Strosahl, and Kelly G. Wilson, *Acceptance and Commitment Therapy: The Process and Practice of Mindful Change* (New York: Guilford Press, 2011).

CHAPTER 5. DO THE RIGHT HARD THINGS (THE RIGHT WAY)

1. Barry Schwartz and Kenneth Sharpe, *Practical Wisdom: The Right Way to Do the Right Thing* (New York: Riverhead Books, 2010), 5.

2. Schwartz and Sharpe, *Practical Wisdom*; W. F. Boh, R. Evaristo, and A. Oudenkirk, "Balancing Breadth and Depth of Expertise for Innovation: A 3M story," *Research Policy* 43, no. 2 (2014): 349–366, https://doi.org/10.1016/j.respol.2013.10.009; K. A. Ericsson, R. T. Krampe, and

C. Tesch-Römer, "The Role of Deliberate Practice in the Acquisition of Expert Performance," *Psychological Review* 100, no. 3 (1993): 363–406, http://dx.doi.org/10.1037/0033-295X.100.3.363.

3. Barry Schwartz, *The Paradox of Choice: Why More Is Less* (New York: HarperCollins, 2004).

4. Kate Brassington and Tim Lomas, "Can Resilience Training Improve Well-Being for People in High-Risk Occupations? A Systematic Review through a Multidimensional Lens," *Journal of Positive Psychology* 16, no. 5 (2021): 573–92, https://doi.org/10.1080/17439760.2020.1752783; Susana Gavidia-Payne, Bianca Denny, Kate Davis, Andrew J. P. Francis, and Mervyn Sydney Jackson, "Parental Resilience: A Neglected Construct in Resilience Research," *Clinical Psychologist* 19, no. 3 (2015): 111–21; Kirsti Haracz and Elysa Roberts, "Workplace Resilience Interventions Show Some Evidence of Positive Effects, Particularly on Mental Health and Wellbeing," *Australian Occupational Therapy Journal* 63, no. 1 (2016): 57–58; Michael Rutter, "Resilience in the Face of Adversity: Protective Factors and Resistance to Psychiatric Disorder," *British Journal of Psychiatry* 147 (1985): 598–611; Mary A. Steinhardt and Christyn L. Dolbier, "Evaluation of a Resilience Intervention to Enhance Coping Strategies and Protective Factors and Decrease Symptomatology," *Journal of American College Health* 56, no. 4 (2008): 445–53.

5. Mark D. Seery, E. Alison Holman, and Roxanne Cohen Silver, "Whatever Does Not Kill Us: Cumulative Lifetime Adversity, Vulnerability, and Resilience," *Journal of Personality and Social Psychology* 99, no. 6 (2010): 1025–41.

6. Alex Mathew Wood, Jeffrey J. Froh, and Andrew Geraghty, "Gratitude and Well-Being: A Review and Theoretical Integration," *Clinical Psychology Review* 30, no. 7 (2010): 890–905.

7. Angela Duckworth, *Grit: The Power of Passion and Perseverance* (New York: Scribner, 2016).

8. Katherine Von Culin, Eli Tsukayama, and Angela Duckworth, "Unpacking Grit: Motivational Correlates of Perseverance and Passion for Long-Term Goals," *Journal of Positive Psychology* 9, no. 4 (2014): 306–12.

9. Amy Wrzesniewski, Clark McCauley, Paul Rozin, and Barry Schwartz, "Jobs, Careers, and Callings: People's Relations to Their Work," *Journal of Research in Personality* 31, no. 2 (1997): 21–33.

10. Amy Wrzesniewski and Jane E. Dutton, "Crafting a Job: Revisioning Employees as Active Crafters of Their Work," *Academy of Management Review* 26, no. 2 (2001): 179–201.

11. Adam M. Grant, "Does Intrinsic Motivation Fuel the Prosocial Fire? Motivational Synergy in Predicting Persistence, Performance, and Productivity," *Journal of Applied Psychology* 93, no. 1 (2008): 48.

12. Wrzesniewski and Dutton, "Crafting a Job," 179–201.

13. Martin E. Seligman, Steven F. Maier, and James H. Geer, "Alleviation of Learned Helplessness in the Dog," *Journal of Abnormal Psychology* 73, no 3, pt. 1 (1968): 256–62.

14. Seligman, Maier, and Geer, "Alleviation of Learned Helplessness in the Dog," 256–62.
15. Daniel Goleman, *Emotional Intelligence: Why It Can Matter More Than IQ* (New York: Bantam, 2012).
16. Thomas Sy, Susanna Tram-Quon, and Linda A. O'Hara, "Relation of Employee and Manager Emotional Intelligence to Job Satisfaction and Performance," *Journal of Vocational Behavior* 68, no. 3 (2006): 461–73.
17. Yvonne Brunetto, Stephen T. Teo, Kate Shacklock, and Rodney Farr-Wharton, "Emotional Intelligence, Job Satisfaction, Well-Being, and Engagement: Explaining Organisational Commitment and Turnover Intentions in Policing," *Human Resource Management Journal* 22, no. 4 (2012): 428–41.
18. Todd B. Kashdan and Jonathan Rottenberg, "Psychological Flexibility as a Fundamental Aspect of Health," *Clinical Psychology Review* 30, no. 7 (2010): 865–78.
19. Anat Prior and Brian Macwhinney, "A Bilingual Advantage in Task Switching," *Bilingualism: Language and Cognition* 13, no. 2 (2010): 253–62.

CHAPTER 6. RETHINK YOUR REST

1. Alex Soojung-Kim Pang, *Rest: Why You Get More Done When You Work Less* (New York: Basic Books, 2016), 2.
2. Anat Keinan, Silvia Bellezza, and Neeru Paharia, "The Symbolic Value of Time," *Current Opinion in Psychology* 26 (2019): 58–61.
3. Charlotte Faircloth, "Intensive Parenting and the Expansion of Parenting," in *Parenting Culture Studies*, ed. Ellie Lee, Jennie Bristow, Charlotte Faircloth, and Jan Macvarish (London: Palgrave Macmillan, 2014), 25–50.
4. Möira Mikolajczak, James J. Gross, Florence Stinglhamber, Annika Lindahl Norberg, and Isabelle Roskam, "Is Parental Burnout Distinct from Job Burnout and Depressive Symptoms?" *Clinical Psychological Science* 8, no. 4 (2020): 673–89.
5. Ben Wigert, "Employee Burnout: The Biggest Myth," Gallup, March 13, 2020, https://www.gallup.com/workplace/288539/employee-burnout-biggest-myth.aspx.
6. Möira Mikolajczak, James J. Gross, and Isabelle Roskam, "Parental Burnout: What Is It, and Why Does It Matter?" *Clinical Psychological Science* 7, no. 6 (2019): 1319–29.
7. Isabelle Roskam, Marie-Emilie Raes, and Möira Mikolajczak, "Exhausted Parents: Development and Preliminary Validation of the Parental Burnout Inventory," *Frontiers in Psychology* 8 (2017), https://doi.org/10.3389/fpsyg.2017.00163; Jody A. Worley, Matt Vassar, Denna Wheeler, and Laura Barnes, "Factor Structure of Scores from the Maslach Burnout Inventory: A Review and Meta-Analysis of 45 Exploratory and Confirmatory Factor-Analytic Studies," *Educational and Psychological Measurement* 68, no. 5 (2008): 797–823.

8. Brad J. Bushman, "Does Venting Anger Feed or Extinguish the Flame? Catharsis, Rumination, Distraction, Anger, and Aggressive Responding," *Personality and Social Psychology Bulletin* 28, no. 6 (2002): 724–31; Brad J. Bushman, Roy Baumeister, and Angela D. Stack, "Catharsis, Aggression, and Persuasive Influence: Self-Fulfilling or Self-Defeating Prophecies?" *Journal of Personality and Social Psychology* 76, no 3 (1999): 367.

9. Soojung-Kim Pang, *Rest*.

10. Sabine Sonnentag and Ute-Vera Bayer, "Switching Off Mentally: Predictors and Consequences of Psychological Detachment from Work during Off-Job Time," *Journal of Occupational Health Psychology* 10, no. 4 (2005): 393; Sabine Sonnentag, Carmen Binnewies, and Eva J. Mojza, "Staying Well and Engaged When Demands Are High: The Role of Psychological Detachment," *Journal of Applied Psychology* 95, no. 5 (2010): 965–76; Sabine Sonnentag and Undine Kruel, "Psychological Detachment from Work during Off-Job Time: The Role of Job Stressors, Job Involvement, and Recovery-Related Self-Efficacy," *European Journal of Work and Organizational Psychology* 15, no. 2 (2006): 197–217.

11. Dalia Etzion, Dov Eden, and Yael Lapidot-Raz, "Relief from Job Stressors and Burnout: Reserve Service as a Respite," *Journal of Applied Psychology* 83, no. 4 (1998): 577–85.

12. Sonnentag, Binnewies, and Mojza, "Staying Well and Engaged When Demands Are High," 965–76.

13. Kathleen Fuegen, Monica Biernat, Elizabeth Haines, and Kay Deaux, "Mothers and Fathers in the Workplace: How Gender and Parental Status Influence Judgments of Job-Related Competence," *Journal of Social Issues* 60, no. 4 (2004): 737–54.

14. Sharon Hays, *The Cultural Contradictions of Motherhood* (New Haven, CT: Yale University Press, 1996).

15. Roy Baumeister, Arlene Stillwell, and Todd F. Heatherton, "Guilt: An Interpersonal Approach," *Psychological Bulletin* 115, no. 2 (1994): 243–67.

16. Gerardo Ramirez amd Sian L. Beilock, "Writing about Testing Worries Boosts Exam Performance in the Classroom," *Science* 331, no. 6014 (2011): 211–13.

17. "Americans Check Their Phones 96 Times a Day," Asurion, November 21, 2019, https://www.asurion.com/press-releases/americans-check-their-phones-96-times-a-day/; SWNS, "Americans Check Their Phones 80 Times a Day: Study," *New York Post*, November 8, 2017, https://nypost.com/2017/11/08/americans-check-their-phones-80-times-a-day-study/#.

18. Larry Rosen and Alexander Samuel, "Conquering Digital Distraction, *Harvard Business Review*, June 2015, 110–13.

19. Blake E. Ashforth, Glen E. Kreiner, and Mel Fugate, "All in a Day's Work: Boundaries and Micro Role Transitions," *Academy of Management Review* 25, no. 3 (2000): 472–91.

20. Wendy Wood and David Neal, "A New Look at Habits and the Habit-Goal Interface," *Psychological Review* 114, no. 4 (2007): 843.

21. Catherine E. Milner and Kimberly A. Cote, "Benefits of Napping in Healthy Adults: Impact of Nap Length, Time of Day, Age, and Experience with Napping," *Journal of Sleep Research* 18, no. 2 (2009): 272–81; Catherine E. Milner, Stuart M. Fogel, and Kimberly A. Cote, "Habitual Napping Moderates Motor Performance Improvements Following a Short Daytime Nap," *Biological Psychology* 73, no. 2 (2006): 141–56.

22. Jennifer R. Goldschmied, Philip Cheng, Kathryn Kemp, Lauren Caccamo, Julia Roberts, and Patricia J. Deldin, "Napping to Modulate Frustration and Impulsivity: A Pilot Study," *Personality and Individual Differences* 86 (2015): 164–67.

23. Pin-Chun Chen, Lauren Whitehurst, Mohsen Naji, and Sara Mednick, "Autonomic Activity during a Daytime Nap Facilitates Working Memory Improvement," *Journal of Cognitive Neuroscience* 32, no. 10 (2020): 1963–74; Sara Mednick, Denise J. Cai, Jennifer Kanady, and Sean P. A. Drummond, "Comparing the Benefits of Caffeine, Naps and Placebo on Verbal, Motor and Perceptual Memory," *Behavioural Brain Research* 193, no. 1 (2008): 79–86.

24. Milner and Cote, "Benefits of Napping in Healthy Adults," 272–81; Mitsuo Hayashi, Naoko Motoyoshi, and Tadeo Hori, "Recuperative Power of a Short Daytime Nap with or without Stage 2 Sleep," *Sleep: Journal of Sleep and Sleep Disorders Research* 28, no. 7 (2005): 829–36.

25. Tricia Hersey, "From a Historic Perspective, Rest Can Be a Form of Resistance," interviewed by Leah Fleming and Tiffany Griffith, Georgia Public Broadcasting, October 8, 2021.

26. Sarah Blaffer Hrdy, *Mothers and Others: The Evolutionary Origins of Mutual Understanding* (Cambridge, MA: Harvard University Press, 2011), 109.

27. Will Kenkel, Allison M. Perkeybile, and Carol Sue Carter, "The Neurobiological Causes and Effects of Alloparenting," *Developmental Neurobiology* 77, no. 2 (2017): 214–32.

28. David Waynforth, "Kin-Based Alloparenting and Infant Hospital Admissions in the UK Millennium Cohort," *Evolution, Medicine, and Public Health* 2020, no 1 (2020): 72–81.

29. David Olds, Lois S. Sadler, and Harriet Kitzman, "Programs for Parents of Infants and Toddlers: Recent Evidence from Randomized Trials," *Journal of Child Psychology and Psychiatry* 48, nos. 3–4 (2007): 355–91; Sandra K. Pope, Leanne Whiteside, Jean Brooks-Gunn, Kelly J. Kelleher, Vaughn I. Rickert, Robert H. Bradley, and Patrick H. Casey, "Low-Birth-Weight Infants Born to Adolescent Mothers: Effects of Coresidency with Grandmother on Child Development," *JAMA: Journal of the American Medical Association* 269 (1993): 1396–1400.

30. David F. Lancy, *The Anthropology of Childhood: Cherubs, Chattel, Changelings* (Cambridge, UK: Cambridge University Press, 2014).

31. Helle Riisgaard, Jorgen Nexøe, Jette Videbaek Le, Jens Søndergaard, and Loni Ledderer, "Relations between Task Delegation and Job Satisfaction

in General Practice: A Systematic Literature Review," *BMC Family Practice* 17, no. 1 (2016): 1–8.

32. Modupe Akinola, Ashley Martin, and Kathy Y. Phillips, "To Delegate or Not to Delegate: Gender Differences in Affective Associations and Behavioral Responses to Delegation," *Academy of Management Journal* 61, no. 4 (2018): 1467–91.

33. Fred B. Bryant and Joseph Veroff, *Savoring: A New Model of Positive Experience* (New York: Psychology Press, 2012).

34. Nick Fox, Heather Henderson, Kenneth H. Rubin, Susan Calkins, and Louis Schmidt, "Continuity and Discontinuity of Behavioral Inhibition and Exuberance: Psychophysiological and Behavioral Influences across the First Four Years of Life," *Child Development* 72, no. 1 (2001): 1–21.

CHAPTER 7. TURN CONSTRAINTS INTO CREATIVITY

1. David M. Berson, Felice A. Dunn, and Takao Motoharu, "Phototransduction by Retinal Ganglion Cells That Set the Circadian Clock," *Science* 295, no. 5557 (2002): 1070–73.

2. Arne Dietrich, "The Cognitive Neuroscience of Creativity," *Psychonomic Bulletin & Review* 11, no. 6 (2004): 1011–26.

3. Claire M. Zedelius and Jonathan Schooler, "Mind Wandering 'Ahas' versus Mindful Reasoning: Alternative Routes to Creative Solutions," *Frontiers in Psychology* 6 (2015): 834.

4. J. P. Guilford, "Three Faces of Intellect," *American Psychologist* 14, no. 8 (1959): 469.

5. Carmen Binnewies and Sarah C. Wörnlein, "What Makes a Creative Day? A Diary Study on the Interplay between Affect, Job Stressors, and Job Control," *Journal of Organizational Behavior* 32, no. 4 (2011): 589–607.

6. Jonathan W. Schooler, Michael D. Mrazek, Michael S. Franklin, Benjamin Baird, Benjamin W. Mooneyham, Claire Zedelius, and James M. Broadway, "The Middle Way: Finding the Balance between Mindfulness and Mind-Wandering," in *The Psychology of Learning and Motivation*, vol. 60, ed. Brian H. Ross (San Diego, CA: Elsevier Academic Press, 2014), 1–33.

7. Martha L. Jones, "Role Conflict: Cause of Burnout or Energizer?" *Social Work* 38, no. 2 (1993): 136–41.

8. Kristin Byron, Shalini Khazanchi, and Deborah Nazarian, "The Relationship between Stressors and Creativity: A Meta-Analysis Examining Competing Theoretical Models," *Journal of Applied Psychology* 95, no. 1 (2010): 201–12.

9. R. M. Yerkes and J. D. Dodson, "The Relation of Strength of Stimulus to Rapidity of Habit Formation," *Journal of Comparative Neurology & Psychology* 18 (1908): 459–82.

10. Byron, Khazanchi, and Nazarian, "The Relationship between Stressors and Creativity," 201–12; Binnewies and Wörnlein, "What Makes a Creative Day?" 589–607.

11. Francesco Montani, Ilaria Setti, Valentina Sommovigo, Francois Courcy, and Gabriele Giorgi, "Who Responds Creatively to Role Conflict? Evidence for a Curvilinear Relationship Mediated by Cognitive Adjustment at Work and Moderated by Mindfulness," *Journal of Business and Psychology* 35, no. 4 (2019).
12. Mihaly Csikszentmihalyi, *Creativity: Flow and the Psychology of Discovery and Invention* (New York: Harper Collins, 1996), 1.
13. Nancy C. Andreasen, *The Creating Brain: The Neuroscience of Genius* (New York: Dana Foundation, 2005).
14. William W. Maddux and Adam D. Galinsky, "Cultural Borders and Mental Barriers: The Relationship between Living Abroad and Creativity," *Journal of Personality and Social Psychology* 96, no. 5 (2009): 1047–61.
15. Markus Baer, "The Strength-of-Weak-Ties Perspective on Creativity: A Comprehensive Examination and Extension," *Journal of Applied Psychology* 95, no. 3 (2010): 592–601.
16. James Baldwin, *Nobody Knows My Name: More Notes of a Native Son* (New York: Vintage, 1993), 61.
17. Christopher J. Burke, Phillippe N. Tobler, Michelle Catherine Baddeley, and Wolfram Schultz, "Neural Mechanisms of Observational Learning," *Proceedings of the National Academy of Sciences* 107, no. 32 (2010): 14431–36.
18. Graham Wallas, *The Art of Thought* (New York: Harcourt, Brace, 1926).
19. Roger E. Beaty, Mathias Benendek, Wilkins Robin, Emanuel Jauk, Andreas Fink, Paul J. Silvia, Donald A. Hodges, Karl Koschutnig, and Aljoscha C. Neubauer, "Creativity and the Default Mode Network: A Functional Connectivity Analysis of the Creative Brain at Rest," *Neuropsychologia* 64 (2014): 92–98.
20. Benjamin Baird, Jonathan Smallwood, Michael Mrazek, Julia W. Y. Kam, Michael S. Franklin, and Jonathan Schooler, "Inspired by Distraction: Mind Wandering Facilitates Creative Incubation," *Psychological Science* 23, no. 10 (2012): 1117–22.
21. Sophie Ellwood, Gerry Pallier, Allan Snyder, and Jason Gallate, "The Incubation Effect: Hatching a Solution?" *Creativity Research Journal* 21, no. 1 (2009): 6–14.
22. Jonathan W. Schooler et al., "The Middle Way: Finding the Balance between Mindfulness and Mind-Wandering," *The Psychology of Learning and Motivation* 60, ed. Brian H. Ross (San Diego, CA: Elsevier Academic Press, 2014), 1–33.
23. Jason Gallate, Cara Wong, Sophie Ellwood, R. W. Roring, and Allan Snyder, "Creative People Use Nonconscious Processes to Their Advantage," *Creativity Research Journal* 24, nos. 2–3 (2012): 146–51.
24. Ut Na Sio and Thomas C. Ormerod, "Does Incubation Enhance Problem Solving? A Meta-Analytic Review," *Psychological Bulletin* 135, no. 1 (2009): 94–120.

CHAPTER 8. REMEMBER TO SUBTRACT

1. Leidy Klotz, *Subtract: The Untapped Science of Less* (New York: Flatiron Books, 2021).
2. Ursula Le Guin, *Lao Tzu: Tao Te Ching: A Book About the Way and the Power of the Way* (Boston: Shambhala, 1997), 31.
3. Gabrielle S. Adams, Benjamin A. Converse, Andrew H. Hales, and Leidy E. Klotz, "People Systematically Overlook Subtractive Changes," *Nature* 592, no. 7853 (2021): 258–61.
4. John M. Darley and Daniel C. Batson, "'From Jerusalem to Jericho': A Study of Situational and Dispositional Variables in Helping Behavior," *Journal of Personality and Social Psychology* 27, no. 1 (1973): 100.
5. Archy O. de Berker, Robb B. Rutledge, Christoph Mathys, Louise Marshall, Gemma F. Cross, Raymond J. Dolan, and Sven Bestmann, "Computations of Uncertainty Mediate Acute Stress Responses in Humans," *Nature Communications* 7, no. 1 (2016): 1–11.
6. Laurie Frankel, *This Is How It Always Is* (New York: Flatiron Books, 2017).
7. Jessica Lahey, *The Gift of Failure: How the Best Parents Learn to Let Go So Their Children Can Succeed* (New York: HarperCollins, 2015).
8. David F. Lancy, *The Anthropology of Childhood: Cherubs, Chattel, Changelings* (Cambridge, UK: Cambridge University Press, 2014).
9. Marie Helweg-Larsen, Stephanie J. Cunningham, Amanda R. Carrico, and Alison M. Pergram, "To Nod or Not to Nod: An Observational Study of Nonverbal Communication and Status in Female and Male College Students," *Psychology of Women Quarterly* 28, no. 4 (2004): 358–61.
10. Olivia Fox Cabane, *The Charisma Myth: How Anyone Can Master the Art and Science of Personal Magnetism* (New York: Penguin, 2013).
11. Holly H. Schiffrin, Miriam Liss, Haley Miles-McLean, Katherine A. Geary, Mindy J. Erchull, and Taryn Tashner, "Helping or Hovering? The Effects of Helicopter Parenting on College Students' Well-Being," *Journal of Child and Family Studies* 23, no. 3 (2014): 548–57.
12. Amy Chua, *Battle Hymn of the Tiger Mother* (New York: Penguin Books, 2011).
13. D. W. Winnicott, *Playing and Reality* (London: Tavistock Publications Ltd, 1971).
14. Tahir Masudi, Helen Capitelli McMahon, Jennifer L. Scott, and Andrew S. Lockey, "Seat Belt-Related Injuries: A Surgical Perspective," *Journal of Emergencies, Trauma, and Shock* 10, no. 2 (2017): 70.
15. National Highway Traffic Safety Administration, *Traffic Safety Facts: 2018 Data: Occupant Protection*, June 2020, https://crashstats.nhtsa.dot.gov/Api/Public/ViewPublication/812967.pdf.
16. Tim Kasser and Kennon Sheldon, "Time Affluence as a Path toward Personal Happiness and Ethical Business Practice: Empirical Evidence from Four Studies," *Journal of Business Ethics* 84, no 2 (2009): 243–55; Jennifer Jabs and Carol M. Devine, "Time Scarcity and Food Choices: An Overview," *Appetite* 47, no 2 (2006): 196–204.

17. Ashley Whillans, *Time Smart: How to Reclaim Your Time and Live a Happier Life* (Boston: Harvard Business Press, 2020), 15.
18. Jordan Etkin, Ioannis Evangelidis, and Jennifer L. Aaker, "Pressed for Time? Goal Conflict Shapes How Time Is Perceived, Spent, and Valued," *Journal of Marketing Research* 52, no 3 (2015): 394–406.
19. Julia Schaupp and Sonja Geiger, "Mindfulness as a Path to Fostering Time Affluence and Well-Being," *Applied Psychology: Health and Well-Being* (August 2021), doi: 10.1111/aphw.12298; Etkin, Evangelidis, and Aaker, "Pressed for Time?" 394–406.
20. Ashley Whillans, Elizabeth Dunn, Paul Smeets, Rene Bekkers, and Michael I. Norton, "Buying Time Promotes Happiness," *Proceedings of the National Academy of Sciences* 114, no. 32 (2017): 8523–27.
21. A. A. Milne and Ernest H Shepard, *Winnie the Pooh* (New York: EP Dutton & Co, 1926).
22. Timothy D. Wilson, David A. Reinhard, Erin C. Westgate, Daniel T. Gilbert, Nicole Ellerbeck, Cheryl Hahn, Casey L. Brown, and Adi Shaked, "Just Think: The Challenges of the Disengaged Mind," *Science* 345, no. 6192 (2014): 75–77.
23. Max Haller, Markus Hadler, and Gerd Kaup, "Leisure Time in Modern Societies: A New Source of Boredom and Stress?" *Social Indicators Research* 111, no. 2 (2013): 403–34.
24. Kirk Warren Brown, Richard M. Ryan, and J. David Creswell, "Mindfulness: Theoretical Foundations and Evidence for Its Salutary Effects," *Psychological Inquiry* 18, no. 4 (2007): 211–37; Rick Hanson, *Hardwiring Happiness: The New Brain Science of Contentment, Calm, and Confidence* (New York: Harmony, 2016).
25. James Clear, *Atomic Habits: Tiny Changes, Remarkable Results: An Easy and Proven Way to Build Good Habits and Break Bad Ones* (New York: Avery, 2018).

CHAPTER 9. GROW CONNECTION THROUGH THE GOOD, THE BAD, AND THE DOWNRIGHT INFURIATING

1. Erika Lawrence, Alexia D. Rothman, Rebecca J. Cobb, and Thomas Nelson Bradbury, "Marital Satisfaction across the Transition to Parenthood," *Journal of Family Psychology* 22, no. 1 (2008): 41; Jean M. Twenge, W. Keith Campbell, and Craig A. Foster, "Parenthood and Marital Satisfaction: A Meta-Analytic Review," *Journal of Marriage and Family* 65, no. 3 (2003): 574–83.
2. Jancee Dunn, *How Not to Hate Your Husband After Kids* (New York: Hachette, 2017).
3. John M. Gottman, James Coan, Sybil Carrere, and Catherine Swanson, "Predicting Marital Happiness and Stability from Newlywed Interactions," *Journal of Marriage and the Family* 60, no 1 (1998): 5–22.

4. Benjamin R. Karney and Thomas Nelson Bradbury, "The Longitudinal Course of Marital Quality and Stability: A Review of Theory, Methods, and Research," *Psychological Bulletin* 118, no. 1 (1995): 3.

5. John M. Gottman and Nan Silver, *The Seven Principles for Making Marriage Work: A Practical Guide from the Country's Foremost Relationship Expert* (New York: Harmony, 2015), 224.

6. Neil S. Jacobson and William C. Follette, "Clinical Significance of Improvement Resulting from Two Behavioral Marital Therapy Components," *Behavior Therapy* 16, no. 3 (1985): 249–62.

7. Andrew Christensen, David C. Atkins, Sara Berns, Jennifer Wheeler, Donald H. Baucom, and Lorelei Simpson Rowe, "Traditional versus Integrative Behavioral Couple Therapy for Significantly and Chronically Distressed Married Couples," *Journal of Consulting and Clinical Psychology* 72, no. 2 (2004): 176.

8. Andrew Christensen, David C. Atkins, Brian R. W. Baucom, and Jean Yi, "Marital Status and Satisfaction Five Years Following a Randomized Clinical Trial Comparing Traditional versus Integrative Behavioral Couple Therapy," *Journal of Consulting and Clinical Psychology* 78, no. 2 (2010): 225.

9. Jonathan Haidt, *The Righteous Mind: Why Good People Are Divided by Politics and Religion* (New York: Vintage, 2012).

10. Jonathan Haidt, "The Emotional Dog and Its Rational Tail: A Social Intuitionist Approach to Moral Judgment," *Psychological Review* 108, no. 4 (2001): 814.

11. Daniel B. Wile, *After the Fight: Using Your Disagreements to Build a Stronger Relationship* (New York: Guilford Press, 1995), 2.

12. Taylor W. Schmitz, Eve De Rosa, and Adam Anderson, "Opposing Influences of Affective State Valence on Visual Cortical Encoding," *Journal of Neuroscience* 29, no. 22 (2009): 7199–7207.

13. Lisa Neff and Benjamin R. Karney, "How Does Context Affect Intimate Relationships? Linking External Stress and Cognitive Processes within Marriage," *Personality and Social Psychology Bulletin* 30, no. 2 (2004): 134–48.

14. Shiri Cohen, Marc S. Schulz, Emily Weiss, and Robert J. Waldinger, "Eye of the Beholder: The Individual and Dyadic Contributions of Empathic Accuracy and Perceived Empathic Effort to Relationship Satisfaction," *Journal of Family Psychology* 26, no. 2 (2012): 236–45.

15. Jorge Barraza and Paul Zak, "Empathy toward Strangers Triggers Oxytocin Release and Subsequent Generosity," *Annals of the New York Academy of Sciences* 1167, no. 1 (2009): 182–89; Carsten K. W. De Dreu and Mariska E. Kret, "Oxytocin Conditions Intergroup Relations through Upregulated In-Group Empathy, Cooperation, Conformity, and Defense," *Biological Psychiatry* 79, no. 3 (2016): 165–73; Waguih William Ishak, Maria Kahloon, and Hala Fakhry, "Oxytocin Role in Enhancing Well-Being: A Literature Review," *Journal of Affective Disorders* 103, nos. 1–2 (2011): 1–9.

16. Markus Heinrichs, Thomas Baumgartner, Clemens Kirschbaum, and Ulrike Ehlert, "Social Support and Oxytocin Interact to Suppress Cortisol and Subjective Responses to Psychosocial Stress," *Biological Psychiatry* 54, no. 12 (2003): 1389–98.

17. Beate Ditzen, Marcel Schaer, Barbara Gabriel, Guy Bodenmann, Ulrike Ehlert, and Markus Heinrichs, "Intranasal Oxytocin Increases Positive Communication and Reduces Cortisol Levels during Couple Conflict," *Biological Psychiatry* 65, no. 9 (2009): 728–31.

18. Neil S. Jacobson and Danny Moore, "Spouses as Observers of the Events in Their Relationship," *Journal of Consulting and Clinical Psychology* 49, no. 2 (1981): 269.

19. Alain de Botton, *The Course of Love: A Novel* (New York: Simon and Schuster, 2016), 217–18.

20. Brennan Peterson, Christopher R. Newton, and Karen H. Rosen, "Examining Congruence between Partners' Perceived Infertility-Related Stress and Its Relationship to Marital Adjustment and Depression in Infertile Couples," *Family Process* 42, no. 1 (2003): 59–70.

21. Shelly L. Gable, Harry T. Reis, Emily A. Impett, Evan R. Asher, "What Do You Do When Things Go Right? The Intrapersonal and Interpersonal Benefits of Sharing Positive Events," *Journal of Personality and Social Psychology* 87, no. 2 (2004): 228.

22. Arthur Aron, Christina C. Norman, Elaine N. Aron, Colin McKenna, and Richard E. Heyman, "Couples' Shared Participation in Novel and Arousing Activities and Experienced Relationship Quality," *Journal of Personality and Social Psychology* 78, no. 2 (2000): 273.

23. Sanford Dornbusch, Philip L. Ritter, P. Herbert Leiderman, Donald F. Roberts, and Michael J. Fraleigh, "The Relation of Parenting Style to Adolescent School Performance," *Child Development* (1987): 1244–57.

24. BJ Fogg, *Tiny Habits: The Small Changes That Change Everything* (New York: Eamon Dolan Books, 2019).

25. Tal Ben-Shahar, *Happier: Learn the Secrets to Daily Joy and Lasting Fulfillment* (New York: McGraw Hill, 2007).

26. Tal Ben-Shahar, *Being Happy: You Don't Have to Be Perfect to Lead a Richer, Happier Life* (New York: McGraw Hill Professional, 2010).

27. James Clear, *Atomic Habits: Tiny Changes, Remarkable Results: An Easy and Proven Way to Build Good Habits and Break Bad Ones* (New York: Avery, 2018).

28. Katy Milkman, *How to Change: The Science of Getting from Where You Are to Where You Want to Be* (New York: Penguin, 2021).

29. Janice L. Driver and John M. Gottman, "Daily Marital Interactions and Positive Affect during Marital Conflict among Newlywed Couples," *Family Process* 43, no. 3 (2004): 301–14.

30. John M. Gottman and Robert Wayne Levenson, "What Predicts Change in Marital Interaction Over Time? A Study of Alternative Models," *Family Process* 38, no. 2 (1999): 143–58.

CHAPTER 10. FINESSE YOUR STRESS

1. Hans Selye, "Confusion and Controversy in the Stress Field," *Journal of Human Stress* 1, no. 2 (1975): 37–44.

2. Richard S. Lazarus, *Psychological Stress and the Coping Process* (New York: McGraw-Hill, 1966).

3. Jeremy Jamieson, Wendy Berry Mendes, Erin Blackstock, and Toni Schmader, "Turning the Knots in Your Stomach into Bows: Reappraising Arousal Improves Performance on the GRE," *Journal of Experimental Social Psychology* 46, no. 1 (2010): 208–12.

4. Nassim Nicholas Taleb, *Antifragile: Things That Gain from Disorder* (New York: Random House, 2012).

5. Taylor W. Schmitz, Eve De Rosa, and Adam Anderson, "Opposing Influences of Affective State Valence on Visual Cortical Encoding," *Journal of Neuroscience* 29, no. 22 (2009): 7199–7207.

6. Sheldon Cohen, Denise Janicki-Deverts, and Gregory E. Miller, "Psychological Stress and Disease," *JAMA: The Journal of the Americam Medical Association* 298, no. 14 (2007): 1685–87.

7. Safiya Richardson, Jonathan A. Shaffer, Louise Falzon, David Krupka, Karina W. Davidson, and Donald Edmondson, "Meta-Analysis of Perceived Stress and Its Association with Incident Coronary Heart Disease," *American Journal of Cardiology* 110, no. 12 (2012): 1711–16.

8. Steven J. Linton, "Does Work Stress Predict Insomnia? A Prospective Study," *British Journal of Health Psychology* 9, no. 2 (2004): 127–36.

9. Elissa Epel, Elizabeth H. Blackburn, Jue Lin, Firdaus S. Dhabhar, Nancy Adler, Jason D. Morrow, and Richard Cawthon, "Accelerated Telomere Shortening in Response to Life Stress," *Proceedings of the National Academy of Sciences* 101, no. 9 (2004): 17312–15; Abiola Keller, Kristin Litzelman, Lauren E. Wisk, Torsheika Maddox, Erika R. Cheng, Paul D. Creswell, and Whitney P. Witt, "Does the Perception That Stress Affects Health Matter? The Association with Health and Mortality," *Health Psychology* 31, no. 5 (2012): 677.

10. Sheldon Cohen, David A. Tyrrell, and Andrew P. Smith, "Negative Life Events, Perceived Stress, Negative Affect, and Susceptibility to the Common Cold," *Journal of Personality and Social Psychology* 64, no. 1 (1993): 131; Anette Pedersen, Robert Zachariae, and Dana H. Bovbjerg, "Influence of Psychological Stress on Upper Respiratory Infection—a Meta-Analysis of Prospective Studies," *Psychosomatic Medicine* 72, no. 8 (2010): 823–32.

11. Sheldon Cohen, Michael L. Murphy, and Aric A. Prather, "Ten Surprising Facts about Stressful Life Events and Disease Risk," *Annual Review of Psychology* 70, no. 1 (2019): 577–97.

12. Cohen, Tyrrell, and Smith, "Negative Life Events, Perceived Stress," 131.

13. Fiona Maccallum, Isaac Galatzer-Levy, and George A. Bonanno, "Trajectories of Depression Following Spousal and Child Bereavement:

A Comparison of the Heterogeneity in Outcomes," *Journal of Psychiatric Research* 69 (2015): 72–79.

14. Doris Fay and Sabine Sonnentag, "Rethinking the Effects of Stressors: A Longitudinal Study on Personal Initiative," *Journal of Occupational Health Psychology* 7, no. 3 (2002): 221; P. A. Hancock and J. L. Weaver, "On Time Distortion Under Stress," *Theoretical Issues in Ergonomics Science* 6, no. 2 (2005): 193–211; Larry Cahill, Lukasz Gorski, and Kathryn Le, "Enhanced Human Memory Consolidation with Post-Learning Stress: Interaction with the Degree of Arousal at Encoding," *Learning & Memory* 10, no. 4 (2003): 270–74.

15. Kelly McGonigal, *The Upside of Stress: Why Stress Is Good for You, and How to Get Good at It* (New York: Penguin, 2016).

16. Susan Stockdale, Kenneth B. Wells, Lingqi Tang, Thomas R. Belin, Lily Zhang, and Cathy D. Sherbourne, "The Importance of Social Context: Neighborhood Stressors, Stress-Buffering Mechanisms, and Alcohol, Drug, and Mental Health Disorders," *Social Science & Medicine* 65, no. 9 (2007): 1867–81.

17. Camara Jules P. Harrell, Tanisha I. Burford, Brandi N. Cage, Travette McNair Nelson, Sheronda Shearon, Adrian Thompson, and Steven Green, "Multiple Pathways Linking Racism to Health Outcomes," *Du Bois Review: Social Science Research on Race* 8, no. 1 (2011): 143–57.

18. Cecilia Cheng, "Cognitive and Motivational Processes Underlying Coping Flexibility: A Dual-Process Model," *Journal of Personality and Social Psychology* 84, no. 2 (2003): 425.

19. Alia J. Crum, Peter Salovey, and Shawn Achor, "Rethinking Stress: The Role of Mindsets in Determining the Stress Response," *Journal of Personality and Social Psychology* 104, no. 4 (2013): 716.

20. Clemens Kirschbaum, Karl-Martin Pirke, and Dirk Hellhammer, "The 'Trier Social Stress Test'—a Tool for Investigating Psychobiological Stress Responses in a Laboratory Setting," *Neuropsychobiology* 28, nos. 1–2 (1993): 76–81.

21. Keller et al., "Does the Perception That Stress Affects Health Matter?" 677.

22. Michele S. Hirsch and Robert M. Liebert, "The Physical and Psychological Experience of Pain: The Effects of Labeling and Cold Pressor Temperature on Three Pain Measures in College Women," *Pain* 77, no. 1 (1998): 41–48.

23. Jeremy Jamieson, Matthew K. Nock, and Wendy Berry Mendes, "Mind over Matter: Reappraising Arousal Improves Cardiovascular and Cognitive Responses to Stress," *Journal of Experimental Psychology: General* 141, no. 3 (2012): 417–22.

24. Barack Obama, "Here's the Full Transcript of Obama's Interview with HuffPost," interview with Sam Stein, HuffPost, updated December 6, 2017, https://www.huffpost.com/entry/obama-huffpost-interview-transcript_n_6905450.

25. Beate Ditzen and Markus Heinrichs, "Psychobiology of Social Support: The Social Dimension of Stress Buffering," *Restorative Neurology and Neuroscience* 32, no. 1 (2014): 149–62.

26. Jennifer L. Brown, David Sheffield, Mark R. Leary, and Michael E. Robinson, "Social Support and Experimental Pain," *Psychosomatic Medicine* 65, no. 2 (2003): 276–83.

27. Simone Schnall, Kent D. Harber, Jeanine K. Stefanucci, and Dennis R. Proffitt, "Social Support and the Perception of Geographical Slant," *Journal of Experimental Social Psychology* 44, no. 5 (2008): 1246–55.

28. Tobias Esch and George B. Stefano, "The Neurobiology of Love," *Neuroendocrinology Letters* 26, no. 3 (2005): 175–92.

29. James A. Coan, Hillary Schaefer, and Richard J. Davidson, "Lending a Hand: Social Regulation of the Neural Response to Threat," *Psychological Science* 17, no. 12 (2006): 1032–39.

30. Michael J. Poulin, Stephanie L. Brown, Amanda Dillard, and Dylan M. Smith, "Giving to Others and the Association between Stress and Mortality," *American Journal of Public Health* 103, no. 9 (2013): 1649–55.

31. Stephanie L. Brown and R. Michael Brown, "Connecting Prosocial Behavior to Improved Physical Health: Contributions from the Neurobiology of Parenting," *Neuroscience & Biobehavioral Reviews* 55 (2015): 1–17.

32. Andreas Bartels and Semir Zeki, "The Neural Correlates of Maternal and Romantic Love," *NeuroImage* 21, no. 3 (2003): 1155–66.

33. Megan Galbally, Andrew James Lewis, Marinus van Ijzendoorn, and Michael Permezel, "The Role of Oxytocin in Mother-Infant Relations: A Systematic Review of Human Studies," *Harvard Review of Psychiatry* 19, no. 1 (2011): 1–14.

34. Elizabeth Sibolboro Mezzacappa, "Breastfeeding and Maternal Stress Response and Health," *Nutrition Reviews* 62, no. 7 (2004): 261–68.

35. Johanna Bick, Mary Dozier, Kristin Bernard, Damion Grasso, and Robert Simons, "Foster Mother–Infant Bonding: Associations between Foster Mothers' Oxytocin Production, Electrophysiological Brain Activity, Feelings of Commitment, and Caregiving Quality," *Child Development* 84, no. 3 (2013): 826–40.

36. Ilanit Gordon, Orna Zagoory-Sharon, James F. Leckman, and Ruth Feldman, "Oxytocin, Cortisol, and Triadic Family Interactions," *Physiology & Behavior* 101, no. 5 (2010): 679–84.

37. Susan M. Johnson, Melissa Burgess Moser, Lane Beckes, Andra Smith, Tracy Dalgleish, Rebecca Halchuk, Karen Hasselmo, Paul S. Greenman, Zui Merali, and James A. Coan, "Soothing the Threatened Brain: Leveraging Contact Comfort with Emotionally Focused Therapy," *PLOS ONE* 9, no. 8 (2013).

38. Shelley Taylor, "Tend and Befriend: Biobehavioral Bases of Affiliation Under Stress." *Current Directions in Psychological Science* 15, no. 6 (2006): 273–77.

CHAPTER 11. TEND TO YOUR HAPPINESS NEEDS

1. Richard M. Ryan and Edward L. Deci, "Self-Determination Theory and the Facilitation of Intrinsic Motivation, Social Development, and Well-Being," *American Psychologist* 55, no. 1 (2000): 68–78; Heather Patrick, C. Raymond Knee, Amy Canevello, and Cynthia Lonsbary, "The Role of Need Fulfillment in Relationship Functioning and Well-Being: A Self-Determination Theory Perspective," *Journal of Personality and Social Psychology* 92, no. 3 (2007): 434–57.

2. Shigehiro Oishi, Edward F. Diener, Richard E. Lucas, and Eunkook M. Suh, "Cross-Cultural Variations in Predictors of Life Satisfaction: Perspectives from Needs and Values," in *Culture and Well-Being: The Collected Works of Ed Diener*, vol. 38., ed. Ed Diener (New York: Springer Science + Business Media, 2009), 109–27.

3. Richard M. Ryan and Edward L. Deci, "On Happiness and Human Potentials: A Review of Research on Hedonic and Eudaimonic Well-Being," *Annual Review of Psychology* 52, no. 1 (2001):141–66.

4. Christopher Peterson, Nansook Park, and Martin E. P. Seligman, "Orientations to Happiness and Life Satisfaction: The Full Life versus the Empty Life," *Journal of Happiness Studies* 6, no. 1 (2005): 25–41.

5. Barbara L. Fredrickson, *Positivity: Discover the Upward Spiral That Will Change Your Life* (New York: Harmony, 2009).

6. Barbara L. Fredrickson and Thomas Joiner, "Reflections on positive emotions and upward spirals," *Perspectives on Psychological Science* 13, no. 2 (2018): 194–199.

7. Barbara L. Fredrickson, "The Role of Positive Emotions in Positive Psychology: The Broaden-and-Build Theory of Positive Emotions," *American Psychologist* 56, no. 3 (2001): 218.

8. Barbara L. Fredrickson, Michelle M. Tugade, Christian E. Waugh, and Gregory R. Samanez-Larkin, "What Good Are Positive Emotions in Crisis? A Prospective Study of Resilience and Emotions Following the Terrorist Attacks on the United States on September 11th, 2001," *Journal of Personality and Social Psychology* 84, no. 2 (2003): 365.

9. Eric L. Garland, Barbara Fredrickson, Ann M. Kring, David P. Johnson, Piper S. Meyer, and David L. Penn, "Upward Spirals of Positive Emotions Counter Downward Spirals of Negativity: Insights from the Broaden-and-Build Theory and Affective Neuroscience on the Treatment of Emotion Dysfunctions and Deficits in Psychopathology," *Clinical Psychology Review* 30, no. 7 (2010): 849–64.

10. Barbara L. Fredrickson and Marcial F. Losada, "Positive Affect and the Complex Dynamics of Human Flourishing," *American Psychologist* 60, no. 7 (2005): 678; Barbara L. Fredrickson, "Updated Thinking on Positivity Ratios," *American Psychologist* 68, no. 9 (2013).

11. Angela Duckworth, *Grit: The Power of Passion and Perseverance* (New York: Scribner, 2016).

12. Rebecca Hewett, Verena Christine Haun, Evangelia Demerouti, Alma María Rodríguez Sánchez, Janne Skakon, and Sara De Gieter, "Compensating Need Satisfaction across Life Boundaries: A Daily Diary Study," *Journal of Occupational and Organizational Psychology* 90, no. 2 (2017): 270–79.

13. Albert Bandura and Nancy E. Adams, "Analysis of Self-Efficacy Theory of Behavioral Change," *Cognitive Therapy and Research* 1, no. 4 (1977): 287–310.

14. Ariana Albanese, Gabrielle Russo, and Pamela A. Geller, "The Role of Parental Self-Efficacy in Parent and Child Well-Being: A Systematic Review of Associated Outcomes," *Child: Care, Health and Development* 45, no. 3 (2019): 333–63.

15. Ed Diener and Martin E. P. Seligman, "Very Happy People," *Psychological Science* 13, no. 1 (2002): 81–84.

16. Robert J. Waldinger, "What Makes a Good Life? Lessons from the Longest Study on Happiness," TEDxBeaconStreet, November 2015, video, 12:38, https://www.ted.com/speakers/robert_waldinger.

17. George E. Vaillant, *Triumphs of Experience: The Men of the Harvard Grant Study* (Cambridge, MA: Harvard University Press, 2012).

18. Gillian Sandstrom and Elizabeth W. Dunn, "Social Interactions and Well-Being: The Surprising Power of Weak Ties," *Personality and Social Psychology Bulletin* 40, no. 7 (2014): 910–22.

19. Ed Diener, Weiting Ng, James H. Harter, and Raksha Arora, "Wealth and Happiness across the World: Material Prosperity Predicts Life Evaluation, whereas Psychosocial Prosperity Predicts Positive Feeling," *Journal of Personality and Social Psychology* 99, no. 1 (2010): 52; Ed Diener and Robert Biswas-Diener, *Happiness: Unlocking the Mysteries of Psychological Wealth* (Hoboken, NJ: John Wiley & Sons, 2011).

20. Roy Baumeister and Mark Leary, "The Need to Belong: Desire for Interpersonal Attachments as a Fundamental Human Motivation," *Psychological Bulletin* 117, no. 3 (1995): 497–529.

21. Barbara L. Fredrickson, *Love 2.0: Creating Happiness and Health in Moments of Connection* (New York: Penguin, 2013), 17–27.

22. D. Watson, "Intraindividual and Interindividual Analyses of Positive and Negative Affect: Their Relation to Health Complaints, Perceived Stress, and Daily Activities," *Journal of Personality and Social Psychology* 54, no. 6 (1988): 1020.

23. Fredrickson, *Love 2.0*.

24. Stephen G. Hofmann, Paul Grossman, and Devon Hinton, "Loving-Kindness and Compassion Meditation: Potential for Psychological Interventions," *Clinical Psychology Review* 31, no. 7 (2011): 1126–32.

25. Cendri A. Hutcherson, Emma M. Seppala, and James J. Gross, "Loving-Kindness Meditation Increases Social Connectedness," *Emotion* 8, no. 5 (2008): 720.

26. Andreas B. Neubauer, Andrea Schmidt, Andrea Kramer, and Florian Schmiedek, "A Little Autonomy Support Goes a Long Way: Daily Autonomy-Supportive Parenting, Child Well-Being, Parental Need Fulfillment, and Change in Child, Family, and Parent Adjustment across the Adaptation to the COVID-19 Pandemic," *Child Development* 92, no. 5 (2020): 1679–97.

27. Paul P. Baard, Edward L. Deci, and Rochard M. Ryan, "Intrinsic Need Satisfaction: A Motivational Basis of Performance and Well-Being in Two Work Settings," *Journal of Applied Social Psychology* 34, no. 10 (2004): 2045–68.

28. Ed O'Brien and Samantha Kassirer, "People Are Slow to Adapt to the Warm Glow of Giving," *Psychological Science* 30, no. 2 (2019): 193–204.

29. Edward L. Deci, Jennifer La Guardia, Arlen C. Moller, Marc J. Scheiner, and Richard M. Ryan, "On the Benefits of Giving as Well as Receiving Autonomy Support: Mutuality in Close Friendships," *Personality and Social Psychology Bulletin* 32, no. 3 (2006): 313–27.

30. Viktor Frankl, *Man's Search for Meaning* (Boston: Beacon Press, 1959), 66.

31. Chiahuei Wu, "Enhancing Quality of Life by Shifting Importance Perception among Life Domains," *Journal of Happiness Studies* 10, no. 1 (2009): 37–47.

32. Richard M. Ryan and Edward L. Deci, "From Ego Depletion to Vitality: Theory and Findings Concerning the Facilitation of Energy Available to the Self," *Social and Personality Psychology Compass* 2, no. 2 (2008): 702–17.

33. Sonja Lyubomirsky, Laura King, and Ed Diener, "The Benefits of Frequent Positive Affect: Does Happiness Lead to Success?" *Psychological Bulletin* 131, no. 6 (2005): 803.

34. Elien Mabbe, Bart Soenens, Maarten Vansteenkiste, Jolene van der Kaap-Deeder, and Athanasios Mouratidis, "Day-to-Day Variation in Autonomy-Supportive and Psychologically Controlling Parenting: The Role of Parents' Daily Experiences of Need Satisfaction and Need Frustration," *Parenting* 18, no. 2 (2018): 86–109.

35. S. Katherine Nelson-Coffey and Sonja Lyubomirsky, "Juggling Family and Career: Parents' Pathways to a Balanced and Happy Life," in *Flourishing in Life, Work and Careers: Individual Wellbeing and Career Experiences*, ed. Ronald J. Burke, Kathryn M. Page, and Cary L. Cooper (Northampton, MA: Edward Elgar Publishing, 2015), 100–118.

CHAPTER 12. BALANCE YOUR PLEASURE AND MEANING

1. N. K. Sandars, *The Epic of Gilgamesh* (Harmondsworth, UK: Penguin, 1972).

2. Daniel Kahneman, Alan B. Krueger, David Schkade, Norbert Schwarz, and Arthur A. Stone, "A Survey Method for Characterizing Daily Life

Experience: The Day Reconstruction Method," *Science* 306, no. 5702 (2004): 1776–80.

3. S. Katherine Nelson-Coffey, Kostadin Kushlev, Tammy English, Elizabeth W. Dunn, and Sonja Lyubomirsky, "In Defense of Parenthood: Children Are Associated with More Joy Than Misery," *Psychological Science* 24, no. 1 (2012): 3–10.

4. S. Katherine Nelson, Kostadin Kushlev, and Sonja Lyubomirsky, "The Pains and Pleasures of Parenting: When, Why, and How Is Parenthood Associated with More or Less Well-Being?" *Psychological Bulletin* 140, no. 3 (2014): 846–95.

5. Ursula Le Guin, *Lao Tzu: Tao Te Ching: A Book About the Way and the Power of the Way* (Boston: Shambhala, 1997), 40.

6. Philip Brickman, Dan Coates, and Ronnie Janoff-Bulman, "Lottery Winners and Accident Victims: Is Happiness Relative?" *Journal of Personality and Social Psychology* 36, no. 8 (1978): 917–27.

7. Ed Diener, Lucas E. Richard, and Christie Napa Scollon, "Beyond the Hedonic Treadmill: Revising the Adaptation Theory of Well-Being," *Am Psychol* 61, no. 4 (May–June 2006): 305–14.

8. Leif D. Nelson and Tom Meyvis, "Interrupted Consumption: Disrupting Adaptation to Hedonic Experiences," *Journal of Marketing Research* 45, no. 6 (2008): 654–64; Leif D. Nelson, Tom Meyvis, and Jeff Galak, "Enhancing the Television-Viewing Experience through Commercial Interruptions," *Journal of Consumer Research* 36, no. 2 (2009): 160–72.

9. Katherine Jacobs Bao and Sonja Lyubomirsky, "Making It Last: Combating Hedonic Adaptation in Romantic Relationships," *Journal of Positive Psychology* 8, no. 3 (2013): 196–206; Nelson, Kushlev, and Lyubomirsky, "The Pains and Pleasures of Parenting," 846.

10. Sonja Lyubomirsky and Kristin Layous, "How Do Simple Positive Activities Increase Well-Being?" *Current Directions in Psychological Science* 22, no. 1 (2013): 57–62; Nancy L. Sin and Sonja Lyubomirsky, "Enhancing Well-Being and Alleviating Depressive Symptoms with Positive Psychology Interventions: A Practice-Friendly Meta-Analysis," *Journal of Clinical Psychology* 65, no. 5 (2009): 467–87.

11. Mihaly Csikszentmihalyi, *Finding Flow: The Psychology of Engagement with Everyday Life* (New York: Basic Books, 1997).

12. Francesco Cirillo, *The Pomodoro Technique: The Life-Changing Time-Management System* (New York: Random House, 2018).

13. David S. Yeager, Marlone D. Henderson, Sidney D'Mello, David Paunesku, Gregory M. Walton, Brian J. Spitzer, and Angela Duckworth, "Boring but Important: A Self-Transcendent Purpose for Learning Fosters Academic Self-Regulation," *Journal of Personality and Social Psychology* 107, no. 4 (2014): 559.

14. Bruce W. Smith, Erin M. Tooley, Erica Q. Montague, Amanda E. Robinson, Cynthia J. Cosper, and Paul G. Mullins, "The Role of Resilience and Purpose in Life in Habituation to Heat and Cold Pain," *Journal of Pain* 10, no 5 (2009): 493–500.

RESOURCES

CHAPTER 1. WHEN YOU'RE LOST, LET VALUES BE YOUR GUIDE

ACT Daily Journal: Get Unstuck & Live Fully with Acceptance & Commitment Therapy, by Diana Hill and Debbie Sorensen

A Liberated Mind: How to Pivot Toward What Matters, by Steven C. Hayes

CHAPTER 2. CHANGE YOUR WORKING-PARENT MINDSET

The How of Happiness: A New Approach to Getting the Life You Want, by Sonja Lyubomirsky

Mindset: The New Psychology of Success, by Carol Dweck

CHAPTER 3. UNHOOK FROM UNHELPFUL LABELS

Choke: What the Secrets of the Brain Reveal about Getting It Right When You Have To, by Sian Beilock

Self-Compassion: The Proven Power of Being Kind to Yourself, by Kristin Neff

Self-Compassion for Parents: Nurture Your Child by Caring for Yourself, by Susan M. Pollak

*Unfu*k Yourself: Get Out of Your Head and Into Your Life*, by Gary John Bishop

CHAPTER 4. SPIN YOUR STORY

Man's Search for Meaning, by Viktor E. Frankl

No Mud, No Lotus: The Art of Transforming Suffering, by Thich Nhat Hanh

CHAPTER 5. DO THE RIGHT HARD THINGS (THE RIGHT WAY)

Emotional Intelligence: Why It Can Matter More Than IQ, by Daniel Goleman

Grit: The Power of Passion and Perseverance, by Angela Duckworth

Practical Wisdom: The Right Way to Do the Right Thing, by Barry Schwartz and
   Kenneth Sharpe

CHAPTER 6. RETHINK YOUR REST

Digital Minimalism: Choosing a Focused Life in a Noisy World, by Cal Newport

*How to Stop Losing Your Sh*t with Your Kids: A Practical Guide to Becoming a
   Calmer, Happier Parent,* by Carla Naumberg

Rest: Why You Get More Done When You Work Less, by Alex Soojung-Kim Pang

The Tao of Pooh, by Benjamin Hoff

CHAPTER 7. TURN CONSTRAINTS INTO CREATIVITY

The Creative Brain: The Science of Genius, by Nancy Andreasen

Creativity: The Psychology of Discovery and Invention, by Mihaly
   Csikszentmihalyi

CHAPTER 8. REMEMBER TO SUBTRACT

*The Gift of Failure: How the Best Parents Learn to Let Go So Their Children Can
   Succeed,* by Jessica Lahey

*How to Raise an Adult: Break Free of the Overparenting Trap and Prepare Your
   Kid for Success,* Julie Lythcott-Haims

Subtract: The Untapped Science of Less, by Leidy Klotz

Time Smart: How to Reclaim Your Time & Live a Happier Life, by Ashley
   Whillans

CHAPTER 9. GROW CONNECTION THROUGH THE GOOD, THE BAD, AND THE DOWNRIGHT INFURIATING

*ACT with Love: Stop Struggling, Reconcile Differences, and Strengthen Your
   Relationship with Acceptance and Commitment Therapy,* by Russ Harris

How Not to Hate Your Husband After Kids, by Jancee Dunn

Love 2.0: Creating Happiness and Health in Moments of Connection, by Barbara L. Fredrickson

Reconcilable Differences: Rebuild Your Relationship by Rediscovering the Partner You Love—without Losing Yourself, 2nd edition, by Andrew Christensen, Brian D. Doss, and Neil S. Jacobson

The Seven Principles for Making Marriage Work: A Practical Guide from the Country's Foremost Relationship Expert, by John M. Gottman and Nan Silver

CHAPTER 10. FINESSE YOUR STRESS

The Myths of Happiness: What Should Make You Happy, but Doesn't, What Shouldn't Make You Happy, but Does, by Sonja Lyubomirsky

The Upside of Stress: Why Stress Is Good for You and How to Get Good at It, by Kelly McGonigal

CHAPTER 11. TEND TO YOUR HAPPINESS NEEDS

The How of Happiness: A New Approach to Getting the Life You Want, by Sonja Lyubomirsky

Positivity: Discover the Upward Spiral That Will Change Your Life, by Barbara L. Fredrickson

Why We Do What We Do: Understanding Self-Motivation, by Edward L. Deci and Richard Flaste

CHAPTER 12. BALANCE YOUR PLEASURE AND MEANING

Happier: Learn the Secrets to Daily Joy and Lasting Fulfillment, by Tal Ben-Shahar

The Happiness Hypothesis: Finding Modern Truth in Ancient Wisdom, by Jonathan Haidt

How to Be a Happier Parent: Raising a Family, Having a Life, and Loving (Almost) Every Minute, by KJ Dell'Antonia

INDEX